PENGUIN BOOKS

THE ONLY WAY I KNOW

Cal Ripken, Jr., was born in Havre de Grace, Maryland. He now lives outside of Baltimore with his wife and two children, and plays baseball—every day—for the Baltimore Orioles.

Mike Bryan, a native Texan, is the author of two books with Keith Hernandez and one with Kirby Puckett. His other books include *Baseball Lives, Chapter and Verse, Dogleg Madness*, and, most recently, *Uneasy Rider*. He lives in New York City.

6/2/99

Joe -
I thought this book would be great for you because you embody so much of what makes Cal Ripkin, Jr. great! Your athletic ability, sincere attitude along with your commitment and dedication to your community will take you far. I've truly enjoyed working with you for the last two years. I'll miss you next year. Good Luck and

Best Wishes to you of thinking of me.

Keep in touch and school!

Send me a baseball schedule!

☺ Ms Drdzc

The Only Way I Know

CAL RIPKEN, JR.

and MIKE BRYAN

PENGUIN BOOKS

PENGUIN BOOKS
Published by the Penguin Group
Penguin Putnam Inc., 375 Hudson Street,
New York, New York 10014, U.S.A.
Penguin Books Ltd, 27 Wrights Lane, London W8 5TZ, England
Penguin Books Australia Ltd, Ringwood, Victoria, Australia
Penguin Books Canada Ltd, 10 Alcorn Avenue, Toronto, Ontario, Canada M4V 3B2
Penguin Books (N.Z.) Ltd, 182–190 Wairau Road, Auckland 10, New Zealand

Penguin Books Ltd, Registered Offices:
Harmondsworth, Middlesex, England

First published in the United States of America by Viking Penguin,
a division of Penguin Books USA Inc. 1997
This edition with a new afterword published in Penguin Books 1998

1   3   5   7   9   10   8   6   4   2

PHOTOGRAPH CREDITS
First section:
The Baltimore Orioles: page 7 (center)
Sports Illustrated: page 8 (above)
Allsport: page 8 (below)
Second section:
The Baltimore Orioles: page 1 (above left, below left)
Walter Iooss: pages 1 (above right), 3 (above left, below right),
6 (below), 7 (above, center left, below left and right), 8
Jerry Wachter Photography Ltd: pages 1 (below right), 4 (above right)
Sports Illustrated: pages 2 (above left and right), 4 (below right),
5 (above right), 6 (above and center)
Allsport: pages 2 (below left and right), 3 (above right, below left),
4 (above left, below left), 5 (above left, below left and right), 7 (center right)
All other photographs courtesy of the Ripken family.

THE LIBRARY OF CONGRESS HAS CATALOGUED THE HARDCOVER AS FOLLOWS:
Ripken, Cal, 1960–
The only way I know / Cal Ripken, Jr., and Mike Bryan.
p.   cm.
ISBN 0-670-87193-1 (hc.)
ISBN 0 14 02.6626 7 (pbk.)
1. Ripken, Cal, 1960– .   2. Baseball players—United States—Biography.
3. Baltimore Orioles (Baseball team)—History.   I. Bryan, Mike.   II. Title.
GV865.R47A3   1997
796.357´092—dc21
[B]   97–9159

Printed in the United States of America
Set in Transitional 521
Designed by Brian Mulligan

For my family, who shows me the way

Chapter One

When I was called to the big leagues with the Baltimore Orioles in 1981, I sat on the bench for the first time in my life and, I have to say, this wasn't what I had in mind for my career. My father was the Orioles' third base coach, but my last name wasn't going to help me win a starting position. It doesn't work that way in the majors; in fact, growing up in a baseball family only made me more aware of how it sometimes *does* work: players—good players—traded or discarded into the minor leagues or relegated to the far corner of the bench, never to be heard from again. Now, it's true that I was one of the top prospects in one of the best organizations in the game, and I felt I'd earned my shot and belonged up here, but I hadn't proved it yet, and lots of players max-out in Triple-A. That's as good as they're going to get. I knew that.

So I chewed more sunflower seeds in two months in '81 than I had in three and half years in the minors; I watched my new teammates, who'd won 100 games the previous season without my help; I thought about what my manager, Earl Weaver, had said about my immediate prospects—"He has some pretty good players in front of him"—and I wondered, How can I ever break into this lineup, and if and when I do, how can I be sure to stay there?

I came up with two answers: play well and play every day. If I do get the opportunity, don't give anyone *else* with the same desire and motivation the same opportunity. I didn't want Earl and the organization to have any reasonable option but to play me. That sounds cold, but mainly it's just old-school, the way my father taught me. In the minors, I knew guys who didn't want to become good friends with other players at the same position who might take their jobs; I knew outfielders who preferred hanging out with the pitchers. That's old, *old*-school, and I didn't feel that way, but I did take a proprietary interest in my position. As a ballplayer, you have to, because until you become established baseball gives you nothing in terms of income or job security, and it can take away your entire professional life in a heartbeat. If baseball didn't invent downsizing, it perfected the practice, which happens at every level on every team every spring.

The truth is, breaking Lou Gehrig's record for consecutive games played was partly an unintentional result of that early and then ongoing determination to keep as much of my destiny as possible in my own hands. Overall, I'm a guy who likes control. I even find myself dissatisfied with the instructions on some brands of microwave popcorn. "Pop on High setting for two to five minutes"? That doesn't do me any good at all. With any new brand or with any new oven—in the houses my wife and I have rented for spring training, for example—I proceed logically, setting the timer for five minutes and listening carefully. When the corn's ready, I check the elapsed time. After one more trial run, just to make sure, I'm all set with this brand. This is the way I go about almost everything, and sometimes my wife or friends or teammates tease me about going overboard. But to me, this is just taking care of business.

I'm instinctively analytical—something else for friends to rib me about. After I did break into the Orioles' lineup as the third baseman in 1982, the year after I came up, Earl Weaver soon moved me to shortstop, and there's been speculation ever since about moving me back to third base. That's a long story, which we'll get into when the time comes, but in 1996, when I did play six games at third in the middle of the season, without preparation, it was disconcerting. In Boston, I found myself standing at the plate after fouling a ball down the third base line and wondering why Tim Naehring, the Red Sox third baseman, was playing so far off that line. Was there some trick to the configuration of the stands at Fenway Park I didn't know about? Should I be playing that far over as well? Those aren't the thoughts you want in the batting box, but they're the kind I can't keep out.

For 1997, I've been moved back to third base permanently. I take this as a new challenge, almost like a second career, because I'm seriously competitive and persistent. I'm determined to play that position as well as I had in the minors, and as well as I had in Baltimore before Earl moved me to shortstop.

Baseball fans from outside Baltimore who tuned in to the hoopla surrounding streak week in September 1995 probably thought that the media and the fans had been on my side from the day I did crack that Oriole lineup in 1982. They probably didn't know that in 1988, when the team was struggling and I was playing with a one-year contract and trade rumors were flying, some observers suggested that perhaps a change of scenery for me would benefit all concerned. Four years later, when I signed my next contract after "protracted negotiations" and during a slump—in the end, I went 73 games without a homer, which was grim—the Oriole front office flashed the terms of the deal on the big screen at the new ballpark at Camden Yards before the game, and I heard more than a few scattered boos. Maybe I did deserve some boos that day, but not because I needed a day off, like some people said. Had I needed a day off the previous year, 1991, when I hit .323 with 34 homers and 114 runs batted in? I guess not. So when the organization makes a financial commitment to a multiyear deal with me, when I'm able to play every day and make contributions to the defense, my instinct during a batting slump is to buckle down, take extra batting practice, and prove the critics wrong.

In short, playing 2,131 consecutive ball games and breaking Lou Gehrig's record had nothing to do with extraordinary talent, which I don't have, or a bionic body, which I don't have either, or a burning desire for the spotlight, which can be fun at times and is really gratifying, but has its drawbacks as well. No, when I look back over those fourteen seasons of consecutive games with the Baltimore Orioles, I have to agree with Billy Ripken's blunt conclusion. Billy knows me because he's my younger brother, and he knows baseball because he's also a major leaguer, and he says I broke that record because I *could*.

What a remarkable two nights those were, September 5 and 6, 1995, an experience that I still feel more deeply in my heart and bones than I can possibly express with any words. I said afterward that it was almost like a dream; over a year later, it still feels that way in my memory. In fact, I hadn't even looked at the videotape of the streak week games until I was working on this book. I didn't want to mess with my memories of that dream. Like my father, I don't naturally or easily wear my emotions on my sleeve, and I worry that I was never able to express fully how extraordinarily touched I was by the response of the fans throughout 1995, and how grateful I was and am. Probably the most eloquent "remark" I made was when I came out of the dugout for another curtain call and touched my heart with my hand. For me, that said it all.

And wasn't it a strange record? After all, I hadn't broken Ty Cobb's mark for base hits or Babe Ruth's record for home runs. I hadn't struck out 5,000 batters. Emotionally, I could understand the fans' excitement; intellectually, I couldn't figure it out, and I still can't. I had showed up and honored the game of baseball by playing as well as I could and as often as I could—every day. I'd been lucky regarding injuries and illness, and I'd hung in there when I'd been criticized. I don't think of myself as an accidental hero, exactly; *unintentional* is the better word. By playing every game I was paid to play, I unintentionally played 2,131 in a row and broke Gehrig's famous record.

What if I'd pulled a hamstring in 1985 or 1988 or 1992 or 1994 and been forced to miss a day or a week? What if I'd gotten the flu and missed a series? Just one absence over those fourteen years and I would have been exactly the same ballplayer—posting the same numbers, earning the same salary, enjoying the same reputation as an iron-man kind of guy who puts in the innings—but I would have been a very different public figure. I might have been working on a new and modest streak of consecutive games, but I wouldn't have been the recipient of tens of thousands of letters, or the shortstop whose name was mentioned in the same sentence with Gehrig and DiMaggio, or the player some people suggested had the responsibility to save baseball in 1995 following the disastrous labor dispute the year before. Nor would I have been the subject of the article in *Sports Illustrated* that depicted me as the lonely and isolated prisoner of the streak. (Actually, "lonely and isolated" would have been really nice some of the time, like when the guy hiding behind the ice machine in the hotel in Texas jumped out, bat in hand, targeting my autograph, not my money. Usually I'm an easy touch, but I felt no obligation to sign that P-72 model at 1 a.m. Although I might have signed. I was so surprised, I don't remember.)

I've been lucky? No, I've been *unbelievably* fortunate. In the promo I shot for Fox Sports' first-time baseball coverage, the sarcastic mailman asks me if I've seen any rabid Dobermans lately out by shortstop and then mutters as he walks away, "Mister I've-Been-Kissed-By-The-Baseball-Fairy." That line was the actor's ad lib, and a good one. I often wonder whether I've been blessed with most of the baseball luck in the Ripken family. After seven and a half years in the major leagues—mainly good years—my brother Billy spent most of 1995 in the minors with the Buffalo Bisons. Billy was as good an infielder that year as he had ever been, as good as most infielders in the major leagues. But his career had been interrupted for months at a time by an assortment of injuries, and he was trapped in the complicated situation that followed the shutdown of the game, so there he was in Triple-A, playing in a ballpark (New Orleans) that features a Port-A-Can in the visiting dugout and riding 6 a.m. flights from that city to Oklahoma City by way of Atlanta. There's no luck there.

My father's minor league playing career ended in 1961, the year after I was born, when a shoulder injury went undiagnosed for three critical months. Today, that injury would be diagnosed immediately and just about rehabilitated in that period of time. Things might have turned out very differently for him. Cal Ripken, Sr., spent his adult life in the Baltimore organization as a minor league player, minor league manager, scout, and then big league coach before he finally got his shot at managing the Orioles in 1987, after Earl Weaver had come out of retirement and then quit again. I think Earl knew that the O's were a team in transition, and he didn't need that frustration. So my dad got the job, but after just one full season and six games into the following one, he was summarily thrown over the side of that sinking ship. The following year he was brought back as the third base coach, then he was fired again four years later. Those episodes were tough on the Ripken family, as they would be for any family. But what if my father had inherited Earl Weaver's team in 1983 and then managed that solid, veteran squad to victory in the World Series, as Joe Altobelli had done? Again, things might have turned out very differently for him. I hope he hasn't spent as much time thinking about that scenario as I have.

With the Orioles, I've seen it all. In the thirteen years before I arrived on the major league scene in 1981, the team had exactly one manager— Earl Weaver. Now, in sixteen years, I've played under seven managers; eight, if you count Earl twice. The organization with the best cumulative record in the major leagues in the sixties and seventies, including eighteen consecutive winning seasons, six appearances in the World Series, and three championships, proceeded to have five losing seasons between 1986 and 1991. In 1988, we lost those first 6 games under the generalship of my father, then 15 more under Frank Robinson for a total of 21 losses to start the season, the record all of us would like to forget. Billy Ripken, a sophomore in the league at the time, became the national symbol of our futility and disgrace, featured on the cover of Sports Illustrated slumped on the bench after another loss, head lodged against his bat in despair. For baseball's most successful franchise during the previous two decades and for my whole family, that was the embarrassing pits.

The national pastime has been through the wringer, too. Not by coincidence, I was called up from Rochester at the conclusion of the fifty-six-day players' strike in 1981, when everyone involved swore to the fans, "Never again!" But "never again" happened yet again in 1985, 1990, and 1994. The year before I came up, Nolan Ryan with the Houston Astros had become baseball's first million-dollar player. When I broke Lou Gehrig's record fifteen years later, the *average* major league salary was more than that. We're talking about a lot of money—not NBA money, but a lot. The salaries reflect the fact that the game is no longer *just* a game, but part of the vast entertainment industry. Salaries grew as the business grew. Still, they were also the reason the owners canceled the World Series in 1994.

For the Orioles and for the game itself, it's been a sometimes bumpy, sometimes controversial ride. For Cal Ripken, Jr., what could I do but lower my head and soldier on, one game at a time? That's my style. Years ago I told a reporter, "Some people will never understand why I go about things the way I do, and that's okay. But I'll keep going about them the same way until it's proven to me that there's a better way." It hasn't happened yet. To this day, the old-school Oriole Way that I absorbed from my father is the only way I know.

Chapter Two

People who know me and know my father also know that this apple didn't fall very far from the tree. In this regard I was fortunate, I think, because my father is a stout tree. He just happened to be the unusual kind that moved around a lot. In 1957, the year my parents got married, my mother, Violet Gross, worked in the office of a local insurance company in Aberdeen, Maryland, and Cal Ripken, Sr., was one of the catchers for the Phoenix team in the old Arizona-Texas League. That was Dad's first year with the Baltimore organization. By the time I was born three years later, he was playing for Appleton, Wisconsin, in the Triple-I League. I was a big baby, at nine pounds two ounces, and Boog Powell, Dad's teammate and two years later the starting first baseman in Baltimore, quipped, "He must have been born wearing his catcher's gear." Dad made it home to see his first son about a week after I was born, when the minor league season was over.

I don't claim any credit, but 1960 *did* turn out to be my father's best as a hitter while playing under Earl Weaver, who was still eight years away from his promotion to the majors. Senior's career batting average in the minors was .253 for ten teams over six seasons, perfectly respectable for a catcher, but the year I was born he hit .281, with nine homers and 74 RBIs. The following spring training, two foul tips in succession winged him on his right shoulder—his throwing shoulder. The first X ray showed nothing; when the pain persisted for three months and got to the point where he couldn't throw at all, a second X ray revealed a dislocation—an unusual kind, because no one had ever heard of foul tips causing a dislocated shoulder. By this time Dad's deltoid muscle had atrophied, and he had a tendon problem as well. The treatment program consisted of rest, with full recovery estimated to be at least several *years*. That's hard for me to comprehend, since I play in an era when most shoulder injuries can be rehabilitated within months, and when entire tendons can be replaced and rehabed within one year.

Practically speaking, if my father wanted to stay in the game he'd have to shift his sights from playing to coaching and managing, and he accepted the organization's offer to become the player-manager in Leesburg, Florida, a Class-D team. After that season ended, he finished out the year in Rochester, New York, where they needed a catcher. (Dad could still catch the ball and handle pitchers; he just couldn't throw well.) The following year he took over as the manager in Aberdeen, South Dakota, where he also handled his final games behind the plate. Altogether, he and my mother and their growing family lived part-time in fourteen towns in ten states over eighteen years: Phoenix, Arizona; Wilson, North Carolina; Pensacola, Florida; Amarillo, Texas; Appleton (Fox Cities), Wisconsin; Little Rock, Arkansas; Leesburg, Florida; Rochester, New York; Appleton a second time; Aberdeen, South Dakota; Tri Cities (Kennewick), Washington; Aberdeen a second time; Miami, Florida; Elmira, New York; Rochester a second time; Dallas, Texas; Asheville, North Carolina, and, of course, Aberdeen, Maryland.

I was fifteen years old before my sister, two brothers, and I spent a whole summer at home in Maryland. That year, 1975, Dad was based in Baltimore while working as a special assignment scout for the Orioles, scouting both the big leagues and top amateur prospects. The following year he became the bullpen coach with the Orioles.

Before any of the four kids were old enough for school, the family traveled with Dad down to Florida in February. Today, the Orioles use an eighteen-wheeler to haul equipment to spring training, and any families making the trip from the Baltimore area are welcome to utilize this service for their own stuff. In Dad's era, everybody was on their own. The blue Buick station wagon was the main Ripken workhorse for years before it finally gave out and was replaced by the white Electra, which we dubbed the "lead sled"; actually, all Dad's cars over the years were the big, American-style sedans he favored and the size his family required.

We'd stay in Florida for a month, maybe six weeks, then load everything up and drive to whatever town Dad would be managing that summer. We towed a big trailer of household items covered with a tarp and with the dismantled swing set bolted underneath; tricyles and bicycles were lashed onto the roof. On the road, we played a lot of license plate games, and we enjoyed hanging out the windows sporting plastic Army helmets attached with elastic bands. We dared them to blow off, and they did, and once or twice Dad even turned the car around to go get one. When things got a little too enthusiastic, occasionally he reached back over the front seat to "correct" one or more of us crammed into the backseats: Ellen, the oldest kid; myself, seventeen months back; Fred, another fifteen months back; Billy, the baby by three years; and Scooby, the mutt who joined us for the last couple of years on the road. We also spent an inordinate amount of time in gas stations with breakdowns, waiting for the water pump or whatever to get fixed. A mechanical whiz, Dad was excellent in his diagnoses, of course.

As the kids got older and had to stay in school in Aberdeen, we skipped the first part of spring training before joining Dad over the Easter vacation. On those "solo" trips over the years, my mother got pretty good figuring out the problem when the car broke down. For my part, I just worried whether the Easter bunny would find us in our motel. I wanted that chocolate. Today, my son Ryan wants his chocolate. We call him Chocolate Boy.

Toward the end of the baseball season, the family had to return home to Aberdeen before Dad did, although when we were smaller we might miss the first week of school. Dad arrived back home briefly in September, but he was soon off again to Clearwater, Florida, where he ran the Orioles' Instructional League camp. That part of his job ran into November, and when we were in elementary school we enrolled down there for a couple of months. But lessons in those classes weren't coordinated with the ones in Aberdeen, so the next two years our teachers drew up lessons, which we took with us. Mom conducted home schooling, in effect.

Returning to Aberdeen for the winter, we'd drive back in tandem with clubhouseman Jimmy Tyler, who had the black station wagon with BALTIMORE ORIOLES painted in orange on the side. It was a kick for the kids to ride with Jimmy part of the way. Before these various trips around the country, one of our getaway chores was to clean the car. One year we ran short of time, and Dad said we could skip the car, but I went out and started vacuuming while he was off on other chores. He heard me and walked out to see what was going on. I remember that episode as one of those moments of early connection between a father and a son. He was proud that I had taken the initiative.

All in all, missing a few weeks of school here or there really wasn't a problem, but friendwise, life on the road was tough on me and my brothers and sister. By choice, maybe, but by necessity, too, the Ripkens have always been pretty self-sufficient. We relied mainly on each other for friendship and activities. Maybe this is why first grade was so traumatic for me: I ran off quite a few times, and still have a vivid memory of waiting until Mrs. St. Pierre was distracted or briefly out of the room before going over to the closet, getting my coat and bag, and running out the door and down the hallway. Mom thought about holding me back a year, but I finally settled in with the help of Mrs. St. Pierre, a really nice teacher who took a special interest in me.

It seems like everyone who knew me as a kid now recalls how precocious I was as a baseball player, but that could be said for all of us Ripken kids. We grew up with baseballs and bats in our hands, but we also had basketballs, footballs, soccer balls, Ping-Pong balls, and bowling balls. We were pretty good at most sports. We were also good at breaking windows. The older we got, the more Dad had to replace, but he only got angry if he determined that the ball had come from inside the room. At home in Aberdeen, he eventually taught us how to cut and install our own glass for the garage windows, which we broke with such regularity he finally opted for Plexiglas.

I remember laundromats around the country, although Mom says that would have been mainly in Asheville, North Carolina, in the early seventies. We kids helped with the wash and entertained ourselves with simple games that became complicated because of our competitive natures. Sometimes we united as a team against an adversary, like in Miami, where we took on the neighborhood kids with rotten mangoes, and one summer in Rochester in a more serious fight with rocks against local kids who were razzing us about our dad's losing streak. Most of the time, though, we vied against each other in laundromats and every-where else.

I was so competitive and annoying that Elly and Fred tried to keep me out of these games at times, but I usually managed to bully or beg my way into the action. In cutthroat hearts, they tried to stick me with the queen, and I tried to fake them out with a show of disgust, then shoot the moon. One year in Miami, my competitiveness caused a trip to the emergency room. I'd been teaching a friend how to play checkers and lured her into some wrong moves that set up a quadruple jump for myself. When I leaped up in joy after that triumph, I slammed my head against the windowsill. Five stitches, according to Ripken lore. A week later another little girl split open the front of Billy's head swinging a bat, and Mom took him to the same emergency room. Nine more stitches.

I was a bad loser and a bad winner, too, and I got what I deserved. During all the coverage of the streak, someone in the family circulated the story that I cheated my own grandmother at canasta. I don't remember that, but I might have occasionally drawn too many cards on her, because I did cheat on everyone else. For years I kept detailed statistics on all these family games, for the sole purpose of trying to prove that I was the best. The only positive note here is that I finally figured out that the only proof of how good you are is if you play within the rules.

When my father's team was playing at home over the summer, I listened in as he talked on the phone to the farm director. I also watched him sitting every morning at the dining room table in our rented house or apartment, typing his baseball reports on the old Smith-Corona. In those days, the organization wanted daily reports on each player, and there were no faxes or modems. Triplicate reports on carbon paper instead, with the box score from the local newspaper attached. Mom took over at the typewriter for the monthly evaluations on every player in the league, using a stack of Dad's notes. That chore took her a day or two, and she could type really fast. Old one-finger, as she teased Senior, was pretty good given his limitation, but she blew him away in a contest we organized, both of them typing "Now is the time for all good men . . ."

At some point Dad would usually take a break from this office work for a quick game of volleyball or basketball. Mom was usually cooking, but if she could join us, three-on-three was a natural: Mom, Dad, four kids. She had a really good two-handed set shot, going back to her days playing half-court girls' basketball in high school. Our big meal of the day was early in the afternoon. My father was and still is a steak eater, so we had steak as often as possible, grilled outside. Dad actually did say "Drink your milk, Cal," the true-to-life line from a series of radio advertisements the two of us did years later for a regional milk cooperative, about which he was teased endlessly. For all our meals at home, he enforced a strict dress code—clean hands, clean shirt, combed hair—and on the rare occasions we went out to a restaurant, he frowned on blue jeans; sometimes Elly had to wear a dress. We had a dress code for bowling and for ball games, too.

Generally speaking, in order to keep my father and me straight, Mom called him Rip or Cal and me Calvin or, rarely, Junior. But most of the time there wasn't any confusion, because by early afternoon Dad was gone to the ballpark—weekends included, of course—and half the time he was gone, period, on a road trip with his team. As my father himself said many times, during the baseball season he spent as much or more time with his players as he did with his family. Then again, almost every baseball manager says something similar every spring training, always leading up to the point that everyone should get along and pull together as a family for six months and wait to pick close friends until October.

When I made the big leagues and Dad was coaching third base for the Orioles, a big deal was made about the father-son relationship. Dad always replied, "They're all my sons." People thought he was just trying to play down the situation, and he was, but he was also stating the truth. He said several times over the years that he spent more time with his players than he did with his own children, and that he feared he had neglected us at times because of his job. But I don't feel that way about Dad's absence. I missed him when he was gone, but he was always *there* in the way that counts. I'm not bitter, nor do I feel some gaping hole in my psyche. I just remember missing him sometimes. One reason I'm so adamant today about spending as much time as possible at home with my own kids, one of the reasons I can't see myself as a manager after I retire, is that I didn't have that time with my own father. He did what he had to do to support his family, and he didn't have many options, but I do, and I'm going to make sure I'm more available for my two kids.

Back home for the winter in Aberdeen, life for us wasn't exactly settled or easy. Even now there's not much money in minor league baseball, and there was less when we were growing up. We were on a budget, like everyone else we knew. When we bought shoes, cost was a definite consideration. Over the winter my father worked about as hard as he did over the summer. He managed a pharmacy, drove a delivery truck, worked at a local hardware store and lumberyard. Sometimes it seemed like I saw even less of him during these months than I had over the summer, when at least he was around the house in the mornings before going to the ballpark if the team wasn't on the road. In the off-season, he was out the door at dawn and then he fell asleep on the couch after supper almost every night, dog-tired.

In the early years in Aberdeen, my parents lived in Dad's mother's old house, then in a succession of rented houses until I was six years old. At that time, Dad's off-season job was with the lumberyard owned by Kessler Livezey. My grandfather had also worked for the Livezey family, and so had my uncle Ollie. (Both of my parents have deep family roots in the Aberdeen area; one of my mother's forefathers fought in that vicinity in the American Revolution.) Dad was something of a supervisor for the homes that Kessler Livezey was building, and one of them became his own—and still is. That three-bedroom frame house was just up the hill from what are now the Amtrak railroad tracks and about three miles from the front gate of the famous Aberdeen Proving Ground, where the Army tested its latest munitions with window-rattling blasts. Thanks to that proximity, sudden loud explosions have never bothered the Ripkens. It's quieter now, my parents tell me, because new people moving in across Chesapeake Bay complained, and the Army came up with some kind of muffling procedure for the explosions.

Dad and I were invited to the base for Ripken Day after I won the MVP Award in 1983, and we saw the famous "Mile of Tanks," which also includes field artillery, missiles, coastal batteries, and a German V-2 rocket—several hundred pieces altogether. We drove the old M-60 tank and the latest M-1, and the M-60 was a go-cart by comparison. Manning the M-1, I hit a target several miles away—or so it seemed. Anyway, I couldn't see it from the top of the tank. The video game display I used for targeting worked to perfection. Plaques from the occasion, featuring each of us looking out of a tank, now hang on the wall in my parents' den.

My grandmother lived with us in this house for the last eighteen years of her life, and she was always complaining to her daughter-in-law that the grandchildren didn't help out enough. My mother had to remind her that we now had an electric oven, so nobody needed to cut wood for the stove. In the summer of 1995, reporters and camera crews—three or four a day for a couple of months—made the pilgrimage to Aberdeen to see the Ripken homestead where my parents have lived for thirty years. They found a house that's about the same as it was after Dad converted the basement into the boys' bedrooms, with windows barred maybe not so much to keep thieves out as to keep us in. Dad has converted the old garage into a rec room and storage area, the new replacement garage is equipped with a first-class shop, and there's new siding on the exterior. Basically, though, the same house. The schoolboy and schoolgirl trophies are still where they were decades ago, along with a few from my later career; the wedding pictures of each of the four kids are grouped around the antique pendulum clock in the den. If the house hasn't changed much by now, I don't guess it ever will.

After we finally moved into our own home, we were settled for eight or nine months of the year. Still the itinerant summers stand out in memory. Elly, Fred, Billy, and I understood that we didn't live like most families. I also thought, at least in the early years, that those were exciting, adventuresome summers. It was neat to have a father in professional baseball. Other kids thought that was neat, too, even though there wasn't any celebrity involved because you didn't see my father with the big league club or on television. As I got older I began to feel left out at school in Aberdeen, but there are a lot worse ways to grow up, I know now.

Today, we Ripkens remain a close family, but we don't see each other all that often, mainly at Christmas and then at a family party Mom throws sometime early in the year, before spring training. At least, Billy and I don't often see everyone else because for almost eight months we're off playing baseball. Some things just never change. I might not actually talk with Elly or Fred for many months, but when one of us does pick up the phone, it's as if we had talked yesterday. Maybe all of us spent so much time with each other growing up and were so dependent on each other for friendship that by now this closeness is taken for granted. I know that the recent widely publicized events in my own life haven't changed the family "chemistry" at all. I seriously doubt whether the streak was ever mentioned at family gatherings in all the years it was slowly building up, and after September 6, 1995, it was ancient history and probably never mentioned again. That's the way we are.

In 1983, after the Orioles had won the World Series and I'd been voted Most Valuable Player in the American League, I was honored with a banquet by the Advertising Club in Baltimore. That was a relatively new experience for me, and I was nervous, and as a way to settle down when I reached the podium, I turned to my parents and said, "I've never said 'Thank you' enough to my parents, especially my mother. She was always there when I needed her. I just want to say how much I appreciate it."

The fact is, Mom was both mother and father a lot of the time. For certain school activities, for father-son events, she had to substitute for Dad, in a sense. Today, a lot of kids are successfully raised in single-parent households, of which there are many more than when I was growing up, but I knew my situation was different from the norm of that era, and there were times when I really wanted my father. At my Little League games, Dad couldn't be there. Mom always was, sitting in the same area along the third base line in the lawn chair she had probably picked up from some discard pile and rewebbed herself. She sat down the line because she didn't want to hear the parents in the bleachers yelling at the kids on the field. By the end of the season, other parents who felt the same way had joined her. I remember one time overhearing some parent console his or her kid after the boy's team had lost to me, the pitcher: "That's okay, his dad's with a professional team. He works with him every day. He's got an unfair advantage." My dad may have been with the Orioles, but my mother was the one keeping score, telling me to keep my head down at the plate, and patting me on the back after the game—a good game or a bad one, it didn't matter. She knows baseball pretty well. She always said (and still says) that half my problem during slumps it that I think too much. Dad says no, I'm adjusting and readjusting, which any hitter has to do. I split the difference on this disagreement. My brother Billy jokes that when he went into the minor leagues and called home for encouragement, Mom would speak up first, then hand the phone to Dad, who would repeat what she'd just said. That sounds about right, if a bit stretched.

My mother always says "Family is *family*," and she should know because she was more than just a substitute for Dad. She was the glue. For all those years, she was usually in charge of the Ripken road show. When you think about those cross-country trips—the longest was in 1965, three thousand miles to Kennewick, Washington, undertaken just a few months after Billy was born—all that packing and unpacking all over the place, the temporary quarters, the pregnancies and babies and arguing kids, the tight budget, the *laundromats*—it must have been difficult for her in many ways. My mother is a wonderful woman, plenty resourceful, down-to-earth, and she had the authority to handle us when she needed it. She could get mad. Coming back from Asheville after Easter vacation one year, she turned around to yell at us for fighting in the backseat, but in the process she also hit the accelerator and almost ran off the road, and that made her even more angry. For that, she cut off our allowances.

My mother says now that she'd have pity on anyone living today like we did, but at the time, those were the facts of life. She didn't like the phrase "baseball widow," because she didn't feel hers was a "negative" situation. It was just the way things were, and you went about your business and got the job done.

My father loved every minute of his work, I'm sure, and he is, by nature, a hardworking man. His motto was, "If you didn't want to work, you shouldn't have hired out." He said this to his kids as we spent hours at the card table on rainy days matching the nuts and bolts he had stored in coffee cans for just such a rainy day, and he said this to his baseball players. He also said to them, "It's like a bank, men. You can't take out more than you put in." I'm sure he still says this at the summer camp he runs. I've gone out there periodically and can testify that it's no-frills, one-on-one instruction. On the ball field he often said, "Practice doesn't make perfect. *Perfect* practice makes perfect." And at some point he doubtless said, "No pain, no gain." In Aberdeen, he took whoever wanted to go to an abandoned high school gym to pitch to us in order to get his arm in shape for throwing batting practice in Florida. He also hit us sharp ground balls on the hardwood floors, which was great practice for future infielders—and for real infielders, because we worked out in that gym a few times when I was in the minors. When a ball nailed one of the kids on the shin, Senior asked what the problem was. "It only weighs five and a quarter ounces," he said. We heard this *all* the time.

Senior has incredible skill with the fungo bat—as far as I know, he's still the only man to hit the loudspeakers hanging from the roof of the Kingdome in Seattle—and with tools and machinery of all sorts. I think his resourcefulness stems in large part from the fact that he became the "man of the house" when he was only nine years old, after his father died in a car crash. His two brothers were much older and already gone from home. With his own kids, Dad was always conscientious in his role as *provider*. He didn't pressure us to get jobs to earn spending money; he wanted us to have all the extracurricular experiences he was denied. As a teenager he worked on a farm, in gas stations, on construction jobs, all of which was good training, as it turned out, for managing in the minors, where the job description can be rather broad: bus driver, mechanic, carpenter, landscaper, mason, general handyman.

Senior carried tools in his back pocket because he never knew when Iron Mike, the dangerous, spring-loaded Dudley pitching machine, would break down. When the organization finally decommissioned one of the oldest of the machines, Dad took it apart, brought it home to Aberdeen, and reassembled it for our use. If the bus driver needed a break from driving, Dad got behind the wheel, and if the bus needed repair, sometimes he could do that, too. If the infield somewhere was terrible, and it often was, Dad would get on a tractor and work the dirt with a drag. When the Orioles moved their spring training complex from Fernandina Beach north of Jacksonville to Biscayne College (now St. Thomas University) in Opa-Locka, a suburb of Miami, Dad was asked to work with clubhouseman Jimmy Tyler and supervise the crew on that construction job. But my father is not one for just standing and supervising. He helped level the infield, seed that grass, and pour the concrete for the dugouts.

Senior is meticulous to a fault. In Asheville, I helped the visiting clubhouseman—my brother Fred—shine the shoes. For money, of course. Every pair had to be perfectly waxed, brushed, and buffed, and they were inspected daily by the boss—Dad, not Fred. When the Orioles traveled to Japan for a barnstorming tour after the 1984 season, the rest of us wore our neckties when we got on the plane and then again when we got off seventeen hours later. Only Senior wore his the whole way, unloosened. Among the Orioles, he's still remembered for that feat. When I came up to the majors, I could drive him crazy by flipping up the bill of my cap, Gomer Pyle–style. At the ballpark, Dad always took two packs of sugar, emptied them into his coffee, rolled up the little packages meticulously, and threw them away. Always the same. However, don't mistake any of this for superstition. Dad has a few of the usual ballplayer superstitions, like sticking to the same breakfast during a hot streak, but he's nothing like Earl Weaver, who had a list of them, according to Oriole folklore. (I seem to have inherited this general disinterest from Senior. I was married on Friday the thirteenth.)

Dad is a *serious* gardener. Many summers he put in a second vegetable patch at the edge of the local soccer field, down the hill from the house in Aberdeen. One time he came home from an Orioles road trip to find his crop of cantaloupes and watermelons leveled to the ground. At first he thought someone had taken to them with a lawn mower, then he realized a groundhog had been responsible. He knew all about these animals from childhood encounters in the woods in the area. Angered, he got up the next morning at dawn (not unusual; he kept farmers' hours, even when he didn't have to) and carried his folding chair, newspaper, thermos of coffee, cigarettes, and shotgun down to the field. Several hours passed, and Dad decided that the animal had gone elsewhere for breakfast. At eight o'clock, with the paper read and the coffee consumed, he was just about to break camp when the groundhog emerged from between rows of corn in the adjacent field and headed directly for Senior's string beans. Dad nailed him with the first shot and then displayed his trophy to the family in the backyard. I wasn't there, but I understand the rest of the Ripkens downplayed the achievement. Mom was upset.

Like I've always said, Dad is the straightest shooter I've ever known. Consider the now-famous hand-crank story, which I did witness. Because my father was absent so often, he did as much as he could around the neighborhood when he was home, and neighbors reciprocated in his absence. One thing he could do over the winter was plow the roads and driveways after heavy snowfalls, because the city crews were slow to get to us. For this he used an old wooden "V" plow towed by a tractor, usually, but once or twice by our car. We kids would stand on the plow to hold it down. One year, he took me and Fred to the nearby barn to get the tractor. With Dad, everything was instruction, and cranking this engine was no different. I was wondering, When am I ever going to have to crank a tractor?—maybe I even made a sarcastic remark—but Dad explained the right way, and the wrong way: windmilling the crank 360 degrees, because if the engine backfires, it might throw the crank off. After no luck cranking the right way, Dad looked at Fred and me and said, "Now, don't you ever do this, but I'm going to windmill it now." Sure enough, the engine backfired and the crank flew off and cracked him right on the forehead. Blood spurted out and Dad reached for a greasy rag. When we got in the car, I thought we were going to the hospital for stitches, but he told me to pull in at the house, where he put on some butterfly bandages. Back in the car, I assumed we were *now* driving to the hospital, but he directed me back to the barn.

He got the tractor started and we plowed the neighborhood streets. So, yes, Dad can be hardheaded, and I'd say I inherited quite a bit of this feature, and I think that some of my subsequent baseball behavior must have been an effort to prove to myself or to him or to someone that I'm a gamer, too.

My dad's stubborn rectitude is why he refused to participate in the annual tomato-growing contests between Earl Weaver and Pat Santarone, the Orioles' veteran groundskeeper in the sixties and seventies. The plants were out in the home bullpen, and Weaver and Santarone were always charging one another with all kinds of foul play, such as urinating on the other's plants. This kind of thing might have been okay in Dad's mind; what he objected to was their practice of snipping off all but a few blooms from each plant. The resulting fruit was a totally false indication of excellence of both the plant and the husbandry, in his opinion. Plus the contest gave too much weight to the size of the tomato, not to the taste. So he let Weaver and Santarone have their contest, but everyone in the Orioles clubhouse waited for the day when Senior brought in the first box of his Better Boys, which he had determined years before to be the best variety for the local climate and soil. We kids spent hours cleaning the tiniest pebbles out of his garden and hauling them to the woods in the reinforced Red Flyer wagon, because we didn't have a wheelbarrow. Today, in the same backyard garden at the top of the rise beyond the swimming pool, the hot tub, and the horseshoe pit, Dad still plants his Better Boys. When that preference leaked out during the streak coverage, he received all sorts of seeds from tomato gardeners pushing other varieties, but he didn't convert.

Dad doesn't believe in converting. He still plays golf with the classic Louisville Slugger Power-Bilt blades he bought in 1957, still smokes his Lucky Strikes right down to the nub, and still looks at things "face value." There aren't too many grays in his world, my mother once teased him. Depending on the situation, he says either "That's water under the bridge" or "That's water over the dam" or "I'll cross that bridge when I come to it."

When I was in high school, he told reporters that he looked on me as "just another prospect," to my mother's mild annoyance. When he called from California to announce the likelihood that I'd be drafted, she replied sarcastically, "I'm glad you noticed." When people started asking my mother some years back if I could or would break Gehrig's record, she asked in reply, "Why not?" Barring injury, she figured it was not only possible but probable. But my father wouldn't address the question at all. What could be the point in even thinking about such a hypothetical inquiry? At the first press conference at spring training in 1995, someone asked me what my father thought of the streak, and I answered in all seriousness, "I don't know."

On the other hand, the warning against judging a book by its cover applies perfectly to my father, who might be a classic case of the guy with the tough exterior but melting inside. I know he loves his kids, and we love him. He is one of those men who have strong feelings about hiding their feelings, and I inherited some of that trait. You can imagine my surprise when he finally let loose with emotion when the Orioles clinched the division title against Milwaukee in 1983. He poured a beer over my head. When the press took notice of this outburst Dad said, "I guess the father in me finally came out." When Eddie Murray and I were in the running for Most Valuable Player that fall, Dad told everyone he'd be just as happy whoever won. In our family we all love Eddie, but I seriously doubt that statement. And then there was the cautionary speech Dad started delivering shortly after I did win the award, stipulating that you have to judge the player over his entire career, not just for a season or two. That's vintage Cal Ripken, Sr. When my mother heard about that remark she told him it sounded "cold" and asked him to ease off. He did. There's even a theory among the Ripken kids that our father has softened up in recent years. Asked in the old days about his greatest experience or some similar question, Dad always said it hadn't happened yet. After September 6, 1995, he told the crowd at a parade in Aberdeen that now it probably had.

Maybe my father could have been a successful major league catcher if he hadn't injured his shoulder. We'll never know, just like we'll never know whether his brother Bill could have had a good major league career. Both of Dad's brothers, Bill and Oliver, played a lot of baseball for the Aberdeen Canners of the Susquehanna League, which played games only on Sunday afternoons. Ollie won the batting title one year. Bill went on to play four years in the Dodgers organization, making it to their Triple-A team in Montreal before quitting because he didn't like the lifestyle. Sometimes players use that excuse when in fact they just aren't good enough, but I hear that Bill probably was good enough. He was working for the bank in Aberdeen when he was recruited a second time by Branch Rickey himself, but Bill turned him down.

Coming up through the minors, I heard a lot of stories about frustrated fathers pushing their sons to achieve something they never did. You might think that my father pushed me into baseball, and pushed Billy, too. You might think that he pushed my brother Fred, and that Fred the motorcycle mechanic moved *away* from the game in response to Dad's overbearing baseball presence. But Senior wasn't that way at all. That remark about judging not just my first two years but my whole career must have been some kind of motivation for me, but I'm not playing the game for him. Nor do I think he has ever lived his baseball life through me. Even if Dad had been able to come to my Little League games, he wouldn't have been one of those fathers screaming for blood. He feels there's too much emphasis on winning at that level. Let the kids play and have fun.

My father would have been the last person in the world to try to pressure one of his sons into playing professional baseball. One of his strongest beliefs is that you should do in life what you enjoy. He believes that a major problem in this society is that too many people are doing jobs they don't really enjoy and find rewarding. Dad has also said he's a blue-collar man and proud of it. "Blue-collar people can be as happy as anyone," he firmly believes, and I agree. He felt a little guilty about all the coverage the Ripken family got during my streak, all of it almost embarrassingly positive. He told reporters there are a lot of good families in the country, and they should get some attention and credit, too.

Dad always said, "Be yourself and prove yourself." The pressure he *did* exert on his children was this: whatever we did in life we should do correctly and to the best of our abilities. He hates anything shoddy or lazy. My brother Billy says I broke Lou Gehrig's record because I could. I might add, on behalf of my father: and because I could, I *should*.

Senior was inducted into the Orioles' Hall of Fame during the 1996 season. At the banquet that preceded the official pre-game installation, he was funny and blunt and foursquare in his remarks, got in a couple of needles here and there, and then said in conclusion that he accepted the honor on behalf of all the equally dedicated men he had worked with in the minor leagues for all those years. Then it was my turn to say something, and I hadn't prepared anything beyond a couple of notes scribbled on a paper napkin. I wasn't even certain I wanted to speak—or put it this way: I knew I wanted to speak, but I didn't know if I could say what I wanted to say. It's difficult for me to talk about my father and what he means to me. So I started with a few stories and jokes, took advantage of the opportunity to needle my brother Billy, who was in the audience, and then referred to my own children, Rachel, six years old at the time, and Ryan, three. They'd been in a bickering mode for weeks, and I explained how one day I heard Rachel taunt Ryan, "You're just trying to be like Daddy." I wanted to break things up but also put some kind of positive spin on the situation. That's the parent's job, right? After a few moments of indecision I had turned to Rachel and asked, "What's wrong with trying to be like Dad?"

When I finished telling this story at the banquet, I added, "That's what I've always tried to do."

Chapter Three

When my father was managing the Rochester Red Wings in 1969 and '70, he'd come into the boys' bedroom on Saturday mornings and shake me in my bed to see if I wanted to go with him to an early clinic he and a couple of his players held for Little Leaguers and their coaches. Fred was uninterested, Billy was too young, and Elly wasn't invited, or so she says, because this was before girls played Little League, but I usually went along, and not for the baseball. Sitting in the stands watching the clinic for two or three hours was boring, but it was my chance to have Dad to myself on the rides back and forth, and I knew he enjoyed having me along. I was nine years old. For my tenth birthday the second summer in Rochester, I took my first plane ride, joining him on the road for games against the Tidewater Tides and Richmond Braves. A real grown-up thing to do. I was with him all the time and wore a full uniform when the team was on the field. The ultimate baseball field trip, as well as my first time away from "home."

By the time we lived in Asheville, North Carolina, during the summers of 1972, '73, and '74, all of us kids were old enough to help out at the park in some useful way, selling candy, working in the clubhouses. I was a batboy as well. Elly couldn't go into the clubhouses, and she resented that, but she swept the bases after the fifth inning, and would occasionally playfully whack the umpire on the butt or kiss him on the cheek. Dad didn't mind; he just told her to keep her eye on the games so she'd know which gesture was more appropriate.

Aside from our chores, however, I was the only one of the three older kids who voluntarily spent much time at the park before the games. I wore my professional-looking batboy uniform at all times. Of course, Dad was conscientious about doing everything right on the field, and he would never have interrupted the pre-game routine in order to play around with me—that's not the Ripken way—but he let me hit some balls and field some grounders before everybody else arrived. However, I had to stand on the *outfield grass* taking ground balls so I wouldn't scuff up the infield dirt for his real players. During batting practice I was allowed to shag fly balls, but I wasn't allowed on the infield, except when the infielders needed me to take their throws, when I was protected by the screens in front of first and second base. (This prohibition was smart policy. One time at Memorial Stadium, when I was quite a few years older, about sixteen, I sneaked onto the infield during batting practice and took a hard shot off my wrist. That hurt, and, worse than that, it was embarrassing. I slunk back to the outfield.) Sometimes in Asheville I donned Dad's old catching gear and got behind the plate for some throws from the BP pitcher—Senior—and these were the hardest pitches I'd ever seen.

When I was finally old enough to take advantage of the baseball opportunities afforded by my father's job, I did so with a vengeance. It also turned out that I already knew more than was expected, so I must have been paying better attention during those Saturday clinics in Rochester than I'd realized at the time. Now I tried to soak up everything I could. I pestered the players for tips, and I questioned them about the smallest details I observed. One afternoon I noticed that Doug DeCinces put on his sanitary socks and stirrup socks and then rolled them differently from my father. I wanted to know why. (Answer: No particular reason.)

During the O's actual games, I was watching, not just goofing off. And at some point I suddenly decided that these Double-A baseball players were making a good living at the game. Dad might be working twelve hours a day twelve months a year to support his family, but most of these guys were single and self-sufficient and, as far as I could tell, living the good life. I was impressed. The question I've been asked more often than any other over the past fifteen years is what I would have done for a career if I hadn't made it in baseball. I can honestly say I've never seriously thought about it, because starting with those three summers in Asheville, all my energy has been focused on pro ball.

Those were really great times. The town of Asheville in the foothills of the Blue Ridge Mountains felt like a home away from home, Dad's clubs were good (a combined 222-193 for the three seasons), and for the last two summers we rented the same house, the former owner's residence behind an old inn. For the first time in my life, I had a separate bedroom. In our backyard, I played hundreds of baseball games against myself, if necessary, or with Fred and Billy for some one-on-one or two-on-one. Against Billy, I got only one out at the plate, and I had to play left-handed in the field. We had two teams, the Orioles against the Reds— the Orioles because they were Dad's team, and they were also good, and the Reds because they were good, too, in the National League. It was easy to root for winning teams. If Dad had worked for the Chicago Cubs, say, who haven't won much during my lifetime, this might have been a serious conflict for a front-runner like me. Among the Orioles, the third baseman was probably my all-time favorite. When I made a great backyard stab I yelled, "Brooks Robinson!"

But the best thing about Asheville was that it happened to have a great Little League program, with good fields and coaches, and with lots of tournaments. I really think those summers were important to my development as a player. We won the state championship one year and went to the southeastern regionals in St. Petersburg, Florida. Dad got time off and the whole family drove down for the games. The team had to collect money door-to-door to meet expenses, even after a local food company donated bus money. As it turned out, the parents couldn't find air-conditioned buses, so we flew down to Florida but drove back in vans. The airline lost my luggage, including glove and uniform. The gear showed up in time for the first game, but I never forgot that close call. When Elly started taking bowling trips—she's an ace, with an average in the 180s, which would theoretically qualify her for the pro tour if she wanted to try—I encouraged her to carry her equipment with her on the plane.

I'm not sure how close we came to going to Williamsport for the Little League World Series, but I do know we won one game in Florida before I gave up the key homer in the final 4–3 loss. That was a high fly, almost a pop-up in my mind, that kept drifting back before barely clearing the left field fence. Distraught, I wanted to blame our fielder for not reaching over and catching the ball, but ended up blaming myself for throwing the pitch in the first place. I was crying along with everyone else.

Great baseball every summer, but then frustration every fall when I'd get back home to Aberdeen and start arguing with my friends about the quality of the league in North Carolina. They had never heard of Asheville and assumed the kids there played on dirt fields. My friends asked me what I'd hit over the summer, and when I said .500 or .600 they put down the competition. That made me mad, of course. No one knew what level I was at because I hadn't showed them firsthand. What's more, in Asheville I had fit in because I was a good player, but I didn't have that advantage back home. As a young teenager, I found this whole situation with my friends—two sets of friends—about as frustrating as anything regarding my life growing up on the road.

Then, after three summers in Asheville, our traveling days were finally over. In 1975, Dad became based in Baltimore to scout for the Orioles before joining the big club the following year. Now I'd be playing all my baseball with my friends and I could show them what I could do. When I made the varsity team as a freshman in high school, in the spring of 1975, they had to quit ragging me, even though I made the team only because we needed a second baseman. I was only fourteen, weighed about 125 pounds, and I was playing against a lot of juniors and seniors. In later years, our manager, Don Morrison, liked to tell the story about the time he was bragging about this "star player" he had coming onto the team as a freshman, and then this star player—myself—tugged on his sleeve and introduced himself in a squeaky, preadolescent voice.

Overmatched at the plate, I was 4-for-about-35 that season. Coach asked me to bunt a lot. One of the stories about that first varsity season that always came up in the streak publicity was the time a huge kid named Steve Slagle flattened me at second base. The ball was a slow bouncer to shortstop, and I was stretching for the throw with my back to Steve, the runner from first. This was a force out situation, there wasn't going to be a double play, but Steve was a football player who thrived on contact and he made an aggressive slide anyway, slamming into my back. In the big leagues, that play might have earned some retaliation, but there's no code at the high school level. Steve thought he was making a heads-up play, and I guess he was. Anyway, I got hit and hit hard, and while flat on my back with the breath knocked out of me I supposedly said, "Don't take me out, Coach. I'm okay!" But what kid wants to come out of any game?

The girls' varsity softball team played their games in the opposite corner of a big field from our games, with no outfield fence for either game. My sister Elly was a star of the girls' team. When a ball from their game rolled onto our field, it was usually her home run. Guys kidded me that my sister had a better arm than I did. I *was* immature physically, and Elly was a terrific athlete, and a year older. We had a lot of good games in the backyard batting cage, up where the horseshoe pit is now. Our mother sometimes expressed regret that her *daughter* had never had the opportunity to play professional ball. And Elly likes to kid that she might have been the third Ripken making some money playing baseball if she had had the opportunity. Sometimes I think she's more than kidding. She would have liked that chance. In high school, she was the All-County third baseman. The team won the state championship her senior year. She lettered all four years in basketball, volleyball, and softball—twelve letters in all, the maximum. She's still passionate about fast-pitch softball—one of her early teams went to the national tournament—but not as much as before back surgery forced her to move to the outfield.

Elly and I not only played on the same field but traveled to the games in the same team bus. Her team was good, and she was often the hero on the ride home. Our team wasn't that good, and I wasn't contributing much, so those were long rides for me. There was also the fact that I was shy and introverted, socially. When Elly's teammates teased me and pinched my cheek, I probably blushed violently. At some point in those years I quit walking home with her, even when our schedules coincided. Now I know this hurt her feelings, but then, it was just too embarrassing.

The good news to report from that freshman baseball season is that I got better toward the end, and for an important reason. For one of the few times, my dad was able to work with me. Although the team wasn't too good, somehow we made the playoffs for our classification, and right before the first game Dad took me into the batting cage in the backyard and we worked on a triggering mechanism that would help me get the bat started sooner. I'd been waiting until the ball was thrown before I made any move at all. I could get away with that in Little League, but not against high school guys who threw harder. In just one session, Dad taught me to turn in my left shoulder during the pitcher's windup. This helped me time the delivery, and it also got more of my body into the swing. In my first at-bat in the playoff game, I stroked a line drive up the middle for a single, and the next time I lined out to center field. Those were the two hardest hit balls I had all year. We developed a baseball confidence on the spot.

In my sophomore year I was once again competitive at the plate—not that this necessarily means much regarding professional prospects. A lot of players hit .500 in high school but aren't considered prospects, for a variety of reasons, including the level of competition in the league. Or maybe the kid has matured quickly for his age but doesn't have the actions scouts are looking for. In my own case, I also hit well in the summer seasons, especially the summer after my junior year, when I played for the Putty Hill Optimists in the Mickey Mantle League based in nearby Parkville. This was a sixteen-and-younger tryout league, essentially an All-Star team that would have been competitive with high school teams stocked with seventeen- and eighteen-year-olds. After I made the Optimists, I was approached by Johnny's, an even better, semi-pro–type team playing in the Babe Ruth League. Johnny's had a great reputation, and I wanted to back out on the Optimists and play for Johnny's instead. In fact, I probably would have done that except that I told Dad what I had in mind, and he set me straight: I had made my commitment to the Optimists, and I would honor it. The Optimists won the district championship in New Jersey and went to the finals in Sherman, Texas, before we lost. And once again, just as in the regional playoffs with my Little League team, I was on the mound for the final loss. Maybe this is why I wanted to be thought of as a position player by the scouts.

The Optimists had games almost every night, but so did the Orioles. Therefore Dad saw almost none of mine, just like he had seen only a few of my high school games. He saw maybe five or six games altogether during those years, and a couple of times he had to leave early. I know I cared about his absence, because when he *was* able to be there I tried too hard and didn't play well. My senior year in high school I struck out a total of four times, I think, and three of those were in one game when Dad was in the stands.

The year I played for the Optimists, I dropped Dad off at Memorial Stadium, drove to my own game, then came back to the stadium to pick him up for the drive home. Waiting for him in the clubhouse I'd talk with Doug DeCinces, Kenny Singleton, Mark Belanger, Eddie Murray, all these guys. Al Bumbry liked to joke that he could tell whether I'd had a good game by the condition of my uniform. If it was dirty, I had some hits; if it was clean, probably not. By that time, I was really into baseball. *Totally* into baseball. Driving home, I peppered my father with questions about the two games, mine and his. I really started to understand how to analyze a baseball game and how to think like a baseball player. Occasionally the Orioles let me work out at Memorial Stadium, and when I was fifteen I cleared the fences off my father. Now Dad was beginning to take me seriously as a ballplayer. Still, the ultimate irony is that he knew much more about me as a soccer player than as a baseball player.

Soccer was the winter game for both of us. He coached two or three different age-group teams each winter, and my senior year I played on his under-twenty-one team, when I was only seventeen. A baseball man of the old school, he might just as easily have been a *soccer* man of the old school if that sport had offered the same professional opportunities. There was a pro soccer league in the Northeast in the fifties and sixties, with teams in Baltimore, Boston, Philadelphia, Trenton, Brooklyn, Bridgetown (Connecticut), and two in New York City, but it was a marginal operation and soon went out of business, partly because it was a summertime league and thus in competition with baseball. The Baltimore Bays played at Memorial Stadium, where the Orioles also played. Growing up, all the Ripken kids played a lot of soccer because Dad loves the game, and loves to teach it as much as he loves to teach baseball. During the World Cup, especially, it's easy to get Senior to analyze the play of midfielders with exactly the same precision and passion with which he analyzes center fielders.

It was on the soccer field my senior year in high school that I was in the biggest fight of my life. Before this game, one of our vans got lost somewhere en route, so we—Fred played on this team of older guys as well—pulled Billy up from his younger team in order to fill out our lineup. At the start of the game I told the other team that the little twelve-year-old kid was my brother, and don't take advantage of him. Immediately, of course, they went right at him with a hard tackle, and words were exchanged. Then a major fight broke out, and Fred was tossed by the referee. In the second half, there were a couple more fights, during which Fred came racing up from our Buick Elektra, where he'd been sitting. He wasn't going to miss out on this action. Dad was in the middle of things, too, trying to break it up to our advantage. Chaos, and the game was finally suspended. The postscript here is that the following summer, when I was off playing rookie ball in the Orioles organization, one of the guys on the other team sued one of our guys for the cost of his dental work. I was subpoenaed, but our lawyers talked their lawyers out of bringing me home. Dad testified, though. The judge dismissed the suit.

That was one of the few fights in which Fred and I were on the same side. More often, we fought each other. When we were little, Elly would sit on my chest and beat me up, and Billy and I scuffled because I taunted him unmercifully before he retaliated in a rage, but Elly was my sister and Billy was four years younger, while Fred and I were close enough in age and strength to have a match. By the time I was nine or ten I was taller but he was stronger, pound for pound. He's built like Dad in that regard: lean, wiry, really strong, and at some point he lifted weights, which made him even stronger. Fred got into *Pumping Iron* in a big way. We fought for a lot of reasons, including silly arguments over TV shows, and sometimes it got a little scary. He'd have no trouble picking up a screwdriver or anything else to throw at me in the heat of battle. Sometimes after we really got into it Fred would say, "I'll get you back." I'd say, "Why don't you get me back right now?" Then he might say, "Well, you gotta sleep sometime."

I wondered, Does he mean that? After all, we slept in the same bedroom. In all our fighting I didn't really want to hurt my brother—I pulled back; I walked away from some fights—and I don't think he wanted to hurt me, but at the time I wasn't absolutely certain. However, I did provoke him, I realize that. A few times I even shattered one of his beautifully constructed model ships.

Finally Dad would take some disciplinary action of his own by ordering us down to what he called the "woodshed," which was the downstairs bathroom. He didn't care whose fault the fight was. He swung the wooden paddle with equal force on both of us. One time Fred hid the paddle, I suspect, because Dad couldn't find it. Okay, he said, follow me out to the garage. So we had to watch with rising anxiety as he deliberately sorted through his scrap plywood to find a piece about the right size, cut a new paddle on his table saw, sanded or maybe taped the handle, and then drilled the holes. Then he took us back inside. And this paddle was bigger than the other one.

I guess the fighting kept Fred and me together. After we got older—fourteen or fifteen—and too big and with better things to do, we went our separate ways, for the most part. I buddied around mainly with some of the high school jocks, while he was off with his pals. Fred told a reporter that he had better physical skills and better instincts than I did when we were kids. Still needling me, after all these years; we've always been good at that. Well, Fred was and is a terrific raw athlete. I have no doubt he could step into the batting cage right now and hit line drives. Everyone in the family remembers the day he climbed onto the high board of the local swimming pool and made a perfect dive. Said he'd been watching the Olympics. He was a good baseball player but preferred soccer, with its nonstop action, and he could kick the dog snot out of a soccer ball (his phrase). Baseball had too much standing around for him.

But Fred was not a *dedicated* athlete. With all the baseball around the Ripken family, maybe he wanted a separate identity. He's a bit of a renegade, too, and one way that expressed itself, I believe, was by *not* playing baseball seriously. We've never talked about the subject in just those terms, but that's what I think. Also, the way it seemed to work out, I got feedback and esteem from our dad through sports, while Fred carved out his niche fixing things and getting into Dad's mechanical interests, with which I have no patience whatsoever. I'd try to care, but eventually I'd take off to go play some game. Meanwhile, our brother Billy took up Dad's athletic *and* mechanical interests; Billy's a really good woodworker.

Like Dad, Fred is pretty much a genius at mechanical work, and he has the perfect family trait for it. He's persistent, and if he sits down to do something, he does it right, like those model ships. He has this innate sense of responsibility and a different kind of competitiveness than I have: he doesn't compete against someone else so much as against himself. Fred's mechanical interests soon led him into motorcycles. My childhood hero was Brooks Robinson; his was Evel Knievel. Today he's a motorcycle mechanic. I don't ride the bikes—I can't; it's in my contract with the Orioles, along with prohibitions against skydiving and skiing and a lot of other activities—but if I did, Fred would be my mechanic, and not just because he's my brother.

I don't guess every high school student gets into soccer brawls that cancel games, but for the most part my high school years were normal and even boring. I was less rowdy than a lot of the guys, although the soccer fight did mark the beginning of a somewhat more aggressive posture. Before that, I hadn't been much of a risk-taker at all. For one thing, I matured late physically. One reason I quit basketball after one season was that the uniform revealed my lack of underarm and chest hair. And if I was on the "skins" team in practice, that was even worse. At the time, I came up with a lot of reasons for playing winter soccer instead—including the fact that I was a better soccer player anyway—but my embarrassment was a big factor. (Football wasn't an option. The uniform covered everything up, but my mother didn't approve of football for any of her sons. She used the fact that we often missed the first week or two of classes in September as a reason that we shouldn't play, but mainly she just didn't want us out there.)

I wasn't likely to go up to a girl to ask for a date, although I ended up with my share of dates, one way or the other. I was a typically awkward adolescent. Just look at the picture of me on my way to the senior prom! (On the other hand, there's a second story behind that picture: I ended up going to our prom with my best friend's girlfriend, and he ended up going with mine. I'm not sure why that happened, but I know we couldn't even go out for dinner beforehand or afterward, because there would have been too much friction.)

I was an Honor Roll student. Math was my best subject, I was always in classes with older kids, and I probably would have studied it in college, although with what career in mind? I don't know. For me, the great thing about math was that there was always a right answer. I could *see* the right answer. Geometry threw me off at first, but then I caught on. For trigonometry and Algebra III my junior year, we had a really good teacher who liked to challenge us with one tough homework problem every night. Early in the semester, the same girl was getting the right answer day after day. She was the only one holding up her hand, but one class the teacher practically said that even she wouldn't be able to solve the next problem. I guess I had less homework than usual that night, and I accepted the challenge. I worked for hours, studied all the books, walked away for a few minutes, came back and studied some more. I was really grinding, and slowly but surely I put it together. At 1 a.m. I wanted to shout when I finally got it right, but I couldn't, because everyone else was asleep.

The next day, I was pretty confident I'd be the only one with the answer. Sure enough, when our teacher asked who'd solved the problem, I looked over at the girl, who did *not* raise her hand. The teacher looked at her, too, naturally, and just as he was about to go to the blackboard to give us the answer, I raised *my* hand. Sure he was surprised. My equations took the entire front blackboard and part of the smaller one on the side wall. It was a great moment for me.

On the baseball field, it was also exciting when the scouts were in the stands. I knew they probably were looking at me, because Aberdeen was not exactly a hotbed for pro scouts. Mike Gustave was the only player who'd ever been drafted out of my high school. That had been in 1974, the year before I made the team as a freshman. When I was drafted four years later Mike was pitching in the minor leagues in the Twins organization, but he never made the majors.

At least one scout talked about bringing in a cross-checker—a supervisor—to come in and take a look at me. Someone said I might even go in the first round of the draft. One observer who wasn't impressed by what he saw of me as pitcher or shortstop was Walter Youse, longtime scout for the Orioles, Angels, and Brewers. This was ironic, because one of Youse's first scouting assignments many years earlier had been to check on the young catcher Calvin Ripken out of Aberdeen, Maryland—my father, who was signed by the Orioles on Youse's recommendation.

Everyone knew that I'd decided to try pro ball rather than take the college route. I was a good student, but my father believes that professional baseball is the best place to develop professional baseball players. I agreed (and still agree). I had an all-consuming drive to get to the majors, and the quickest way to achieve that was to go straight into the pros. I told my coach I wasn't going to college, and I never solicited colleges' attention, although a few letters and queries came through anyway. West Point was interested in me as a soccer player; my mother liked to think they were interested in my academics as well.

I first caught the attention of the scouts on the basis of some strong pitching performances my junior year, and for two seasons it seemed to me that they always came to watch when I pitched, which was every other game. A few did see me play shortstop, and they saw me hit, but most thought of me as a pitcher. This bothered me a little. I had a good fastball—eighty-seven miles per hour, according to one clocking—and a 7-2 record with a .79 ERA my senior year, but I also hit .496 and led the team in hits and RBIs—set the school record, in fact—and played a good shortstop as well. I had reasonable speed. In soccer, I was even considered fast, and playing baseball for Putty Hill I had 21 steals in 22 attempts, and the one time I was out I didn't slide.

Officially, the Orioles had me penciled in as a pitcher-shortstop. Tom Giordano, the scouting director, was thinking of me mainly as a pitcher, but Dick Bowie, the scout, thought I could play every day, and he thought this even more after giving me a private workout at Memorial Stadium in which I hit the ball hard and fielded well. Earl Weaver had also seen me hit some balls in Memorial Stadium, and I heard he was interested in me as a regular player because I had some pop in my bat. When my large size as a shortstop became an issue in Baltimore years later, people thought this disagreement had started before I'd even signed with the team. But I don't think my size was a factor at all back then. I was about six-foot-two, maybe a little taller, and I weighed about 185 pounds. No one knew I'd end up two inches taller and thirty-five pounds heavier.

I told everyone who asked that I'd play anywhere, but I preferred shortstop. So did Dad. Probably a majority of the players on every major league roster pitched in high school, mainly because they were the best athletes, so Dad accepted the fact that I was considered a pitcher, too. However, and speaking as the teacher–evaluator–organization man he was, he explained that if I started as an everyday player but didn't make the grade, I could always go back after a couple of years and try to succeed as a pitcher. But if I started as a pitcher and didn't make it, I was probably out of professional baseball. You can lay off from pitching if you maintain your basic arm strength, but you can't lay off from hitting because there's no substitute for hitting. Facing minor league pitching after four or five years of no hitting at all since high school is really difficult. Numerous big league pitchers have played other positions until they were in their twenties—in 1995, Nerio Rodriguez was a catcher in the Orioles organization; the following year he pitched a few innings for us in the big leagues—but I can't think of one player in recent decades who pitched until he was twenty-one or twenty-two and *then* converted to the field. Michael Jordan's minor league career is instructive on this point. I'm amazed Michael was able to hit even .200 against good Double-A pitching. That's a tribute to his natural talent. I don't think there's any question that the only reason he wasn't able to hit a lot higher was the lost years. Of course, Babe Ruth was initially a pitcher, but that was seventy-five years ago, another era, and no analogy at all. He was a hitter all along. In 1918, Ruth was 13-7 as a starting pitcher with Boston while also leading the majors in home runs, with 11.

Dad wasn't pressuring me about playing a position. He just pointed out the facts and then asked, "What do you want to do?" I took his advice at face value. I wanted to play every day, not so much because I could return to pitching, but because I liked the action. I wanted to be in the lineup. Pitching is great when you're pitching. You're in total control, and there's no better feeling. In high school ball, you pitch or play your position in the field every other game, but in the pros, you start every fifth game. What do you do on the other four days? As a reliever, you pitch more often but fewer innings. And I'm not just making this point now that I've played 2,300-plus consecutive games. I already felt that way when I was seventeen years old.

By the way, and for the record, I think I'd have had a good shot at being a major league pitcher, if not "The Best Pitcher You *Never* Saw," as the headlines sometimes read years later. I had a good fastball, a very good curve, a slider, and a pretty effective change-up taught me by George Bamberger, the O's pitching coach at the time. And I had command of these pitches. Size doesn't always translate into power, but I've got to believe that all the size I put on after I became a pro, combined with greater arm strength, would have translated into a little more speed on the fastball. I probably could've broken ninety.

My senior year, the Aberdeen High School Eagles played for the Class-A state championship about a week before the June draft. I was tired and pitching on one day's rest and I wasn't sharp, and in the fourth inning we were losing 3–1, and the opposing bench jockeys were razzing me about my prospects in the draft. Then I saw the storm clouds rolling

in. Like in the majors, high school rules require five innings for an official game, so I stalled by throwing over to first base. I wasn't counting,
but our manager, George Connolly, told everyone I threw over nine
times. Anyway, the rain arrived and saved the day. In the make-up
game, I was rested and strong, struck out seventeen, threw a two-hitter,
and the Eagles were the state champions. The bench jockeys didn't have
much to say that day.

I didn't know how the Orioles plotted their draft choices, and I didn't
really care. I didn't judge the draft as a contest between me and some
guys in California or Texas. I thought I'd go pretty high, and I didn't
know what the Orioles' priorities were, nor did I know they'd end up
with four picks in the second round. Deep inside, I wanted to be drafted
by the O's, but any organization would have been okay. There are no
guarantees; with trades and everything, you don't know where you're
going to end up anyway. You just need a starting point, and that's what
the draft is. So I drove off for school the morning of the draft not
knowing where I'd be playing baseball one month later. Dad was in
California with the team. I can't report a lot of details about the big
day because it's not one of those indelible moments—in fact, I've
almost forgotten it. I *think* someone from the office brought me the
news at school, but I don't really remember. My mother came to school
but never found me. In any event, the Orioles drafted me as their third
pick of the second round, the forty-eighth selection overall. Bob Horner
out of Arizona State was the first pick in the nation. The Orioles took
third baseman Bob Boyce in the first round, then Larry Sheets and Ed
Hook ahead of me in the second round. The organization had those four
second-round picks because three had been awarded in compen-
sation for losing players to free agency for 1977. If Baltimore hadn't
had those picks, another organization might have taken me, and I'd
probably be playing somewhere else today.

We didn't have a big dinner that night, or any other celebration.
When Dad returned home from his road trip, he conveyed his pride
with a handshake and a look and a certain pat on the back. When we

gathered at home to sign the contract, the Harford County *Aegis* was on hand to record the event. My signing bonus would be paid in two equal installments; I put the first $10,000 in the bank that same day. I was a professional ballplayer, with plans to give the game five or six years. If that career didn't pan out, I'd enroll in college as a twenty-five-year-old. In fact, my signing agreement with the Orioles included a full four-year scholarship to the school of my choice, if things didn't work out on the field.

Has the statute of limitations run out on that clause?

Chapter Four

I'll never forget the first game I played in Paintsville, Kentucky. It was Opening Day, 1978, for the Highlanders in the all-rookie Appalachian League, and their management had draped red-white-and-blue banners everywhere, and the mayor, the mascot, and the band were all at the park. But there were just three little sections of stands about four rows high, and they weren't full. There wasn't much of a field, either, to be very frank. The dugouts couldn't have been twenty feet long, and there were weeds up to the knees of the relief pitchers in the bullpen. Typical low–minor league playing conditions, in short: charming but definitely on the primitive side. Plus I made three errors and wasn't much better at the plate.

Back at the motel, I picked up the phone to call home in Aberdeen. Now, if you listen to Brooks Carey, my roommate that summer, he'll say I moaned and groaned and told my parents I wanted to come home. Brooks exaggerates, just like he exaggerates when he describes the scene at the park in Paintsville. I never said I wanted to go home and I never thought about calling it quits—no way—but those first two or three weeks in rookie ball were a low point, there's no doubt about it. Brooks tried to encourage me, and he reminded me that the infield conditions in Paintsville, particularly, were poor, but I was scuffling. I wasn't quite eighteen years old, baby-faced, barely shaving, and I'd never been away from my family for any length of time. I had some very *unpolished* talent, and I was going from being a star back home in Maryland to playing in a league in which everyone, especially the seasoned players coming out of college, was much closer to me in talent and performance, if not considerably better.

Jesse Orosco, for example. In Elizabethton, Tennessee, where the lights were about fifteen feet off the ground and not white, either, but yellow, we faced Jesse, who had two strong college years in California under his belt.

"Is he throwing hard?" someone asked in the dugout.

"It sounded like it," I answered. Jesse was throwing seeds I barely saw. (*Seed:* vernacular for a fastball thrown so hard it looks mighty small approaching the plate.) Jesse was one of those college pitchers who totally outclass their rookie league competition.

Making matters worse for me, Tom Giordano saw some of those early games of the Orioles' franchise in Bluefield, West Virginia. Although he never said a negative word, I pictured him thinking about me, *See?* I told you to stick with pitching. Some of our pitchers might have wondered the same thing. They'd see me messing around on the sidelines and say, "Hey, you could pitch." Brooks Carey said that Al Widmar, the pitching coach, teased his own staff by saying, "We're in trouble. The shortstop has the best stuff on the team." But I was a player, not a pitcher! I felt I'd been talented enough to be drafted in the second round, and I knew the Orioles weren't going to waste a high draft choice out of loyalty to my father. I didn't think I was given any more opportunity or treated with more patience than anyone else. Still, I wasn't proving my talent, so maybe some people were beginning to wonder. I probably called home once a week that summer, maybe more early on. Dad would ask about the symptoms—popping up; beating the ball into ground—and deliver the appropriate version of the stock answer: get back to basics.

After the first few weeks, I got my feet on the ground in Bluefield and settled down for the final five or six weeks of the short season. Dad got down to see me one game, and Elly saw a couple of games. My final .264 average was okay, with no homers, seven doubles, one triple. I'd hit a homer in our first intrasquad game and thought, Hey, this is easy. I was popping them out in batting practice with regularity, and I did ricochet a few drives off the wall in left and a few others off the *top* of the wall. But none over it. If just one of those drives had bounced over instead of back onto the field, things would have been a little easier for me in the beginning. I was disappointed by this lack of power, but Dad assured me that power comes with waiting on the ball, and most young hitters have trouble waiting. As it turned out, one of my offensive highlights that summer was the blooper I dropped in off the otherwise overpowering Orosco to win the game on August 24, my eighteenth birthday. The second baseman and right fielder blew their communication on the play. When Jesse joined the Orioles in 1995, I kidded him about that game-winner seventeen years earlier. He remembered it just like I did.

In the field that summer, I started out with a series of multi-error games, so the final fielding statistics were on the ugly side: 32 errors in 63 games. Accuracy on my throws was the main problem, and I was learning when to come in for the short hop, when to lay back, when to do everything. Meanwhile, Bobby Bonner had also joined the Baltimore organization that year. He was a really polished shortstop out of Texas A&M, light-years ahead of me as a fielder, and Mike Boddicker never let me forget it. Like Orosco, Mike was another one of those dominating college pitchers. He came out of the University of Iowa, and I don't think he gave up a hit in the innings he pitched for us—a man in a boys' league, literally. He was soon moved up to Double-A Charlotte, and he immediately dominated the Southern League as well. The next year Mike set the league record for most strikeouts in a game, 18, against Knoxville. Eventually he went on to have a great career with the Orioles, and I'm glad he did, but he really teased me for the few weeks he was in Bluefield, saying things like, "You aren't going anywhere as long as

Bobby Bonner's in this organization. You're going to die in the minor leagues."

The thing is, that's what I thought, too, when I first saw Bonner in the field. I told our manager, Wilbert "Junior" Miner, that it looked like I wouldn't be playing much shortstop on this team. Junior told me not to worry because Bonner would be leaving for Charlotte soon. He did leave following our mini-training camp, and Mike followed him shortly. But Mike teased me even from Charlotte. When he wrote one of our teammates with shipping instructions for some stuff he'd left behind, he included a postscript: "Tell Cal there's still hope. Bonner's on the D.L. with a bad knee."

Brooks Carey and I were good friends that season and throughout most of my three years in the minors. We shared apartments or were road roomies all the way up, and one year in winter ball as well. In the beginning, Brooks was way beyond me in maturity (depending on how you define maturity). He was a senior out of Florida State, but he was in a different kind of state that summer in the Appalachian League—a state of shock. In a college program like Florida State, you play on good fields and suit up in good clubhouses. Now here he was a so-called professional baseball player warming up in the weeds, as he put it.

"Where am I?" Brooks asked in mock horror one day, probably in Paintsville. "Am I hallucinating?"

In Bluefield, Brooks slept in a bathtub in a motel room for two weeks until he joined me in a boardinghouse when Boddicker moved up to Charlotte. Larry Sheets and Tim Norris, a couple of other players fresh out of high school, also stayed there. Tim was from the Baltimore area. He'd been drafted in the fourth round with great high school stats, and he had a baseball scholarship to Clemson, just in case. We'd met for the first time at Memorial Stadium when the Orioles had a private tryout for local players about a month before the June draft, then for a second time when the team had a Family Night for its draftees. The following morning I joined Tim, his mother, and his girlfriend in their car for the long drive to Bluefield. I guess I wasn't too excited. I slept most of the way.

As lifelong Oriole fans, Tim and I were a natural match and spent hours that summer analyzing the big league team from a distance. The Orioles were good in 1978. Heck, they were always good, although the Yankees won their third straight American League East title. Tim is also as intense a competitor as I am. In pinball, pool, backgammon, hearts, and bowling we had to beat each other. Whoever won that particular game was the champion of the world.

Our boardinghouse in Bluefield was owned and operated by the elderly Mrs. Short. Her house had three bedrooms upstairs, one with twin beds. There was no air-conditioning, but you didn't need it because Bluefield is in the foothills of the Appalachian Mountains, and it's relatively cool in the summer. If the temperature does get to ninety degrees they serve free lemonade downtown, by way of apology. At least they used to. Mrs. Short placed a fan in every bedroom, and in the living room she set up what she called a wind machine, which might have blown her down if she had tried to stand in front of it. She was a frail little lady even then. I understand that Mrs. Short was still renting her three bedrooms in 1995, at the age of eighty-eight. During the streak coverage some enterprising reporter tracked her down, and she told him that altogether she's had four hundred, maybe five hundred boarders since she took in her first one after her husband died in 1960. Some of these boarders she remembers, some she doesn't, others she does remember but wishes she didn't. She mails Christmas cards to her favorites, and she points to the corner bedroom and tells visitors, "Cal Ripken slept here."

Tim, Larry, Brooks, and I treated our landlady with respect, and I think she liked us. She said we were the only boarders she had ever agreed to cook for. We asked her if she could have a large meal ready at 3 o'clock, and she said she'd do it until the first time one of us didn't show up, and then she'd quit. We showed up. We were quiet when we came in late after games or very late after a road trip, although she was usually up anyway, waiting. She never went to our ball games, because of her arthritis, but sometimes she and her dog would join us on the front porch to talk about the game. I think the four of us paid her $25 per person per week, which also covered two loads of laundry. Our take-home pay was about $400 a month, so we actually saved some money.

It might surprise you to learn—it surprised me—that Mrs. Short's baseball players were better behaved than the college students she sometimes housed. That's what she said. The only time the ballplayers cut up that summer was on our road trips, especially when we were leaving a town on getaway day. For the last night, management usually packed the whole team into three or four motel rooms to save money. These crowded conditions usually led to all-out wrestling matches. I've never wrestled on a team, but I love to wrestle, and I'm tenacious and strong—more so now than when I was eighteen, but I could hold my own with most of the guys even then. We messed up some of those motel rooms, I have to admit, and some luggage got destroyed, although I don't think we were ever chewed out.

Overall, though, we behaved. For one thing, Junior Miner was strict about beer. The way I figured it, in the minors the beer regulations depended on the manager, and "No beer" was Junior's rule. One late night on the road we begged him to let us buy just one. "One lousy beer, Junior. Come on." Finally he gave in, with the understanding that this would be the only time he'd allow it for the entire season. When we walked out of the convenience store, Junior broke out laughing: each of us was carrying one *quart* of beer. He was a great guy. He was a father-type manager, which is just what rookies need. Junior died in 1990.

Back home in Maryland that fall, I bought a Ford LTD, only to find out that my credit wasn't good enough for the Texaco credit card I needed to go along with it. Mom wrote a long letter explaining that I'd paid cash for my car and that the Ripken family had supported the company for almost thirty years. A compromise was reached: I could have the card if my parents cosigned.

After just a week or two, Tim Norris and I rolled out of Baltimore again, this time in separate cars heading for our first Instructional League in St. Petersburg. For the next couple of years, we followed each other back and forth between Baltimore and Florida, stopping every time at the same motel in Savannah, a full day south on Interstate 95. The fact that I'd been invited to the Instructional League was a good sign: the organization saw some potential in me. As the name implies, the purpose of this fall league is instruction, so there are usually two guys assigned to each position in the field. You split the playing time in the 45-game schedule and get instruction when you're not in the game. But that year the other player scheduled at shortstop on my team, "Cat" Whitfield, came down with a sore arm, I believe. Overall, I got a number of good breaks in the minors, including other guys' bad breaks—injuries—that opened up opportunities for me. I always seemed to be on the right team at the right time. Because of Whitfield's injury I got to play every inning of every game. My fielding improved, and even though the pitching was better than I'd faced in Bluefield, including pitchers from the high minors working on various things and other good pitchers coming out of rehab programs, something started clicking for me at the plate. When I hit a homer, I never heard the last of it from the guys on the team who had seen me struggle with my power over the summer. After no homers in that bandbox in Bluefield, which was only 365 to dead center—a glorified high school field, really—I hit two or three out of this huge field at the Mets' former complex, which we called Yellowstone Park. I took as much extra batting practice as I could, and in the field I took millions of fungoes from Tim Norris. Occasionally I even threw BP myself, although the coaches frowned on that.

I met Will George, a pitcher who'd been drafted out of high school in New Jersey by the Orioles the year before. He'd spent 1978 in Miami. Will immediately told Tim Norris and me about his own rooming-house experience in Bluefield the year before we were there. The owner of Will's house had been an elderly woman in the habit of walking around in her negligee. The next year the team dropped her from the roster of acceptable landladies. But mainly Will, Tim, and I talked about baseball because we had the same desire to make the majors. When I called Dad back home in Aberdeen, Will would listen to my half of the conversation and claim to get a lot out of the partial dialogue. We watched *This Week in Baseball* and *The Game of the Week* and talked about everything we saw. We ate, drank, and slept baseball. As a pitcher, Will grilled me about hitting and the thought processes of good hitters. I was a long way from being an expert, but I told him what I knew. About the only thing we didn't discuss was the notes I'd kept in Bluefield on all the pitchers and their pitch sequences, which I still have in a box somewhere. It was hard to keep track of the names, because we were facing different pitchers all the time, and their names weren't on the backs of the uniforms, but I tried to be diligent, at Dad's urging. I didn't tell the guys about these notes because the subject was kind of embarrassing. No one else was doing this. I kept notes on the pitchers throughout the minor leagues and for the first few years in the majors, until the Orioles' coaching staff started including the equivalent figures in the information prepared for the media.

That was a solid, beneficial six weeks of baseball in St. Petersburg, highlighted by my dad's visit for a couple of weeks. We worked on technical things on the field, played golf, ate meals—all in all, spent more time together than we'd ever been able to before. This irony struck me hard: if I made the grade in professional baseball, especially if I made it with the Orioles, the game that had taken my father away so much when I was a kid would bring us back together again as adults.

Back in Aberdeen for the winter, I lived at home and worked as a substitute teacher at my old high school. The pay was $40 a day; I needed gas money. I taught a history class once or twice, and health class, where I thought I did a pretty good job handling the adolescent jokes and remarks during sex education, but mostly I got the gym classes, which was fine with me because I got to play a fair amount of basketball, my second-favorite sport (except when I'm playing, when it comes in first).

The good work in Florida in the fall carried into the following spring, 1979, at my first minor league spring training camp. The Oriole minor leaguers trained at Biscayne College, about twenty miles from the big league camp at Miami Stadium. The college dorms were nice, and so was our locker room, which was used by the Miami Dolphins, but the field was dubbed Iwo Jima. I don't know whether Senior could have done much for it with his drag. When we weren't in baseball camp that spring, a group of us—myself, Will George, John Shelby, Willie Royster, Drungo Hazewood, the occasional odd man—would sneak off to play basketball on the outdoor courts in north Miami. This was during March Madness, if it was called March Madness back then, and we were pumped to play hoops. We played on a lot of "dunk courts" with eight-foot baskets. Goal-tending was legal, so those were rough games around the boards, with hands and arms banging against the rim. Returning to camp covered with bruises, we told the coaches we'd been out jogging. If it had come down to it, we could have argued that we were just continuing the tradition started in the early seventies by Don Baylor, who organized a team of Orioles that challenged all comers in the spring.

I was assigned out of spring training to the Orioles A-ball team in Miami. This was the logical next step for me, even though I struggled at the plate the first few weeks in Miami and picked up the same doubtful feeling from Tom Giordano that I'd had in Bluefield. Maybe I was paranoid, and the Orioles scouting director didn't say anything in so many words, but the feeling I got from him was, I told you so, you should have signed on as a pitcher. But then things started clicking again with the help of another bit of good fortune, not the kind that makes a career, but enough that I remember it distinctly. I'd been swinging M-110 bats from my first day in the minors (in high school, I used Dad's old wood bats that I'd discovered in the attic; if it was really cold, I switched to aluminum), but for the second half of the season in Miami I received by mistake a shipment of M-159s. I'd never been a big one for experimenting with a lot of different bat models, but this M-159 had a skinnier handle than the M-110, and I liked the feel of it from the first practice swing. In batting practice I was really popping the ball.

The length and the weight of these Louisville Sluggers were the same—thirty-five inches, thirty-two ounces—but in the M-159 more of that weight was in the barrel, and I formed the mental image of a bat that had a little bend in it during the swing, a little snap, almost like with a whippy golf club. I liked the bat and I liked the image, and that same night, July 2, with the game tied 0–0 in the top of the twelfth inning in West Palm Beach, I drove a pitch from Joey Abone over the left field wall. Abone had thrown the entire game and was tired, but so was I. It was my first home run in the minor leagues (Instructional League doesn't officially count), and the only reason the crowd didn't go wild was that there wasn't a crowd. They'd gone home. Then something happened to the lights on the field, and during the blackout I sat on the bench wondering if the homer counted if we didn't finish the game. Fortunately they came back on, we won the game 1–0, and I had my homer. (And I had my bat. The P-72 I switched to in the majors and still use is basically the old M-159—same handle, slightly bigger barrel. The only difference is I've added one ounce to the weight.)

The much bigger deal that season was the wrist injury to Bob Boyce when he was hit by a pitch—another injury to another player that indirectly worked out perfectly for me. Boyce had been the Orioles' number one pick the previous year and the MVP in the Appalachian League playing for my team at Bluefield. He looked great. He was the organization's third baseman of the future, but this injury in Miami set him back (as it turned out, Bob never made the majors) and created a problem for the team. We had two shortstops that year, myself and Steve Espinoza, and one of us would have to move over to replace Bob at third. I seemed to be the logical choice—but, again, I don't think this decision was based on the fact that I was getting taller and heavier every month, and therefore not the traditional image of a big league shortstop. That hadn't become an issue yet.

At shortstop, I'd still been having some problems putting together all the elements of the play: catching, setting up, and throwing in one more or less continuous motion. With balls in the hole or behind the bag, the shortstop doesn't have time to break down the play into separate parts; it's all or nothing, all at once. But at third base, the ball gets to you faster off the bat, and those extra microseconds make all the difference. The required actions can be singled out and separated: catch or block, regroup, throw. You have some time. I played third base very well from the minute I went over there in Miami, and I wasn't gun shy. Almost immediately I took a ball in the throat, but I shook it off. That move to third base turned out to be natural and I think it was important for me at that stage of my development. When I eventually returned to shortstop, I was ready.

I also became really relaxed at the plate in Miami, got four more home runs in the big ballparks we were playing in, and led the team in most categories. But there were still some whispers that my last name was more important than anything else in my career in the Orioles organization. Here I was almost over the hump, I thought, with a good shot now to make the majors in some capacity, but I *still* heard some rumblings about the unfair advantage of my last name.

In Bluefield the year before, our gang had saved money at Mrs. Short's house. In Miami, finances were tight on $700 a month. I shared an apartment with Tim Norris. Tim's father was a caterer who sometimes sent us crabs from Maryland, and Tim knew something about cooking, but it was strictly meat and potatoes. I had the bunch of recipes my mother sent off with me every time I drove south, but I didn't use them much. Tim was the cook, I was the bum. The apartment didn't even have a TV, but we did fine just playing cards, working puzzles, and talking baseball. The recreation highlight was probably the afternoon I bowled a 300 and Larry Sheets a 299. At least, those were the scores on the computerized printout we presented to Tim. He had a difficult time believing this, naturally, since all of us were just average bowlers.

And all of us wrestled, of course. One night I started messing with Brooks Carey on the tarmac outside the stadium. He tried to beg off on the grounds that he was scheduled to pitch the following night against Daytona Beach, but I wasn't buying that. Before he knew what was happening, I had him down, pinning his arms with my knees, working on his chest. The next day on the bus up to the game, Brooks told me that I'd hurt him. He said his chest was tight. That was his word: "tight." I told him he'd be okay, but warming up for the game he said his chest was still tight, and he intended to tell Lance Nichols, our manager, that I'd beat him up in the parking lot the night before. Now I was getting nervous and asked Brooks not to tell Lance.

"Throw change-ups," I suggested weakly, maybe harking back to my own experience two summers before with the Putty Hill Optimists. Nursing a sore back, I threw mostly change-ups in the final playoff game we lost in Texas.

But Brooks said he was going to teach me a lesson. "I'm going to Lance," he said, "and you're going with me."

"Wait a minute," I countered. "Just go out for one inning and see what happens."

Brooks agreed to do that, and what happened was . . . not much, from the perspective of the opposing hitters. Brooks struck out about a dozen guys and threw a shutout. After that episode, he somehow figured I owed him, while I had it the other way around. That game was one of the best showings of his young career.

Late that summer I was called up to Double-A Charlotte. If there's an opening, it's common for players to be moved up a notch at the end of a season to give them a taste of the next level. It's a good challenge, but also pressure-packed. You don't have much time to prove that you're ready for what may be the real promotion the following spring. I was nervous in Charlotte that month, and I had the misfortune to drive some balls out of my new park in my first batting practice. I say "misfortune" because that success seduced me into uppercutting for homers from then on. I also dislocated my pinkie diving into first base and missed a few games, and I was playing only off and on because Russ Brett was there at third base. Bottom line: a .180 batting average in 61 at-bats over three-plus weeks of games, with 3 homers.

I wasn't happy, but I wasn't overly concerned, either, and then, in Instructional League that fall, yet another injury opened up another door. Russ Brett got hurt, and that let me play all these games at third base. In Charlotte the next season, 1980, I had third base all to myself and played every game—144—plus the playoffs, so I figured I had earned the bonus I had negotiated for myself. The way it works in the minors is that the organization mails you a letter in the off-season stating your salary for the coming year—a take-it-or-leave-it proposition. When I received my offer of $900 a month, I thought I deserved a little bonus of some sort. Dad said if that's the way I felt, I should write Tom Giordano and make my case, and I did, asking for $1,000. After a couple of letters back and forth, the negotiations ended up where they'd started, and I mailed off a final letter expressing my "disappointment." So I was pretty surprised when I walked into the office in Charlotte to sign the contract and saw that the monthly figure was $1,100.

That was the first time I'd ever started every game in a season, and this was also my breakthrough season, powerwise, although I wasn't totally surprised. For one thing, I was filling out at the rate of five pounds a year. I was now six-three and 195 pounds, pushing 200 pounds. I was much stronger than I had been the year before, living proof of what Dad always said: "The difference between .240 and .290 is strength." Actually, I believe the difference *can be* strength, and it can be other factors as well, such as learning to wait on the pitch, or having a quicker bat. But strength never hurts, that's for sure. The strong guy can hit the ball off the handle and still muscle it over the infield; the weaker hitter can't do that. And if the stronger guy hits the ball with the sweet spot of the bat, it has a better chance of clearing the fence, obviously. Also, the fences were shorter at Crockett Park in Charlotte than they had been in Miami, and it seemed to me that the ball carried better, too. Finally, a lot of people in baseball believe a hitter needs at least a thousand professional at-bats before he understands what's going on and can begin to demonstrate his true level of talent. His first year, a guy is doing what got him drafted in the first place. In Instructional League and his second year, he's working on new things and might actually be worse statistically than the first year. The third year, he's beginning to put things back together and should be showing real progress. In the fourth year, he's almost ready, or maybe he is ready. That's just about the way it went for me, and this formula for success hasn't changed, despite the fact that players may now be rushed to the big leagues sooner. Are they bona fide major league hitters before their fourth or fifth year of professional baseball? Not really.

In Charlotte, I hit high gear. I worked hard on waiting, waiting, *waiting* on the pitch and broke through with 25 homers, breaking Drungo Haze-wood's old team record of 24 from the previous year. However, I didn't set a new record because Drungo now had 28 home runs himself. Hitting third in the lineup, I had a great deal worked out that season with John Shelby, who was either leading off or hitting second. I told John, "If you get on, I'm taking pitches until you steal." Then I'd drive him in. I had 78 RBIs that year, and a lot of them were John Shelby, who said I was the first hitter who'd ever taken pitches for him. I probably was, because when you're still learning how to hit, as most guys are in the lower minors, by definition, you hate to give up strikes and get behind in the count. In addition, pitchers like to throw fastballs with a base stealer on first, and the strategy of swinging "first pitch fastball" has worked well for lots of good hitters. But I was confident enough that year as a hitter to take some pitches and risk falling behind in the count if it would move the runner—Shelby—into scoring position.

John and I also had a contest going for the team leader in doubles. We ended up tied, we thought, but then the media guide distributed during the following spring training had me down for 28, one more than John. Apparently one of his doubles had been discounted, for some reason. When he saw that, he lowered the boom on me, claiming that I'd pulled rank with my last name. He *stayed* on me about that. Playing basketball in Baltimore years later, he'd make a great play against me and then say quietly, "Payback." Or maybe it was payback for something else. John and I were always ragging each other. He even got on me at Bluefield when I was making all the errors the first couple of weeks. Generally speaking, you don't rag a guy about his performance on the field, but John didn't hesitate to kid me about being tired of all the extra work required of him in center field, picking up the balls that had rolled between my legs.

John's a great guy, almost always in a good mood. He even came around to liking his nickname, T-Bone, which somebody in Bluefield laid on him. Before that everyone had called him by his middle initial, "T." Guys ribbed him with the modified "T-Bone," which had nothing to do with steaks, and John finally accepted it. That's what his current minor league players call John, who's managing in Double-A San Antonio after a good career with the Orioles and the Dodgers, mainly.

T-Bone had this thing about shoes. He was very close to his shoes, especially a pair of Converse sneakers he'd brought from home, Lexington, Kentucky. He took care of them like he would a pair of dress shoes. At a beach party in Miami he was trying unsuccessfully to body surf when I tossed one of those sneakers at him. I thought it would float. It didn't, and he went haywire. When he finally found the one shoe in the surf, I tossed in the other one, which he never found. "Look, I'm not a barefoot man," he said when he walked out of the surf. "I need my shoes." He was genuinely unhappy with me, so from that point on I felt some responsibility for keeping him in good cleats—we wore the same size—and I was usually able to deliver, compliments of either my father or Frank Robinson. Overall, John didn't take to the ocean, but we did have one other beach episode two years later, when we were playing winter ball in Puerto Rico. I'll never forget this one. John had heard about the undertow off the beach in front of our apartment. People were always being pulled out to sea, T-Bone had heard on good authority, but this day I talked him into trying a modest wave. However, his timing was late and he got tumbled pretty good and slammed down on the bottom. When he finally came to the surface he was turned around facing out to sea, convinced in his mind he'd been dragged a mile offshore to certain death. He started screaming, even though he was standing in water only up to his waist. He was hollering but I was laughing, because I was standing right behind him. John jerked around and saw me, saw the beach, got angry, said "That's it, I'm out of here," and went back to the apartment to wait for the game.

John worked as hard at his profession as anyone. A converted infielder playing center field, he spent as much time shagging fly balls as I did fielding grounders. He was one of the very few outfielders I ever saw who would make the pitchers clear out of center field during batting practice so he'd have open territory to shag balls, all the way from left-center to right-center. He felt he needed all the work he could get, and he felt that shagging during BP is the closest you can come to game situations. Fungoes are okay, but different. The ball doesn't come off the bat the way it does when thrown by a pitcher. Even when he got to the majors, John would leap at the wall during BP, trying to take away doubles and homers. How else was he supposed to practice those plays?

T-Bone was one of my best wrestling and basketball buddies. He was quicker and a better jumper and probably stronger pound for pound, but I was bigger and had a lot of leverage. If he blocked me one-on-one for some payback, I tried to make him pay up double soon enough. Needless to say, he was an excellent guy to have on your side during a brawl. One in particular comes to mind, a story I have to set up with a flashback to Bluefield two years before, when I got hit on the wrist after the previous batter had homered. I didn't make a move because I was on the ground and didn't realize the pitch had been intentional, but John charged out of the dugout toward the mound because he did know. This was his second year in pro ball, everyone else's first year. What did we know about anything? When John found himself out there all alone, he made a sudden ninety-degree turn and headed for home plate, where he pretended to check me out.

Now, two years later in Charlotte, Tommy Smith and T-Bone hit consecutive homers in a game against the Memphis Chicks. When I came up next, the first pitch from Greg Bargar was over my head. *Behind* my head. By this time I did know the ropes a little bit. After two homers, that kind of pitch is intentional and requires redress. I was going to the mound, help or no help.

I have a temper. That year I threw some bats and I smashed some helmets. I'd already had a fair amount of conflict with the umpires. I was intolerant of what I thought were bad calls; I'd tell the umps what I thought. Some of them didn't like me, and I don't blame them, because I did get out of hand once or twice. I was immature and unfairly blamed them for standing in the way of my desire to get to the big leagues. In fact, I'd already gotten in one argument that same game. I was screaming at the home plate ump when Jimmy Williams, our manager, hurried out. I thought he was coming to my defense, but Jimmy had had enough of my tantrums and chewed *me* out instead. If I got thrown out and fined by the league, he was going to double the amount.

But when Bargar threw behind me, I had no choice: I was on my way to the mound. I got to Bargar about the time the Chicks' catcher Tom Wieghaus caught up with me. Then the cavalry arrived, led by Shelby and Drungo Hazewood. Someone took a punch at Drungo, a large, perfectly muscled guy who'd won a full scholarship in football to USC, who would play a year in the USFL after his baseball career ended. He was big and fast and something to watch scoring from first on a double. After that punch, the focus of the brawl became Drungo's attempt to get revenge on the Chicks' player. He, myself, and four other players—but not T-Bone—were thrown out of the game. In the clubhouse, I was laughing. Lots of fun, nobody hurt, the fans had gotten into it, helped by the fact that it was 25-cent beer night. But Drungo wasn't laughing. He threw on some street clothes—no shower—and then stopped in front of a display of two bats mounted on hooks on the wall. He grabbed one and snapped it like a toothpick. I saw it happen, but don't ask me *how* it happened. I've seen replays of guys snapping the bat over their knee, but Drungo didn't snap this bat *across* anything, and he didn't hit it *against* anything. He just *twisted* and it snapped like a toothpick. Then he stuck the barrel into his pants and ran down the hallway to the entrance to the Chicks' clubhouse, where he pounded on the door shouting at the other guy to come out. Two cops were posted, but they did nothing. After a couple of minutes, Drungo went around to another entrance to the visitors' clubhouse and started pounding and shouting. Someone summoned Jimmy Williams from the game, and Jimmy had to lock Drungo into the owner's office until he cooled down.

"Outstanding," John Shelby said. That was his favorite phrase for a good brawl, a good play, a good meal, anything at all. That whole year was outstanding, although the facilities at Crockett Field were certainly not: wooden stands and roof, funky clubhouse, window air conditioner in the manager's office, a bigger one for the clubhouse, which barely worked. Half the showers barely or never worked, but we didn't really care. The place had a certain charm, we were good as a team, a lot of us were coming into our own as players, and we had a great manager in Jimmy Williams. Jimmy and his wife now live north of Baltimore, and they play a lot of golf with my parents. Before joining the Orioles organization, Jimmy had played all his baseball with the Dodgers, where, in fact, he'd been a roomie with my Uncle Bill in Dayton in the Triple-I League in 1948. It must have been easy for Jimmy to move from Los Angeles to Baltimore, from Dodger Blue to the Oriole Way, two model organizations.

Jimmy was careful not to give all his attention to the better prospects on the team. On any Double-A or Triple-A team, everyone knows who's probably going to the big leagues and who's not, but if a manager is blatant in his favoritism, he'll lose the rest of the guys. So if Jimmy wanted to work with me or John Shelby, say, he'd make sure that three or four other players were also included in the drill. That's a little thing, but a smart one. We learned a lot from Jimmy on our bus rides that year with Charlotte. On every team I played on in the minors, the manager traditionally had the right front seat. After a game, someone would usually go up to Jimmy in his seat and ask, "Skip, what did I do wrong here? What happened?" or Jimmy might call someone up and say, "Here's what you did wrong on that play." Soon there'd be five guys talking and listening. And sometimes the conversation veered in odd directions, like when Jimmy told us about the three revolutions he'd played in during winter ball in the late fifties, one each in Venezuela, Cuba, and Panama. In Caracas, Jimmy thought the airplanes flying over on New Year's Day were still shooting off fireworks, but the puffs of smoke were antiaircraft fire. In Cuba, he was in Havana when Castro took over in 1959. After an unscheduled break of a couple of weeks, Jimmy was talking with Camilo Pascual, who was sitting in the stands with a friend during a doubleheader. This friend turned out to be Camilo Cienfuegos, one of Castro's troika and a big baseball fan. Jimmy and the revolutionary shook hands and Jimmy asked, with the help of Pascual's translation, how the revolutionary fighters on the beach had felt about the baseball games in Havana. Cienfuegos said that they had wanted to bomb the ballpark, but they couldn't find a convenient time when no one would get hurt.

Chapter Five

In Charlotte, Larry Sheets was back in baseball after a voluntary absence. That's kind of a famous story, at least in the Baltimore organization. Playing with us in Bluefield, Larry had hit a homer in his first game and led the Appalachian League in power numbers most of the summer, but this performance was almost expected because he was the twenty-ninth pick in the country after playing high school ball in a little town in Virginia. From that kind of school, he was lucky to get any attention at all. The break he got was at the American Legion state tournament where he was MVP, with the scouts watching. He was our best hitter and slugger that year, without a doubt, but then he quit the pros to stay home in Virginia, go to college, and play basketball.

The two of us made for an interesting contradiction: I knew what to expect socially as a minor leaguer and was never homesick, but I had to adjust to the better quality of baseball; Larry was very comfortable playing the game—dominating, even—but he didn't fit in socially with his teammates. Since he didn't drink beer, he was often the designated driver when any of his teammates wanted go out on the town. More important, Larry was uncomfortable with what he saw as the cutthroat nature of the baseball business. He got upset when one of the players sneaked into the Bluefield office to find out the signing bonuses everyone had received. I mentioned earlier that some guys in the minors are reluctant to befriend others playing their position. Larry was uncomfortable with this kind of attitude. He saw professional baseball as dog-eat-dog, life-or-death, and he didn't feel that kind of commitment, even though he was our best player. So he left, and in 1979 *Sports Illustrated* ran a brief story about the big guy who had walked away from a promising baseball career. They titled it "Safe at Home."

A year and a half later, in 1980, Larry returned. He'd found out he missed playing the game. The Orioles were happy to have him back and started him at Bluefield again, but then moved him all the way up to Charlotte in Double-A when it became clear he could still hit. The organization also moved him to catcher. That must have been Earl Weaver's idea. Earl salivated at the idea of a left-hand-hitting catcher with power. Larry also played some left field and some right field—anywhere at all to avoid playing first base, his natural position, because the O's had a guy named Eddie Murray playing that position on the major league club. In his first three seasons in the majors, Eddie had already hit 79 home runs. In 1980 he was going to add 32 more.

I hadn't seen or talked to Larry Sheets in eighteen months; he'd missed all those great basketball games in Florida in spring training. But that seems to be the way it is in baseball. Missing friends come and go and come back, and you just pick up your friendship right where you left off. Larry's arrival in Charlotte was especially timely, because I needed more guys to wrestle. I wanted nothing to do with Drungo Hazewood, my roomie for the month I spent with Charlotte the year before—he could slam me around with ease, football-style—and my roomie in 1980, Will George, was having a hard time getting his strength back after coming down with mononucleosis. He was also trying to rehabilitate his shoulder. Give Will credit, he had pumped iron over the winter, trying to get ready for me in 1980—so he said, maybe only half jokingly—and in spring training I could see the difference in his body. But if he thought he was going to come in and kick my butt, it didn't happen. I was still able to sandwich him between the box springs and the mattress. What can I say? I was pretty strong, even with the minimal weight work I did at that time, with good leverage because of my height, and I've always had energy to burn.

Someone said I had more wrestling holds than Gorilla Monsoon, but that wasn't really true. I wasn't a "technical" wrestler. I was just playing around. I had the energy and enjoyed the physical interaction. By coincidence, Will, Larry, and I lived in a two-bedroom suite at the Days Inn in Charlotte where some of the World Wrestling Federation competitors also lived. The owner of the baseball team, Francis Crockett, owned the contracts of a bunch of these guys, who were really nuts. They made the Double-A baseball players look tame. Brooks Carey and a roommate lived next door to us, and the wrestlers were always sneaking into their place through the sliding door, beating them up, tossing firecrackers everywhere. That was a bit more than I had in mind.

On the field in Charlotte, Larry Sheets was unhappy about his hitting. He had pounded the ball in Bluefield, but now we had lots of discussions on the bench after Larry had just gone down swinging on another change-up. I was rolling along pretty good. How could I take the fastball down the middle and then drive the slider on the outside edge to right field for a double? Well, sometimes I took the first pitch so John Shelby could steal, but the main answer was that I had become confident enough to start looking for pitches, and if you're looking for a breaking ball or a change-up and the pitch is a fastball down the middle, you have to take it with less than two strikes. You have to have that kind of discipline. It's the only way to hit successfully in big leagues, at least for me.

While I worked on learning the pitchers in the league, I also tried to learn the hitters on the other team. By the third or fourth game of a series, I had a pretty good idea whether they were looking first pitch fastball, whether they were really looking for other pitches with an idea in mind or were just up there guessing. Brooks Carey and I talked a lot about the opposing hitters. If you're playing third base, knowing the hitters isn't as important as it is for the shortstop, second baseman, and center fielder, but it still helps a third baseman in certain situations. (In a couple of years, when Earl Weaver returned me to shortstop, my experience in learning the hitters proved to be invaluable while I was getting my feet on the ground in my new position.)

Somehow Dad got away from the Orioles for one of our games in Charlotte and presented me with an award for making the All-Star team with Miami the previous year. With him watching, I made two errors at third base. Figures. In the end, though, we won the Southern League championship that year, beating Memphis 3–0. I homered and Brooks Carey threw the shutout. All around, Charlotte was the best year I had in the minors, and one of my most enjoyable in baseball, period: great team, great teammates, great manager, great fans, and I had a great feeling about my future in the game. I loved Charlotte, but I never wanted to go back there to play baseball.

Now I was flying pretty high. John Shelby, Drungo Hazewood, Bobby Bonner, and Mike Boddicker, who had even started one game for the O's late in the year, and I were considered among the organization's best prospects. Larry Sheets had announced that he was going back to college for his junior year. For the second time, he was going to sit out at least a season. Larry says now he isn't proud of the way he went about things in the minors, but he did what he felt he had to do, and everything worked out. He got his college degree and, eventually, his major league career as well. For myself after the 1980 season, no guarantees, but things looked good. Really good.

Then something strange happened. For some reason I never learned, I didn't get invited to Instructional League. I was going to Caguas, Puerto Rico, for winter ball under manager Ray Miller, but I could have played a couple of weeks in St. Petersburg before flying to the island. When I'd been in Instructional League my first two seasons, it seemed like most of the winter ball guys stopped over for a couple of weeks on their way to the islands. Maybe the organization had two other third basemen who needed the work more than I did, and it wasn't a big deal when I wasn't invited, but I did get a little annoyed. I wanted to play baseball.

Some guys treat winter ball as preparation for spring training in the States, but I took it seriously. I did fly home for Christmas for four days—that long weekend was in my contract—but otherwise I was into the baseball. I was burning to get to the big leagues, that's not an exaggeration. I felt I was closing in, and this was another opportunity to show what I could do. I played baseball eleven months of the year, maybe even more, cramming in a tremendous number of ball games: over 600 in my three full years of minor league and winter ball experience. This was the way I wanted it, because in my mind playing was learning. For me, there was no other way to reach the majors.

It was unusual for me to be invited to play winter ball because I was coming out of Double-A, while almost everyone else would be Triple-A or big leagues. I felt it was almost an honor to be able to play with Jose Cruz and all the other good major leaguers on our team. Rickey Henderson and a bunch of other great players were in that league—good, good competition. And the owners in Puerto Rico want to win. They make moves really quick. If you're not doing the job, they bring someone else in. I felt a little heat, and in the beginning I was a little overmatched, but Ray Miller had a trick up his sleeve. After a couple of weeks I realized that Ray had been putting on a lot of hit-and-runs with me, and every time he did I hit the ball hard. After four or five of these plays, I realized that I was getting a breaking ball almost every time. Finally I went up to Ray and asked him why. He laughed and explained that he put the play on with good pitchers on the mound, guys like Eric Show, who would probably want to throw the breaking ball down and away on a hit-and-run count, and who were good enough to put the ball where they wanted to. The hit-and-run always makes the batter concentrate on making solid contact—the play is a good way to help certain batters break a slump, and lots of players put on the hit-and-run *them-*

selves, especially against a pitcher who gives them trouble—and Ray wanted to see how I'd handle the must-swing situation against good pitchers. He seemed impressed that I remembered those pitches, but I thought, If you're paying attention, who wouldn't remember them?

I said the owners down there want to win. Before the seventh game of the final round of the All–Puerto Rico playoffs against Santurce, I was sick with the flu, and had a temperature of over a hundred degrees. Our owner, Dr. Bonomo, a renowned ophthalmologist with patients from all over, talked me into taking a B-12 shot. I don't know if the treatment worked, but I played against Eric Show and we won the game. As the winner in Puerto Rico, we normally would have been entitled to go the Caribbean World Series, but they didn't hold it that year, for some reason. Just as well, maybe, because those playoffs last forever. I flew home instead with the trophy for Most Valuable Player on the team. The trophies they handed out in winter ball were enormous, about four feet tall for team MVP, even bigger for league MVP. (I was third in that balloting.) I was concerned that I might have to buy an extra seat on the flight just for the prize, but the team packed it into three smaller boxes.

My mother didn't know what to do with this huge trophy. I jokingly said that maybe she could do something with a matched pair. I was pretty cocky at the time: I had my eye on one season in Triple-A, maybe one more season of winter ball, then the major leagues with the Baltimore Orioles. That's about how it worked out, too: I did win a second team MVP award the following winter, and Mom did get her matched pair of four-foot trophies. Today they stand on either side of the big-screen television in the den.

When I stepped onto the field of my first major league spring training camp in 1981, Bryant Gumbel was standing by with a *Today* crew to record the Ripkens' father-son story. This was the first time Dad and I had been on a baseball field together in an official capacity. We played down the event, of course, and saw very little of each other off the field, even though we were staying only four floors apart at the Dupont Plaza Hotel. We had a couple of meals together, but that was about it, because Dad was running that camp. The media flocked to the first intrasquad game in which I played on one team and Dad managed the other one. After I smoked a few pitches, Earl Weaver and my father exchanged barbs about the quality of the pitches. Had Senior instructed his pitchers to serve up fastballs right over the middle, to make his son look good? Earl wanted to know. Not very likely, Dad said, but not in just those words.

Despite a pretty good camp and Jim Palmer's accolade that I was now the best athlete on hand, I was eventually cut and assigned to the minor league camp, and from there to the Triple-A team in Rochester. I wasn't disappointed. If you're going to be shifted to the minor league camp, it might as well be sooner rather than later, so you can be certain to get in your full complement of at-bats. Also, I'd known I wasn't going to make Orioles straight out of Double-A anyway. It's true that Eddie Murray had played less than half a season in Rochester at the end of 1976, but I wasn't Eddie Murray. Also, the club had had openings in 1977, when Reggie Jackson and Bobby Grich left for free agency, and it didn't have openings in 1981. As far back as I can remember, Dad had sat down one day every winter and listed the roster of the forty players invited to spring training and a second list of the twenty-five players he thought would still be around with the Orioles on Opening Day. He had compiled other lists for the minor league teams. In 1981 I was on the long list for the spring camp, but not on the short one for the final team. There wasn't a spot for me.

When Earl brought the news, I prepared to go to Rochester, get rid of the nickname Ray Miller had given me ("J.R.," a reference to my status as a "junior" and also to the character on *Dallas*), and put up some numbers and give the big leaguers something to think about. You always hear about minor leaguers watching the big leaguers to see if a spot might be opening up, but it works the other way, too. Major leaguers know whether somebody is tearing up Triple-A. When I left the major league camp, Ray Miller said my having a good year in Rochester might help the big club win 105 games. I hoped so.

Before I left that camp to drive north from Miami Stadium to the minor league camp twenty miles away, I asked Earl if I could go into the cage to take some cuts, and he said sure. Right off, I pulled something in my right shoulder, and it really hurt. Minutes after I'd been reassigned, here I was with a serious-looking injury. I'd missed a few games in both Rookie and A-ball because of a shoulder sore from overuse as I tried to correct my throwing problems, but this timing was unbelievable. The trainers put me on a regimen of rest and treatment. No hitting, no throwing. I hated the not-knowing feeling.

In the training room at the minor league camp, I let everyone else go in front of me for treatment because most of them could do *something* on the field, while all I could do was run. That was my whole day. Therefore I was the last guy on the field for the workout, and I could see that some guys thought I'd pulled an "attitude muscle"—one that hurts mainly because you have an attitude about something and just don't want to play. You can never be certain in a particular case, but I think I've seen some attitude muscles. For myself, though, I wasn't unhappy being in the minor league camp. Really.

After a couple of weeks, I heard that the organization might put me on the disabled list before the season started. The DL? I went straight to Tom Giordano and objected that this wasn't part of the deal. I was doing everything the trainers and doctors had told me to do, but this decision was being made before I'd even had a chance to test out the shoulder. I asked the doctors if I could start swinging the bat, just to find out where I stood. They said okay, and in the cage I popped the ball pretty well, and the same guys who thought I had an attitude muscle now changed their minds. After I passed that test, the medical staff decided I could play in *parts* of three games to see whether I could go north and start the season with the Red Wings. I didn't hit the ball well in those games, but every grounder had eyes. I was 5-for-7, maybe 5-for-8, which was good, but mainly I didn't have any pain, so they let me break camp with the team. Then we ran into snow in Rochester before the first game, and I was worried again, this time about my shoulder stiffening up. But we played, and the shoulder felt pretty good. I made an out the first two times, then homered on a line drive over the left field fence—I thought Mike Smithson was coming inside with the pitch, and he did.

Then came one of the biggest surprises of my young career. With the game tied in the ninth inning, Doc Edwards, our manager in Rochester, pinch-hit for me. I didn't say anything—I couldn't—but I also couldn't help thinking, Wait a minute. I hit a home run my last at-bat! I sat on the bench wondering as Tom Chism blooped a hit over shortstop to tie the game, which we went on to win.

Other than the homer, for a week or so I struggled. I couldn't even hit Doc in BP, and cold weather kept us from getting our usual number of cuts, so one day I said to my roomie Floyd Rayford, "Rafe, if I throw BP for you, would you throw for me?" Sugar Bear—Floyd's nickname—said sure, so we were out there by ourselves at 1:30 p.m., throwing seventy-five to a hundred balls apiece, then shagging them in the outfield. We lost maybe a dozen a day over the fence, but the club never said anything. The work helped, because I got unbelievably hot. Doc Edwards never pinch-hit for me again. On April 27, I had three homers in one game against Charleston, and I was looking for every pitch from Mike Paxton. The first one was a 2-and-0 fastball, an obvious pitch to look for, at least in Triple-A. The next time, we had guys on second and third, first base open. I looked for the curve on 2-and-1, another obvious calculation because Paxton would remember what he had thrown on the previous 2-0 count. I got the curve. The third pitch was a slider over the heart of the plate.

The next night, I got a standing ovation before my first at-bat, but when I struck out on a check swing on a slider in the dirt with men on base, I heard a few boos. That got my attention. In Charlotte they never booed the home-team players. In Rochester they did—one difference between the North and the South, I guess. The fans up there are knowledgeable, love their baseball, and sometimes can be kind of hard, but fair enough, because they're used to good baseball. Sometimes you hear that Triple-A is a holding station, the way the game is organized now, with many roster-filling guys joining the real prospects. That's true to an extent, but organizations want their legitimate prospect at shortstop, say, to play with a quality second baseman, even if they don't have a legitimate major league prospect at second. So the roster fillers need to be good, and that's why you get guys who have played in Triple-A for six, seven years. They're good ballplayers who provide a good example and competition for the prospects. Triple-A is like a summer job for these guys, who perform a valuable service in the scheme of things.

I had no more problems with my shoulder. Looking back at that first and last injury of any significance in my career, I think it might have actually helped me. It was probably a signal of overuse; I might have needed that two-week rest coming off winter ball and what had been a three-year program to make the big leagues. This accelerated pace had worked for me, but it didn't work for everyone. Allan Ramirez is an example. Allan had a great year for us in Charlotte in 1980, and for the first two weeks in Puerto Rico he was all-world. Then his arm gave out. He got to the big leagues for a cup of coffee in 1983, but that was it, and I've often wondered whether Allan pitched too many innings in 1980, from which his arm never recovered. That's the danger of winter ball, and baseball people are divided about sending pitchers to winter ball to strengthen their arms. I believe a pitcher has only so many innings in his arm. While I was in Puerto Rico, the Braves sent Gene Garber to get in work as a starter. That was fine, because Garber had been a reliever during the season, pitching fewer than 100 innings. But many starting pitchers have blown out their arms after throwing a lot of innings in the States, then a lot more down in winter ball.

●　　　●　　　●

Nineteen eighty-one was the year of the first long strike by the major league players, starting June 12 following some court actions, and overlapping the famous strike by the air traffic controllers. In baseball there was talk about maybe using replacement players if the major leaguers didn't get back to work soon. In Rochester we continued to play, and one afternoon I got a call from Mark Belanger, who was nearing retirement with the Orioles and was active in players' issues. I knew Mark from all my years around the O's organization. He told me that I would be an obvious choice as a replacement player because I was, by then, maybe the most prominent minor league prospect for the Orioles, and he wanted to know what I would do if the organization asked me to play. I told Mark not to worry, that I wasn't going anywhere. I would never be a replacement player, and that was that.

The way that strike in the big league turned out, *not* making the Orioles was another break for me. If I'd been with Baltimore when the rosters were frozen for the strike, I'd have been stuck for almost two months with no organized games to play. According to the rules, I couldn't have gone back down to play in Rochester, and my development would have stalled. Plus I would have missed the world-famous thirty-three-inning game in Pawtucket on April 18. The temperature was in the thirties, the wind was blowing straight in, nobody could reach the commissioner, apparently, and I guess the umpires didn't know there was a curfew in the International League. Pawtucket tied the game with a sacrifice fly in the bottom of the ninth, then they tied it again in the bottom of the twenty-first on a fly ball that was blown all the way back to the infield. We had guys who'd been pulled out by Doc Edwards at 10 o'clock and had time to get drunk and sober up *twice*. That was my teammate Brooks Carey's joke, anyway. It became so cold it was practically impossible to play. Someone procured an empty oil drum and built a fire in one end of our dugout. Finally, and after we had a guy thrown out at the plate in the top of the thirty-second, the umpires stopped the game after Pawtucket's at-bat. We had played for eight hours and seven minutes. Two months later, on June 23, the two teams picked up where they'd left off, now playing in front of TV crews from all over. I singled in the top of the thirty-third (making me 2-for-13 for the game) but didn't score, and Dave Kokza won it for Pawtucket with a single in the bottom of the inning. Good riddance.

Meanwhile, back in the major league strike, the two sides finally settled after fifty days and 712 canceled games. I wasn't following those negotiations. I understood they could affect me in future years, but my main concern was *getting to* the major leagues in the first place. It's sad, though, to look back at Mark Belanger's widely quoted remark to Lee MacPhail, president of the American League, at the 6 a.m. press conference on July 31 that announced the settlement. Mark said, "Lee, we can never let this happen again."

On August 8, Doc Edwards told me in the clubhouse that I'd been called to Baltimore. The major league clubs had been allowed to expand their rosters by two players. Jeff Schneider and I were the choices for the Orioles. I knew about the new positions, of course, and I'd been hopeful because I was playing well, but still it was a surprise. A few of us had a little celebration after that last game in Rochester, and the next morning I loaded my LTD and was out of there. Mom and Dad were excited, of course, and so were Billy, Fred, and Elly. They knew how hard I'd worked for this chance. For the rest of the year, I lived at home and commuted to my new job with Dad.

Nothing special was said on the way to work the first day, a Sunday, just "play within yourself." At Memorial Stadium, Jimmy Tyler, the O's clubhouseman who had known me my whole life, conspired to hang my uniform with the number 8 in Dad's locker on Coaches' Row, and Dad's uniform with the number 47 was on some hooks off on the wall. Some guys are particular about their number, but I didn't care. I was just happy to have any major league uniform with any number. In the minors I'd worn 16, 7, 12, and 5, respectively. If I'd thought about it, which I didn't, I might have preferred 7 with Baltimore, because that was Dad's number throughout his years managing in the minors, but Dad also preferred that number, which he got in a few years when

Belanger retired. And really, the number made no difference to me. I just wanted a big league jersey with any number at all.

When everyone quit laughing at Jimmy Tyler's joke, reporters asked my father if this was a dream come true for him. I knew what Senior would say, and he didn't disappoint me: "I don't dream. People say you have to have dreams, but what's the use of dreaming if you can't do the job?" And he insisted, as he always had, that the father-son relationship is not a factor in the big leagues. In Little League, yes, if the dad is the coach, but not here. If I hadn't known, I learned that lesson the hard way when I called Dad just that—"Dad"—within earshot of some players, who then had a mocking refrain of their own every time the two of us were together. "Dad! Oh Dad!"

They teased me pretty hard, and at the ballpark "Dad" immediately became "Senior" or "Number 47" to me.

My first big league action? Trotting out to second base as a pinch runner for Kenny Singleton in the twelfth inning against Kansas City. I'd never been on that kind of stage before. A minor league stadium isn't even *close* to the same experience. It was a thrill, but at least I didn't lose my head over the situation, because second baseman Frank White put on a pickoff play immediately. The umpire said "Safe!" and Frank said, "Just checking, kid." John Lowenstein immediately drove me in with a drive down the right field line, and I was a happy kid, still not twenty-one years old.

At the same time, I was afraid this wasn't "for real." The Orioles didn't have a place for me to play, not full-time, which was what I wanted. Doug DeCinces was the third baseman, and a very good one. His back had been a problem that year, and so had his shoulder, and no one could be sure he'd be ready to play after the strike layoff, but I wasn't likely to push Doug aside if he stayed healthy. As it turned out, he played great, and I mean great, while I was miserable sitting on the bench chewing my sunflower seeds. Earl Weaver had always been excellent about defining the role of every player and making every player feel he's part of the team. But I wasn't even a "role player." I was just additional infield insurance. I can't imagine anything worse than coming to the ballpark unsure what I was going to be doing that night, and that was exactly my situation when I was called up in 1981. Those were the innings when I began to think that if I ever got in the lineup, I wasn't coming out.

After September 4, I had no plate appearances at all because we were in a pennant race, and I guess Earl Weaver didn't trust me enough. That was the year of the split seasons, and in the American League East, the Orioles had finished two games back of the Yankees in the first half, before I showed up, and with me watching we finished two games back of Milwaukee in the second half, tied for fourth. We had the second-best overall record, but we were knocked out of the playoffs by the format. In the National League, neither Cincinnati nor St. Louis, the two teams with the best overall records in their divisions, made the playoffs.

The whole time, I felt *somewhat* a part of the team. The other guys on the bench quickly enrolled me in their various games and pranks, and I gladly went along. It was something to do. Still, would I have been better off playing in Rochester than mostly watching in Baltimore, especially if I wasn't watching for some good reason? I wondered. After the '81 season, and even though I was no longer with Rochester, I was voted rookie of the year and top major league prospect in the International League. In Baltimore, I had 5 hits in a grand total of 39 at-bats, with 1 walk, no extra-base hits, no RBIs. Playing in the field in parts of 18 games—12 at shortstop, 6 at third base—I made 3 errors. My instructions from the organization were to return to Puerto Rico for a second time and play some shortstop.

By this time my confidence was sort of beaten down. It had been a couple of years—Charlotte at the end of 1979, my second year in the minors—since I'd had a period of uncertainty. It was important for me to have some success *somewhere*, and I also knew the club might give me a look at shortstop in spring training the next year. I knew Earl wanted to see what I could do. That position was a whole lot more open than third base, because Mark Belanger was thirty-seven years old and hurting, and the two main candidates, Lenn Sakata and Bobby Bonner, were young guys with whom I might end up competing. After all, Earl had even started me nine times at shortstop, out of the blue. I wasn't *completely* cold at the position because I'd played a few games at short in Rochester when Bonner had come up for Sakata before the strike, but I wasn't exactly up to speed, either. I'd be able to do the job, I felt, but my choice at that time would have been third base. I was *totally* comfortable there. In Puerto Rico, I'd try to become more comfortable at shortstop, too.

Ray Miller was our manager in Caguas again, and he knew I was supposed to play some shortstop, but he had me playing third base, third base, third base for the first couple of weeks of the season. Finally I said, "Ray, I thought I was going to get a chance to play a little shortstop here. That was one of the reasons for coming down, wasn't it?" He said, "Don't worry about it, kid." At the time, I was a candidate for the Triple Crown in Puerto Rico, and someone must have made the decision that I was ready for the big leagues, because, if I remember the timing right, the day after I asked Ray what was happening with shortstop, the Orioles traded third baseman Doug DeCinces to California for Dan Ford, an outfielder. Ray must have known what was up. Jeff Schneider, who had come up with me from Rochester, was also in that trade. He never made it into a game with the Angels. The twenty-four innings he threw for Baltimore in 1981 turned out to be his entire career.

Doug DeCinces always felt there was more to that trade than met the eye, going back to his role in the strike as the player representative for the American League. Looking at what happened to the other players who figured prominently in the strike, you have to believe Doug's analysis may have been right. Bob Boone, catcher for the Phillies and the National League representative, was seldom played by Dallas Greene in the second half of the '81 season, then he was traded to the Angels. Mark Belanger, American League pension representative as well as the Orioles' player representative, signed with the Dodgers as a free agent. DeCinces was traded to the Angels. Of the four main players associated with the strike, only one, Steve Rogers of Montreal, the National League pension representative, wasn't with a new team the following year. But Steve Rogers was one of the best pitchers in the league; he'd win the Cy Young Award in 1982.

After the '81 season, Earl Weaver had told Doug that he respected him for standing up for the players, that he had no hard feelings, and that Doug would play third for the Orioles in 1982, with me at shortstop. Two hours after the trade was announced a month or so later, Earl called Doug on the phone, and Doug brought away from that conversation the conclusion that management had made that trade, not Earl. What's more, Doug believes, Earl had already decided *then*, way before the 1982 season started, that he was retiring after the season. The day after the trade, some glitch threatened the deal, and Doug got a call at home from Edward Bennett Williams himself, the first conversation they'd had since the settlement of the strike. EBW, as we often called our owner, wanted to assure Doug that he'd be the starting third baseman if the deal didn't go through, but Doug knew, from his talk with Earl, that the team wanted me to play third base. So Doug politely suggested to Williams that he *make* the trade work. He did.

All in all, a baseball career can't fall into place much better than mine did. The trade was good news in another way, too, because now I wouldn't have to compete with Doug for the third base job. If Earl had moved me to shortstop, I wouldn't have had to compete with him, but I wasn't sure Earl was going to move me. And if he did, I would have had to compete for shortstop.

Doug and I went back a long way. My father had been his manager for two years in the minors, first at Dallas, then at Asheville, and considered him as yet another son, which made him like my stepbrother. Most famously, he was the player who grabbed me in Asheville and hustled me into the dugout when a kid with a rifle fired a wild shot from beyond the center field fence that whistled past us while we were playing pepper.

Rumors of competition between Doug and me had started almost the day I arrived in Baltimore in August. He was particularly sensitive to the situation because of what he went through when he took over when Earl benched Brooks Robinson in 1976. Brooks was revered in Baltimore, of course. His replacement—Doug—was booed when his name was announced; he got hate mail; he had to change phone numbers. Doug didn't want me to feel we were in competition, and he knew how much he'd learned from Brooks, and he knew the importance of teaching. In Baltimore, veterans had often helped mold the guys they knew would eventually take their jobs. Lee May took Eddie Murray down the first base line to work on pop fouls. So as the rumors circulated, Doug told me, in effect, "Don't listen to these guys. Just play your game. Whatever happens, happens."

I appreciated Doug's attitude, and he continued to help me every way he could. However, our relationship may have changed just a little when I came up, with a little tension added because I represented at least a minor threat to his position. Or maybe that was just my perception. Anyway, as I've said, he played great and gave me no chance, and this performance raised the distinct possibility that I might have *lost* any competition between us the following year. And Doug himself had been returned to Rochester twice before he finally took Brooks Robinson's job. Don Baylor and Bobby Grich had lingered for at least one extra year in the minors with great numbers, waiting for an opening on the Orioles. I knew all these stories, so even though I was sad to see Doug leave the Orioles, I also knew the trade was a huge opportunity for me. One way to look at it: third base was now mine to lose. When I got the news of the trade from Ray Miller, I wasn't going to get all sentimental about Doug. My first thought was, It's my position now.

Chapter Six

With Earl Weaver, whatever was going through his head came out his mouth. At least, that's the way it seemed to me. In this respect, we were opposites. And in my official rookie season, 1982, some of what was coming out of Earl's mouth wasn't very nice. I hit the ball pretty well in spring training and, with my mom and sister in the stands, I went 3-for-5 in a big Opening Day victory against Kansas City, including a two-run homer off Dennis Leonard in my first at-bat (a nice trifecta for me: Opening Day dingers in Charlotte, Rochester, and now Baltimore). Then I went into a deep, deep slump: 4-for-55. In the minors I'd had a moderate number of walks. Now I had *one* walk. Why bother to walk me? I couldn't even hit my Dad during batting practice, which I'd been doing since I was a teenager.

Every day, Earl or batting coach Ralph Rowe had me out for extra BP. Earl wanted to work on my position in the batter's box. I was used to standing well off the plate, then striding into the ball, as we say, toward the plate. People thought I was *too* far off the plate, but remember, I'm tall and have long arms. Diving toward the plate like I did, I had no trouble reaching the outside corner. I didn't feel that was the problem at all—it never had been—but Earl wanted me to stand close to the plate like Frank Robinson had done. Frank had handled the inside pitch from that vantage, and Earl thought I could adopt the same approach. In BP, he'd climb up on the bar across the back of the batting cage—otherwise, he wasn't tall enough to see where the pitches were relative to the plate—and coach me to move up on the plate, always move up on the plate. Then he'd say, "See, now the outside pitch is down the middle."

"Yeah, Earl," I'd say, "but now I can't hit the *inside* pitch. It's too close."

"Oh, that'll come. That'll come. The important thing is there's no place on that plate they can pitch you now."

"Earl, I don't feel comfortable with the inside pitches." I wasn't debating him. I was a rookie, not even twenty-two years old, while he was maybe the most famous, definitely the most notorious, manager in baseball. He'd been a manager in the Baltimore organization since 1957, and for the Orioles since 1968. My father was his third base coach, whom Earl had put in charge of spring training. Those two had a lot of mutual respect, so I wasn't about to argue with Earl Weaver. I was just sheepishly responding to his points, for the most part.

On another issue, however, Earl and I saw eye to eye, at least at first. I was patient at the plate, especially facing a pitcher I didn't know. I didn't just *give* him the first strike, but I usually wouldn't swing at the first pitch, either. I wanted to get some idea what he had. I'd go deeper in the count to get a feel, especially if no one was on base, so I'd have an idea what to expect if I came up later with men in scoring position. I had first gotten comfortable taking a lot of pitches in Charlotte two years before, often waiting for T-Bone Shelby to steal a base. Now with the Orioles, I didn't know many of the pitchers, obviously, so I got in the habit of taking the first pitch. Back in spring training somebody had written a story about this—they counted the number of consecutive at-bats in which I did it—and Earl had defended me. Give the kid time, he said, adding that Ken Singleton had made a pretty good living following the same strategy. But when the season started, the pitchers caught on, of course, and as the slump went on game after game, that first pitch was usually a fastball for a strike. Then came the slider for strike two, swinging or taking, then a check swing when I'm down in the count and I'm back on the bench, struck out or grounded out and looking bad.

In addition, I was looking for breaking balls, because that's what I had seen all the time in the minors. But in the majors, the first thing the pitchers want to know is if you can handle the major league fastball, and they'll throw it until you hit it. Then they want to know what you can do with the inside pitch. Eddie Murray patiently explained all this to me, but still I sometimes outsmarted myself looking for breaking balls. I'd say to Eddie, "I'd wish they'd throw me the curves they throw you," and he'd say, "I wish they'd throw *me* the fastballs they throw *you*." One day he framed the point a little differently. "Boy, would I love to be you," he said. "Anytime you're struggling, all you have to do is look fastball." I listened, but I guess I wasn't learning. I'm surprised I didn't try one of Eddie's favorite tricks for breaking out of a slump: video games. Our trainer Ralph Salvon's son-in-law ran some arcades, and the Orioles ended up with a couple of games, including the very popular Asteroids that Eddie felt was great for his concentration and hand-eye coordination. But I was never even tempted to give it a try.

Taking some pitches, trying to be patient and learning the pitchers, I was digging myself a huge hole instead. I'd practically been given the third base job when they traded Doug DeCinces, I'd had a great season in winter ball, I felt I was ready for my official rookie season, I had that home run on Opening Day and had gotten everyone's hopes sky high— but now, the pits. Everybody on the team wanted to help, of course, and guys reminded me that even Willie Mays had gotten off to a horrible start, but all this advice and consolation worked out negatively with me. I was overanalyzing and overwhelmed. I just couldn't hit the ball, and I was out-thinking myself (and not for the last time, perhaps). In the batting cage, my father tried to simplify things. "You know how to hit," he'd say. "You got to the big leagues without all these guys, right? Let's get back to the basics." Easier said than done, right then, and slowly but surely I was driving Earl Weaver crazy. In his calmer moments he'd say, "Look, you take the good ones and swing at the bad ones." A couple of times he was more blunt, exploding on the bench after I'd returned after another weak out, "Take the *#@! pitch right down the middle, swing at the *#@! pitch over his head or in the *#@! dirt! How's he ever going to hit that way?"

Earl was right; that's the definition of a slump. Or one of the definitions. Those explosions were under his breath, just barely loud enough for me to hear. I knew all about Earl's tantrums, of course—in the minors we had always kept abreast of the latest Weaver outbursts—and I talked about the situation with Rick Dempsey, our catcher and my roommate the following two years. Rick had had many run-ins with Earl before I arrived on the scene. Earl would yell at him and Rick would yell back, "You think I'm not trying? I don't need you screaming in my ear. If you don't think I'm good enough, don't put me in the lineup." One time the catcher actually threw his shinguard in the general direction of his manager, a famous episode around Baltimore. A funnier one was the time Rick found out he wasn't in the lineup against Ferguson Jenkins. When he stomped into Earl's office demanding to know why, Earl pulled out his statistics on match-ups. He was one of the first managers to keep these numbers in great detail, and he showed Rick the hard facts of life: four K's the last game he faced Jenkins; he'd never hit him, period. "I'm due," Rick countered. Earl said, "I've seen too many of those 'due-fers' turn into O-fers. Now get out."

Eventually, after years of combat, Rick developed a theory that Earl wasn't really yelling at him, but at the pitchers, indirectly, in a way he could get away with. That's what Rick decided as a form of self-defense, that managers don't yell at the pitchers, figuring they're too sensitive to handle it—Jim Palmer might have been an exception to the rule—but Earl could yell at him and know the pitchers would hear it. The pitcher is responsible for the pitch selection, in the final analysis, so if Earl criticized Rick, Rick figured that he was actually criticizing the *pitcher*, but from a safe distance. The theory among most of the Orioles was that

Earl vented his frustrations on guys who wouldn't be hurt by the accusations, who would even be motivated—like Dempsey, like Jim Palmer, who eventually wrote an entire book about his battles with his manager. Other players Earl would leave alone entirely. He never once yelled at Eddie Murray, from what I understand. I guess he was afraid that yelling would be the wrong thing to do—and I think he was correct about that. Plus Eddie was the best hitter on the team and the best clutch hitter in the league. Why yell? He didn't need that kind of motivation.

I finally decided Earl *did* intend for me to overhear his angry mutterings, maybe like he intended for the pitchers to overhear his tirades against Rick Dempsey, but a couple of times he also tried the soft sell, inviting me into his office before the game and telling me not to worry about going back to Triple-A because he didn't have anyone else to play third. "Doug DeCinces is gone," he said, "you're all I've got." This approach didn't make me feel much better, but I wanted to believe him because I had in mind that they might give me 100 at-bats to get something going, a couple of dozen games. After that, well, even Mickey Mantle had been shipped out his first year.

Rich Dauer, our second baseman, tried to encourage me by telling me all about his own rookie slumps—two slumps, in fact—and about Earl's reaction. When Rich was called up in September 1976, he was 4-for-39. The following year, he struggled again and at one point was a combined 5-for-80 in the major leagues. Earl had called Rich in and said, "We've got to do something, we've got to figure something out." Rich had a great answer: "Don't worry, Earl, I'll get three hits tonight." Even though he didn't get three hits that night, Earl stuck with him. What could he do? He knew Rich was going to hit once he got his feet on the ground, and, according to Rich, Earl believed I'd hit, too. But he was losing patience. Both of us were.

The pressure was almost as bad that April as it had been at the end of the previous year, when I knew Earl would pinch-hit for me with Terry Crowley or Jose Morales in a close game, and I might have only two at-bats to do something. That's terrible pressure, but in 1982 Earl also

84 Cal Ripken, Jr.

reminded me I was playing a good third base, which was true, and he knew I was working hard.

At some point early that season, my old friend T-Bone Shelby tried to help me out with some horseplay. The Orioles had traveled up to Rochester for the traditional exhibition game against our Triple-A franchise, where T-Bone had started the season. Inside my locker in the visiting clubhouse I found a stack of local apartment brochures—a not-so-subtle hint that I might be looking for a place in 'chester someday soon. I knew who had left those brochures there, and I knew why: more payback from T-Bone. This might still have been about doubles, but I suspect it was about a prank of mine a few seasons back. I knew T-Bone was looking forward to a full winter off, and I found some official Orioles stationery and typed a letter telling John to report to spring training weeks ahead of the normal time. I signed it as one of the front office executives and mailed it to John's home in Kentucky. It was a great practical joke, I thought, well-conceived and -executed, but something tipped him off, and he patiently waited a year or two for this opportunity to get even. I had to hand it to him, the apartment brochures were a great joke.

One day at the batting cage Earl surprised me by saying, "Okay, stand where you want to stand." My dad was pitching, I took my favorite position off the plate, and after a dozen pitches I realized they'd all been on the outside corner and I had been slapping them to right field. Dad has good control, he could put the ball where he wanted to, and I suddenly realized what was going on. Earl must have *told* Senior to throw every pitch on the outside corner to prove to me that I couldn't hit it with any power from where I was standing. Clued in, I started diving out to get that outside pitch—exactly the same thing I'd do in the game. I *anticipated*, and I started pulling the ball on the outside edge over the left–center field fence.

Earl said, "I guess you really can hit the outside pitch." Then he said, "But you know what I mean. When you've got a tough pitcher out there and he's nibbling on the outside corner and the umpire might be giving him a little extra, and you've got a 2-0 count, right when he goes into his windup, why don't you sneak up on the plate and that outside pitch is right in your power?"

I said "Okay, Earl," even though shifting my stance during the pitcher's windup was a foreign concept. As it turned out, not long after I finally broke out of that slump, I was facing the Blue Jays' Ken Schrom, a young pitcher with really good control. The game was lopsided in our favor already, so when Schrom went 2-and-0 on me, I decided to try Earl's tip about moving up on the plate. The pitch was on the outside edge but I pulled it over the left field fence. Back in the dugout I told Earl I had crept up that time, and he said, "Oh, good! Good!" But I've stepped forward like that only a few times in the following fifteen years. (What I *have* done more often is moved in or out, up or back in the box—not during the windup, but initially—depending on the match-up against a particular pitcher. The most recent episode was in the 1996 playoffs, when I was standing almost on top of the plate à la Frank Robinson. I felt I had to do something to combat the hard breaking balls on, or just off, the outside corner from righthanders Charles Nagy and Orel Hershiser of the Indians and David Cone of the Yankees. I adopted the new position to force the action, and it seemed to work okay.)

I don't recall the exact date Earl played that trick on me during BP, but I know it was on May 1 when he ran out to argue the balk call against Jim Palmer that had moved Reggie Jackson from second to third base. While Earl was busy kicking dirt on home plate, Reggie called me over to the bag and said, "Look, don't let everyone else tell you how to hit. You could hit before you got here. Just be yourself and hit the way you want to hit. They traded DeCinces to make room for you, didn't they? They think you can play. They *know* you can."

In 1970, Reggie had had one of his few off years, and he went to winter ball with Frank Robinson because he'd been told that Frank was good with young players. Reggie gives Frank credit for teaching him how to manage his excitable personality and his temper. Their conversations in Puerto Rico had been much longer than our brief exchange standing at third base, but he had learned from Frank that the right words can help a player. They definitely can. I think Reggie had a similarly positive impact on several other young players.

When Reggie called me over, I was afraid at first that he was going to give me more technical advice, the last thing I needed, but what he said was perfect. Dad and Eddie Murray and others had been telling me the same thing, but coming from a guy of Reggie's stature at the time, and also as a player from another team, it just clicked. When word spread about the Jackson story, Eddie saw the opportunity to apply the needle. He pulled me aside, reminded me that he'd been saying the same thing, and said, "Hey, I can play the game, too. I don't care about getting my name in the paper, but I can play."

Maybe Reggie's timing was perfect because I'd already decided to quit worrying so much, play my best, and let the chips fall. If I was sent down, I was sent down. It wouldn't be the end of the world, and I'd be back anyway. The next day I responded with two resounding scratch hits and saw Reggie, who wasn't in the lineup, nodding his head and laughing in the dugout. My batting average jumped to .141. Then the following day I was beaned in the fifth inning by Mike Moore, and that turned out to be an important turning point, without a doubt.

In my first at-bat against Mike, who was also in his rookie year playing with Seattle, I had waved at a breaking ball and hit it off the end of the bat back to the mound. I'm stubborn, of course. If a pitcher got me on a certain pitch, I vowed he wasn't going to do it again. I went up the next time determined to prove I could hit Mike's curve. He'd have to get me out on a different pitch. I can't count the number of times that approach produced a hit in my early years in the game, because the pitchers kept going back to the same well. They wanted to make me prove I could hit a pitch, and I patiently waited for the opportunity. In the minors, especially, but also in the majors sometimes, I would wait two or three at-bats for the curve on the outside corner, then hit it hard somewhere, usually.

In the majors, it probably didn't take long for me to get the reputation as a hitter who looked for pitches, more so than most hitters. Some people even call this guessing. I call it *figuring it out*, and my own experience was my guide. A simple example: If I got a base hit on a fastball my first time up, the second time I could safely look for something else. Sooner or later in that at-bat, I'd get it. The calculation gets much more complicated than that, and you also have to determine who's really calling the game, the pitcher or the catcher. The two positions can think very differently about setting up batters. It's part of the game I really enjoy.

In any event, the way I hit, often looking for pitches, I have to have confidence in my judgment that this *is* a breaking ball. Recognize the spin, anticipate the break. When any batter is going great, it seems easy to pick up the spin almost the moment the ball leaves the pitcher's hand. When you're struggling, you don't see the ball or the spin as well. This is another definition of a slump. On Moore's first pitch in that second at-bat, I read curve ball, not because it was a curve ball but because I *wanted* the curve. I waited for the break . . . waited . . . waited . . . then suddenly realized this pitch was *never* going to break. It was Mike's ninety-four-mile-per-hour heater, and it clocked me right in the back of the head. Put me flat on my back; put a dent and a crack in my batting helmet as well. I was sent to the hospital for the standard "precautionary X rays," which were negative. Our general manager, Hank Peters, sent the helmet back to the company because it wasn't supposed to break like that. (I tried to find that helmet, but it disappeared. I'd like to have it back.)

I knew I couldn't let anyone think that this beaning was going to affect me negatively. If word spreads that you can be intimidated by high inside pitches, you're going to see a lot of high inside pitches. But if you can prove that the intimidation actually backfires against the pitcher, if you become a *better* hitter, you may see less of those brush-back pitches. In retrospect, a lot of people decided that the beaning woke me up. That's possible. I like to think that it made me an even more determined hitter.

On a mission following the beaning, helped along by the encouragement from Reggie Jackson and also by Earl's agreement that I should hit the way I was most comfortable, I finally broke that rookie slump and bit by bit pulled myself out of that deep hole. Earl told me in his office that all he wanted was for my average to go up, that he wasn't concerned about home runs. But I knew he did expect home runs from his third basemen because every manager does. Especially Earl. At the start of the season I might even have gotten into an uppercutting mode, trying for homers. Now in batting practice I worked hard on swinging level and hitting line drives, letting the homers take care of themselves. With a young player, sometimes a slump in the actual games produces a slump in batting practice, too, because you're trying too hard to prove that at least you can hit BP pitches. The approach in BP should be entirely different than the approach in a game, but the tendency during a slump is to try to look good in BP by hitting homers off sixty-mile-per-hour straight balls. Now I was careful to stay within myself, in BP and the games. I cut out all the bad habits and got back to the basics of driving the ball gap to gap. The Orioles left for a West Coast swing, and by the time we were back I was smoking and my average had gone up ninety points.

The slump was the first surprise my official rookie season. The second one came on July 1 at Memorial Stadium when I walked into the clubhouse for the Cleveland game and saw the 6 by my name on the lineup board. The number 6 is shortstop. I played 5—third base—and logically assumed Earl had made a mistake. I didn't notice that he had written 5 by my roomie Floyd Rayford's name. Then Lenn Sakata, who had been playing shortstop, came up to me in the clubhouse and said, "You know you're playing shortstop?"

"I am?"

"Yeah."

"No, that's just a mistake."

"No, you're playing short."

I found Dad; he confirmed the move and said don't worry, I'd be fine. Earl and the coaches had talked about the move, and Dad had told them I could handle the job. Right before the game Earl called me in and said, "Look, just make the routine plays. Don't try to go beyond yourself. If the ball's hit to you, I want you to make sure to catch it. Take it out of your glove. Get a good grip on it. Make a good throw to first base. *Okay?*" That's *exactly* how he was speaking to me, almost like I was a Little Leaguer. I'll never forget it. Then he continued, "If he's safe, he's still on first." He paused, I was wondering what exactly he was driving at, then he continued with his voice rising until he was almost yelling, "But if you catch the ball but then throw it over Murray's head, then not only is the runner safe, but *he's also on* *#@*! second base!*" That was a pet peeve of Earl's, similar to one of Senior's, who always said, "If you drop it, I don't care if it takes all day, pick it up the first time because if you hurry you'll fumble it again and compound the mistake." Both Senior and Earl were simply instructing the Oriole Way: don't give the other team any extra bases; make them earn everything they get. Basic, but effective.

Given what has happened in the following fifteen years, that sudden decision by Earl Weaver to move me from third base to shortstop in 1982 has probably been dissected more closely than any other episode in my career. Earl had always prided himself on his baseball judgment regarding who could do what, and when, and how. Everyone else in the game thinks they're great at these judgments, too, but Earl had the track record to back him up. He'd say, "They claim the manager might influence six or seven games a year. Well, *tactically*, maybe so, but what about his choice of the roster in spring training, when he sets up the team? The manager influences *all* of the games then, making sure he has someone for each and every situation that comes up in the ball game."

I agree. That assessment is one of the manager's key jobs. It makes sense that Earl was upset when the organization overruled him by trading Doug DeCinces to make room for me at third base. He disliked that deal on two counts: first, he wanted to keep DeCinces; second, he wanted me at shortstop, not third base. He'd been thinking about me at short ever since he'd seen me as a potential draftee fielding ground balls and clearing the fences at Memorial Stadium hitting off my father. Elrod Hendricks told a lot of reporters about the conversation he overheard on the field about that same time between Tom Giordano, the Orioles' scouting director, and Weaver. That exchange went something like this:

"Pitcher."

"Shortstop."

"Pitcher."

"Shortstop."

Earl's thinking regarding me and shortstop was straightforward. He didn't care whether I looked the part of the prototype. He didn't care whether other great shortstops were nicknamed "Scooter" and "Pee Wee," and he didn't care that I was "Rip" instead of "Runt." Apparently I reminded him of Marty Marion, one of his favorite players in St. Louis. Marion was tall, at six-two, but skinny, like I was when I was a kid in Bluefield. They called Marion "Slats" or "The Octopus." By 1982, I was pushing six-foot-four, 210 pounds. Earl didn't care whether I was acrobatic like Ozzie Smith, who was setting a new standard for the position while playing in the National League. Earl had always said he wanted three things out of his shortstop, and only three: make the routine play; turn the double play; make the third and final out. Maybe he was even suspicious of acrobatics on the grounds that with anyone but Ozzie, they lead to wild throws over Murray's head and a runner on second base. Earl wanted dependability from shortstop and, if possible, some pop. Ideal would be the baseball equivalent of Magic Johnson, a big guard who could drive the length of the court but also post up a forward. When DeCinces went on to hit 30 home runs in California in

1982, while I hit 28 in Baltimore, Weaver did the math and moaned that he could have had 58 home runs from the left side of the infield, definitely enough to win the division for us that year, since we came close anyway.

Bobby Bonner had been Mark Belanger's heir apparent at shortstop, highly touted from his first day in Bluefield, fresh out of Texas A&M. Bobby was about as smooth a fielder as there was. When we were on the same field in Bluefield, he made me look like a klutz. Three years later in Rochester, I was still in awe of Bobby's natural ability. Hard line drives got past the mound that Bobby stopped behind second base. He threw bullets from his knees deep in the hole. One day I was playing in close at third when a high chopper bounced over my head. When I looked back expecting to see the ball roll into short left field, there was Bobby, catching it while running full speed toward the line. Then he threw back across his body on a dead run to nail the fast runner at first. Amazing.

Earl knew all about these plays, of course, but he also knew about the one that, according to many people around the Orioles at that time, turned him against Bobby. That had been toward the end of 1980, when Bobby had stepped in for Mark Belanger and Lenn Sakata off and on. He'd made a few other errors, but the clincher came in a game in Toronto when Eddie Murray hit three home runs, including one in the top of the eleventh. In the bottom half of that inning, with Lloyd Moseby on second base, Barry Bonnell hit a bullet right at shortstop. On the wet, slick artificial turf, Bobby never got his hands down. Tie score, and the Blue Jays won the game in the thirteenth. My father said it was practically an impossible chance, but Earl didn't see it that way. The scene in the clubhouse afterward wasn't nice. Mike Boddicker, who had also been called up at the end of that season and had a locker near Bobby's, right around the corner from Earl's office, heard the explosion from Earl: "Where the hell did we get this guy? He's supposed to be our best shortstop prospect? He couldn't catch anything!" Earl went nuts, and if Mike could hear the tantrum from his locker, Bobby could hear it, too. Quite a few players said that he crumbled on the spot and never recovered. Mike said he saw it in Bobby's eyes.

I don't know. I wasn't there. All I know is that Bobby and I had been featured on a baseball card as "Baltimore Orioles Future Stars," and regarding Bobby, I agreed. I thought he was going to be the next great shortstop in the big leagues. He had outstanding tools, but Earl lost confidence in his *everyday* dependability to help a *winning* ball club in the majors, which is the only place it counts. Earl could live without pop from his shortstop's bat—Belanger had 20 home runs for his entire career—but he insisted on dependability.

Mike Boddicker also thought that Earl's tantrum in Toronto was one of his tests of a player's character. Doug DeCinces thought that, too, because he felt he'd been given his own test by Earl—and passed it. That's an instructive story that I'll pass along because it says a lot not only about Earl and Doug, but about the Oriole teams of that era. It happened in 1978, my first year in the minors in Bluefield, Doug's fourth year with the Orioles in Baltimore but his first full season as the official successor to Brooks Robinson, who had retired the previous fall.

Suddenly Earl was unhappy with his offense, so he decided to try Eddie Murray at third base, DeCinces at second, Lee May at first. He could count on lots of homers from those three, but could they field? Two of the three—Eddie and Doug—were playing out of position, basically. Doug didn't respond during the experiment. He'd broken his nose in spring training, never got on track to begin with, and now he was bouncing between third and second, making some errors, not hitting. One day, with guys on first and second, two out, Mark Belanger fields a ball behind the bag but can't get it out of his glove and tries a backhanded flip to Doug covering second. The toss goes wide and Doug is off the bag when he catches it, stumbles, and turns to see the lead runner, Buddy Bell, going for home. His throw to the plate is high and Bell is safe on a bang-bang play. Earl runs to the mound screaming, and Doug looks over at Mark wondering why Earl's so upset. Mark shrugs. Maybe it's the fact that it had been an 0-2 pitch.

When the inning is finally over, Earl is still angry on the bench, and Doug asks Lee May why. Lee just points at Doug.

"Why me?"

"I don't know. He just picked you out."

So Doug turns to Earl and says, "Hey, you talkin' to me?" And Earl comes after him and jabs his finger in his chest. That's when Doug grabs Earl's hand and says, "You do that again and I'll knock the $#%@ out of you." Earl goes, "Oh, yeah? Smith! You're on second," hollering to Billy Smith, a role player for the Orioles for a couple of years. Doug says, "You tell Smith he can play second the rest of the #@^&* year. I'm tired of your little games."

Doug really blew up. He admitted it later, but he also figured he'd gone through enough difficulty trying to replace Brooks Robinson, now he was trying to convert to second base because Earl had asked him to, and he gets chewed out on a play that wasn't even his fault, that was messed up to begin with. Elrod Hendricks and a couple of other guys, maybe a security guy in the dugout, had to hold Doug back.

As it happened, that was the first game of a doubleheader, and Earl called a team meeting between games. He talked about tempers and sometimes pushing players too far. In Doug's mind, Earl almost apologized for the incident. He said he didn't hold grudges, he was here to win, he expected his players to be here for the same reason. For the second game, Doug started at first base with Jim Palmer going for his 200th victory. In the seventh inning, Doug doubled off the right field wall and drove in two runs. Then he was amazed when Rich Dauer trotted out to pinch-run for him. Dauer was in his second season, the likely second baseman of the future, but he couldn't outrun Doug. At least Doug didn't think so, and as he came off the field, Lee May could see that he was steaming and met him on the top step of the dugout. Lee wouldn't even let Doug stop to pick up his glove. He escorted him straight into the clubhouse and said, "Remember, Earl doesn't hold any grudges."

In Doug's mind he could have folded right then, but he didn't. In

Doug's mind, Bobby Bonner did fail his own similar test from Earl two years later. Doug and a lot of the Oriole players from that generation had the notion that Earl's thinking regarding his own temper tantrums was this: If you can't deal with me, you can't deal with bases loaded, top of the ninth. If you can't handle *my* pressure, how can you handle the pressure of the game?

Maybe, but again, I don't know. The theory sounds nice, but a lot of people have tried to figure out Earl Weaver. I know he used all kinds of psychological warfare, and Bobby Bonner himself told reporters covering my streak fourteen years later that he knew from that day in Toronto when Earl exploded that he wouldn't be playing many games for this manager. And he was right. After playing a little in 1982, he didn't play at all the following year and asked to be traded. That didn't happen. In 1984 he was sent instead to Rochester, where he had his best year at the plate. Now he was a minor league free agent with other baseball offers in hand, but he had something else in mind. Already a born-again Christian, publicly regretting the wild ways of his youth, Bobby moved with his family to Zambia, where, the last I heard, he's still working as a missionary.

I don't think Earl maliciously tried to hurt Bobby Bonner or any of his ballplayers. He could be friendly or he could be so wrapped up in something else that he'd walk right past you in the clubhouse and never say a word. Or he could just ignore you altogether. With injuries, he was always pushing, pushing, *pushing* guys to get back: "Can you give me a day? Can you give me an inning?" He even had a public run-in with Mark Belanger over the severity of Mark's back injury. But I don't think he had a doghouse—DeCinces started the game the day after his battle with Earl, and he started for the next three years, before he was traded—and as far as I know Earl never lied to his players. He could be tough, no doubt about it, and some of the players may not have liked his methods, but they got the truth from him, I think, and they respected him for that. If you weren't getting the job done, Earl would tell you, like he was telling me during that rookie slump, and if he decided you *couldn't* get the job done, he'd get rid of you. But something else about

Earl few people know about: as end of the season approached, he called guys into his office and asked if they had any incentives in their contracts that they still hadn't made—innings played, mound appearances, at-bats, etc. Here's where the baseball side and the business side can mix. Without passing judgment on whether Earl was right or wrong, policywise, I think it's really cool. I think it was his way to say thank you for the player's time and effort.

In 1982, two years after Bonner's famous error in Toronto, Lenn Sakata was the main shortstop, with Bobby Bonner playing a little—very little. In June, the team fell behind Boston and Milwaukee—but not by much, only five games. I was finally hitting pretty well, climbing out of that hole I'd dug myself, when Earl decided to make the change at shortstop. He thought I could play the position and deliver some offense as a bonus. Floyd Rayford replaced me at third, for the time being. Earl said about the experiment, "If it doesn't work, Cal can always go back to third, where we know he can do the job."

At that stage, I was prepared to move, even though I was happy to be the third baseman of the future for the Orioles. I was playing my position about as well as I could, about as well as anyone else in the league at the time: six errors in 69 games. And I was now hitting. Would this new position and the extra responsibilities throw me into another slump? The thought crossed my mind, as it must have crossed Earl's. This is a pretty bold move, I thought, but I'm game if he is. I'd played fewer than 10 games at shortstop since A-ball in Miami. I knew the rudiments of the position, but it was almost like starting over. On the field I was very deliberate, like Earl said, focusing on the routine play, slowly gaining confidence with the others. Every time a new play came up that I handled, I told myself, Okay, that's one more you know you can make. Pretty soon most of them were taken care of. Working with two second basemen—Dauer and Sakata—didn't make things easier, but all of us made the adjustments.

Dauer and I talked a lot about positioning. He warned me that the coaches trying to move me around from the dugout couldn't really see where I was to begin with. "They can't really see how deep you are," he said. "They can't see the angles. They can't see what pitch is called. If you have any doubts, play as straight up as you can. Don't get too caught up in overshifting. If they move you and you don't like it, nod your head, move, then when they're not looking, go back where you were." I also think Senior finally convinced people to leave me alone to work out my positioning with help from Richie. Dad had a lot of confidence in my baseball sense and instincts, and I slowly got enough confidence to start cheating on batters, but only if I had a really good sense of where they'd hit the ball, not just a guess. If I didn't have a good idea, I didn't get fancy. (I still don't.) Soon enough, I was calling the coverages at second base. Dauer was all for it.

Immediately after the move to shortstop I hit maybe half a dozen homers, but then I went into a tailspin, not quite as bad as the slump in April, but almost, and adapting to shortstop might have had something to do with it. Playing third, I had gone into the dugout thinking only about hitting. Playing shortstop, I was sometimes thinking about a play or situation that had just occurred on the field. When I didn't reach a ball, I wondered if I should have. But slowly I settled in, and after the season, Earl Weaver summed up by saying that I had played well, that maybe I hadn't gotten to every ball Belanger would have reached, but that I had gotten to some that quite a few other shortstops around the league would have missed. And don't forget, Earl reminded everyone, it's easier to find a third baseman who can hit 28 homers. (In theory, that's right, but the Orioles haven't had consistent power out of third base in the last fifteen years.)

On May 29, about a month before he moved me to shortstop, Earl gave me the second game off in a doubleheader against Toronto. My roomie Floyd Rayford started that game at third base. It turns out that was the last time I wouldn't be in the starting lineup for fourteen years . . . and counting.

Chapter Seven

On September 26, the next-to-last Sunday of the 1982 season, the Orioles were three games behind the Brewers, playing the third game of a big series against the division leaders in Milwaukee. We had split the first two games and were leading in the bottom of the eighth inning on Sunday, 3–2. Bob Skube was on third base for Milwaukee with one out, Cecil Cooper batting. Cooper hit a fly to medium deep center field— deep enough to score Skube and tie the game, it looked like, but T-Bone Shelby made a perfect throw to catcher Rick Dempsey for the bang-bang third out of the inning. We held on for the win, and T-Bone's play was subsequently celebrated as one of the great ones in Oriole history, maybe saving a pennant drive. However, I don't think the story behind that throw ever made the sports pages.

T-Bone had been called up from Rochester at the end of the season, although his arm was hurting and he wasn't able to do very much. In fact, he was scheduled for elbow surgery following the season. Weaver called T-Bone into his office shortly after he arrived and asked if he could make one throw if he had to. "One" was the reply, and Earl said okay, he'd remember that. John saved his arm. He didn't practice. He did make just one meaningful throw in September, and it saved that ball game on Sunday. Our dugout went wild, of course, and then after we'd won the game in the ninth, guys tried to carry John off the field. In the clubhouse, he was surrounded by more reporters than he'd probably seen in his life, and he looked a little confused by all the hoopla. All he had done was throw the guy out. Sure his arm was sore, but still, just one throw. Just one game.

Finally I realized what was happening and walked over and asked John, "You don't know what you did, do you?"

"No."

John knew we were in a pennant race, but he didn't know how crucial that game—and every game—was. No one had told him, and John is a really low-key guy. T-bone would say later what a lot of the guys on that team have said over the years: the final series of that season, the four games against the Brewers in Baltimore the following weekend, was the most exciting baseball of his career. I agree, and I include the World Series the following year and the series against Toronto at the end of the '89 season. That weekend was just . . . outstanding.

To get to the point that the final series of the season meant anything, we had to make up for a bad streak in the early dog days when we lost 16 out of 23 and Howard Cosell wrote us off on *Monday Night Baseball*. Spurred on by the inspirational speech on "contest living" from our owner, Edward Bennett Williams, we put together a patented Orioles hot streak, winning 17 out of the next 18. EBW delivered that speech once or twice a year, it seemed like, always when his team was struggling, but he was so commanding and eloquent that the guys listened every time. One of his main ideas was always that in baseball the team can lose sixty games a year and still have a great season. Coming from the courtroom, where every case is a season in itself, our litigator-owner seemed amazed by this feature of baseball. After Williams spoke, Earl Weaver got up and talked for an additional twenty or thirty minutes. It was like a convention in the clubhouse that afternoon. Earl reminded us that the Orioles had always won in the past with hot streaks in August and September, and this year would be no exception.

We did get really hot, won two of those three games in Milwaukee, then closed out the season with a second consecutive huge weekend series against the Brewers, this time in Baltimore. But we were still three games behind with four to play. Win them all, and we win the division title; lose one game, and we were history; there would be no tie.

Earl Weaver had officially announced his retirement weeks earlier, there had already been an emotional farewell ceremony a couple of weeks earlier, and now, win or lose, the fans in Baltimore were pumped up to send Earl on his way. The energy in the stands that weekend was incredible to begin with, and after we swept the first two games in a doubleheader—Storm Davis, just twenty years old, nicknamed Cy Clone (as opposed to Cy Young), won the second game—it was pande- monium in the stands and the clubhouse. Then on Saturday afternoon Sammy Stewart and Scott McGregor threw a six-hitter and we won going away, 11–3, and the huge crowd went absolutely crazy.

Now we were tied with the Brewers with one game to play, winner take all for the pennant on Sunday, with a great match-up of Jim Palmer against Don Sutton, two of the best pitchers for the past decade. The stands were full of brooms, ready for the sweep and the title. But it didn't happen. Robin Yount, who would win the MVP that fall, hit two homers for the Brewers, and Ben Ogilvie made a great sliding catch on a slice by Joe Nolan in the eighth inning, which broke our back.

On the last day of the season, we fell short. I was disappointed, of course, but the disappointment wasn't deep. That had been such an exciting stretch run, and our fans were really proud of us. They wouldn't even leave the stadium, demanded curtain calls, and then more curtain calls. Wild Bill Hagy, our burly, bearded, cabdriving cheerleader, came down from his section in the upper deck, where he and his stalwart gang were known as "The Roar from Thirty-Four," to lead the cheers from the roof of the dugout. The whole stadium chanted "WE WANT EARL! WE WANT EARL!" and finally the Certified Genius trotted back onto the field, tears in his eyes, to lead one last O-R-I-O-L-E-S cheer. Totally exhausted, a bunch of us sat on the floor of the clubhouse talking about how incredible the scene had been. Storm Davis ended up playing in three World Series (one with the Orioles, then two with Oakland), but that weekend in Baltimore made Storm an Orioles fan for life; just ask him. I was a rookie and figured this was the way baseball was supposed to be, and always would be, at least in my hometown. We always won, or came close, so I'd have plenty more of these great times. It was the Oriole Way. That's what I naively believed.

Earl enjoyed joking years later, "If I'd only moved Ripken to shortstop earlier. We'd have won the pennant that year, too." With the benefit of hindsight, I agree: we probably would have won if we'd started the season with me at short *and* Doug DeCinces at third. Too bad life doesn't work that way. After starting off in the bad slump, I worked the average up to .285 before it settled back to .264 at the end, but with 28 homers and 93 RBIs. Earl loved those power numbers, and they were good enough to get me in the running for Rookie of the Year, with Kent Hrbek the main competition, and also Gary Gaetti. They'd had strong years. And Wade Boggs, Von Hayes, and Tom Brunansky were also rookies in '82. At the All-Star break, it had been almost a foregone conclusion that Hrbek would win the honor, because he started off fast and made the American League All-Star team. Kent wound up hitting .301 for the year, but my other numbers matched up well— more games, home runs, doubles, RBIs, and runs—and I think the baseball writers put a lot of emphasis on my position at shortstop. The voting was also probably weighted in my favor because my team had taken the race to the final day of the season, while the Twins were out of it.

The night the vote was going to be announced, I waited in the townhouse in Cockeysville, north of Baltimore, which I had just bought. John Blake, our PR guy, had gotten me excited by asking permission to give my phone number to the American League office. That was a good sign, I thought. A bunch of my friends from Aberdeen were on hand for a party. My brother Billy was there, too. He'd been drafted by the Orioles and played in Bluefield that year.

It was about eleven o'clock when the phone finally rang, and everyone got quiet.

"Hello?"

It was Jack Lang, executive director of the Baseball Writers Association of America, and he said one word by way of a greeting: "Congratulations." I gave everyone the thumbs up and the party began. How could my rookie year have gone any better? Only if we had won the division and then if my father had been named the Orioles' new manager for 1983, replacing Earl.

Joe Altobelli got the job instead, but no one could fault that choice. Like Senior, Joe was a big part of the Oriole Way. He had managed eleven years in the minors for the organization, including six in Rochester, and he had helped set up the spring training camps with Senior. My dad had played for Earl in Appleton, Wisconsin, in 1960, the summer I was born, and they had a great deal of mutual respect, but Earl had close ties with Joe, too, who had played for Earl in Rochester as a veteran, working a lot with the younger prospects. When Earl found out the organization was looking for a Rookie League manager in Bluefield he recommended Joe Altobelli. Earl was always proud of that phone call.

Ray Miller had also been a deserving candidate for the job in Baltimore, and Frank Robinson, too. I was disappointed Dad wasn't promoted, but I wasn't upset or hurt by Joe's selection. My father was still young—forty-seven years old. He had plenty of time.

With the coaching staff, Joe made no changes for the following year, and none of much significance on the team. The best thing he did with that talented group was let us play, and we rolled from the first day of spring training. I know that some of the veteran players were also determined to show that they could win without Earl Weaver. I didn't think about that at all, and don't believe it was really a factor. I think we won the World Series that year because we looked back on our lousy start in '82 and were determined not to lose the ground early that would be hard to make up in August and September. I also believe that the incredible emotion from that final weekend the previous year catapulted us into 1983.

Floyd Rayford agrees with me. He told me that he'd known right after the final game against the Brewers that this group of guys would be back the following year, and that we'd win everything, and that's why he was so upset not to be part of it.

Floyd was cut from the squad during spring training and returned to Rochester. I was going to miss him, because he'd been my road roomie my rookie year. I have no idea why we were assigned together. Maybe it was because our last names started with "R" and we both liked to wrestle. Floyd was just one of those guys people love to pick on. It's true, and he'll say the same thing. Eddie Murray picked on him all the time, pounding Sugar Bear's ribs. Me, too. Our pitching coach, Ray Miller, tried to come to his defense, because Floyd performed some backup catching that year as well as playing third base. Ray was right, but we ignored him. Some nights Floyd must have played with sore ribs.

What happened to Floyd the following year is another example of how things can work out in baseball if you're not careful and lucky as well as talented. In those early years in Baltimore, every one of these stories that I saw or heard just reinforced the conviction I already had: keep playing every day, and never look back. After Sugar Bear was cut, Leo Hernandez was going to be our third baseman, but this wasn't necessarily a disaster for Floyd. If he played well in Rochester, he could come back. And he did play well. He hit .360 for the first couple of months, which was way, way higher than he'd ever hit before. He said it reflected his motivation to get back to the team he was sure was going to the World Series, and his hitting probably would have earned him that trip to Baltimore except for one major catch: he'd have to clear waivers before the Orioles could bring him up from the minors. He could only clear waivers if no other team wanted him, but other teams would have wanted Floyd. So there was no way Floyd could play for the Orioles in 1983. No way at all. Instead, our general manager, Hank Peters, traded him to St. Louis for a player to be named later. When we needed outfield help, Hank got Tito Landrum to close the deal. Tito had been playing great for Louisville, and he played well for us, too, and won the fourth game of the playoffs against the White Sox with a tenth-inning home run in a scoreless tie.

The following spring, the Rayford trade was reversed: Tito went back to the Cardinals, Floyd returned to the Orioles. The funny-looking sequence of events hurt Floyd's feelings. Hank Peters pointed out that he wouldn't have played in the majors at all in 1983 if he hadn't been traded to St. Louis the first time, but Floyd *knew* that Orioles team was going all the way, and he wasn't there to be part of it. The following two years he played some with us in Baltimore, but then in 1986 disaster struck. One day in spring training, Rick Dempsey missed the bus to somewhere and Sugar Bear was pressed into service as the catcher. With Mike Flanagan on the mound, a foul tip caught Floyd on the right thumb. It was one of those flukey things, but Floyd's career went south, as he put it. Today he manages the Batavia Clippers, Philadelphia's A-ball franchise in upstate New York, and he lives in the off-season in Maryland. He has never been to the new ballpark in Camden Yards.

But at least Floyd made it to the big leagues. After I went up to the Orioles, I never again saw my old minor league friends and roomies Will George, Tim Norris, and Brooks Carey on a baseball field. None made the big leagues at all. It's tough for pitchers, no doubt about it. A good pitcher who doesn't break down will almost certainly make it to the big leagues, if not necessarily stay, but so many do break down. The game is probably tougher on pitchers psychologically, too. I know these three guys felt that way, because they told me so all the time. They'd say, "Look at you. You only have two or three guys *at most* competing for an infield position, but the Orioles have *fifty* pitchers in the minors, and how many do they need every year in Baltimore? Maybe a couple." They pointed out the burden of having an opportunity just every fifth day. The regular player can bounce back from an 0-for-5 the following night, but after getting shelled, a pitcher has to wait almost a week to redeem himself. When a hitter has four O-fers in a row, everyone says, "Hey, everybody has slumps." But after three or four bad games in a row, a pitcher's stock may go down.

I understand their points in that long-standing argument, and on one point I do totally agree: pitchers are much more vulnerable physically; their arm is all they've got, so they live with a greater fear of career-threatening injury. Otherwise, I disagree. A slump is a slump, for hitter or pitcher. The hitter has to rely on the pitcher to make a mistake in order to see a good pitch to hit, while the pitcher's mistake is *his* mistake. Pitchers control the game and their success rate is at least seventy percent. Excellent hitters succeed thirty percent of the time, and I'm not even sure they'd average .500 in *batting practice* if fielders were playing their positions.

This argument will go on as long as baseball is played, and no one will win. All in all, it comes down to this: you're in competition with yourself, mainly, to develop and improve, and with other players as well, and the challenge of making the majors is tough for everybody.

Will George played with us in Rochester in 1981, then he was sent back to Charlotte, then he was traded to Detroit. The next year he was released by the Tigers and signed by the Miami Marlins, an independent team. Will's contract was bought by the San Diego Padres, and he played Double-A for them before he hurt his arm—not for the first time—in 1984, and became a player-coach in their system. That was the end of the road, playingwise. Some of our friends from the minors think that things started going sour for Will when he got mononucleosis after the '78 season. They said he never got his strength back, although I never heard Will say that himself. He then worked as a minor league pitching coach in several organizations, including the Orioles, before becoming a scout for the Miami Marlins, the expansion club in the National League.

Tim Norris, my first friend in professional baseball, really, the high school graduate from Maryland I drove to Bluefield with, got off to a rough start, but by the time he got to Charlotte in 1980, two years later, he was throwing pretty well. When I went up to Rochester in 1981, Tim returned to Charlotte, then came down with tendonitis and was sent to Hagerstown for rehab, where he pitched as well as he ever had, from what I heard long-distance. But Tim knew his days were numbered, with the O's at least, when he was told in spring training in 1982 that there wasn't a spot for him in Charlotte. The story of his career was making the papers back home in Baltimore, with management people saying he had a weight problem, maybe a concentration problem. Tim said he wasn't getting the opportunity to pitch. It was a standoff.

Finally the organization moved Tim to Charlotte for the last month of '82, and to everyone's surprise, including his own by that time, he threw a couple of good games. But the following spring the Orioles told him again that they didn't have a starting spot for him in Charlotte. Tim had asked for his release a couple of times so he could catch on with somebody who might be able to use him. He didn't want to be strung along by the Orioles until he was twenty-five or twenty-six years old, when nobody else would be interested. Now he asked for his release again, because he'd decided he wasn't going back to A-ball. He got the release, and the Orioles also set him up with a team in Italy, but his wife was pregnant, so Tim went home to Maryland to see whether the phone would ring. It never did. When I saw Tim the first time after he'd gone home for good, he said he'd expected a letdown, but actually a big weight had been lifted from his shoulders. He works today with the same printing company he joined when he quit baseball, and he also coaches a "select" Little League team—the best players. I'm sure he's very good.

It's strange seeing guys in later years who worked side by side with you in the minors but never made the majors. It's even worse when the player isn't positive that a lack of talent had been the problem. But at the same time everyone knows going in that the odds are against you. About two percent of all the players who sign professional contracts actually make the big leagues for even a single game; I guess many of the other ninety-eight percent do a lot of looking back. Tim Norris told me that if he had it to do over again, he would have put himself up for the draft as a first baseman. With Eddie Murray in place, the Orioles wouldn't have been interested, but the Tigers had told Tim they were ready to draft him at that position.

And then there's Brooks Carey, who called me Bubba, which he said was a Key West thing. His family has owned a radiator and auto parts store in the Florida Keys for years, the only one between Key West and Key Largo, Brooks said, and I took that to mean it was a really good business. Brooks got off to a pretty good start his first few years. His problems came later, in 1981, when he pitched in winter ball and, altogether, 300-plus innings over a twelve-month period. This might be another story about the dangers of winter ball for starting pitchers, because Brooks's arm was never the same. As he put it, "I was trying to flick it up there with my thumb." Halfway through the '81 season, Tom Giordano told him either he could say he wanted to go home because his arm wasn't feeling good or the Orioles would have to release him. Brooks went home and rested, but in spring training 1982, his arm was sore. They gave him three cortisone shots, his arm felt great, and the next day he was traded to Cincinnati for Joe Nolan, a catcher. I didn't see him before he left Miami.

The first thing they did in the Cincinnati camp was send Brooks off on a timed sixty-yard dash, and he tore his left hamstring. "I didn't pull it," he told me, "I tore the thing in half." That put him out of commission until the last month of the season, when his arm was sore again, as bad as ever. One day early in spring training the following year—1983—Brooks was left behind to throw on the side while the rest of the Reds squad traveled to games. Walking toward the minor league clubhouse, he saw Fred Norman walking toward him. Freddie was on the Reds' coaching staff, and Brooks knew him from somewhere. Before Freddie could say a word, Brooks said to him, "Hey, Freddie, is this your first spring training as a coach?" When Freddie nodded, Brooks said, "Let me ask you a question, just out of curiosity. Have you ever had to tell someone he was released?" Freddie gave him this amazed blank look, and Brooks said, "No, I didn't think so. Well, here's how you do it. I'm going to pretend like I'm you and I say, 'Brooks, your arm's not what we thought it was, and we're just going to have to let you go.' "

Freddie Norman hugged Brooks and told him he couldn't know how much he appreciated that. But Brooks did know. He knew that Freddie had been sent over to deliver the news, and he knew how bad Freddie would feel having to deliver it. Brooks had tears in his eyes.

In the following few years I saw Brooks a few times here and there, but then we went quite a while without talking until he showed up at spring training in 1992, maybe '93. We talked a little in the tunnel after one game, but the next day I saw Brooks in the stands and asked someone to bring him into the dugout—spring training, remember— and the first thing I did was grab him in a headlock, just to prove I could still do it. We sat there for seven innings, bringing each other up to date. Brooks is now running the family auto parts business in the Florida Keys. I didn't remind him then, but I remembered when he'd say to me about the majors, "I just want to get up there for one game."

I never knew what to say in reply. I did know that one game would never have been enough for me.

With Floyd Rayford gone, my roomie in 1983 was Rick Dempsey. This was right at the tail end of the roomie-on-the-road era in major league baseball, before single rooms became the norm. With Earl Weaver gone from the Orioles, Rick must have needed someone on the team to drive him to distraction and figured I could fill this role with my wrestling. So he asked me to bunk with him, and I said yeah, and I think I gave him his money's worth. If I caught him sleeping at an inappropriate hour, I made a sandwich of Rick between the mattress and the box springs, a move I had perfected against Floyd Rayford. Sometimes I used the mattress to stuff Rick in a corner of the room. One time in spring training he hid under a table and found a hammer on one of the chairs. When I came after him, he swung the weapon at my feet, and he wasn't playing around, either, like I was. Sometimes things degenerated into something close to a fight between Rick and me, and he always blamed me, saying I had too much energy for my own good. I did have a tremendous amount of energy, and I still do, but at that time I was in my early twenties while Dempsey was a worn-down catcher eleven years older. (Just joking, Rick.) However, Rick could dish it out, too. I wasn't there for the classic example, but I heard about it in the clubhouse. Everyone on the Orioles heard this story.

First, some background. In the majors, it's traditional for veterans to pick up the check for new guys; if everyone has about the same seniority, it's traditional for everyone to pitch in on the check. On the Orioles in that era, three guys in particular were notorious for somehow stepping out on the check, or not having any cash on them when the time came. This was the standing tease, and Tippy Martinez, Lenn Sakata, and Mike Boddicker were happy to play into it. And they saved money to the extent that it was true. Those three guys shared an apartment in Key Biscayne during spring training one year—to save more money, presumably. One night after they'd just stiffed Rick and the rest of us on another check, he raced to their place and hid in a closet. Don't ask me how he got in, I don't know, but he did. After his three targets came back to their place, and when the opportunity arose, Rick snuck out of the closet and threw the circuit breaker for the whole place. After the three of them got the lights back on, they sat down to a game of penny-ante poker, which for them was high stakes. Rick was back in the closet, and from his position down a hallway, peering through the slats of the door, he could see them in a mirror. When the game got rolling, he tossed a hairbrush into the room, disguised his voice, and announced an armed robbery.

Panic broke out, and Rick swears he held them at bay from that closet for thirty minutes. He swears that Lenny Sakata was on his knees, praying. Finally he got all three of them into another room, took the money off the poker table, and made his escape. Rick was and probably still is prone to exaggeration, and there seem to be some holes in the plot line he gave out after the fact, but we know there's some truth to this tale because the story about the three Orioles robbed at gunpoint in their apartment complex made the newspaper the next morning. Our friends had called the cops. Total reported loss: $500. But when they got to their lockers in the clubhouse, they found their money from the poker game waiting for them—$50. Rick never let them forget it.

All in all, I'd say those Oriole teams from 1982 to 1985 or '86 were as loose as any I've played on. For myself, I joked around a lot in the clubhouse, but my more elaborate hijinks were away from the park, mainly at the hotels on the road. Rick Dempsey teamed with me, hoping that I'd burn off some energy and save him some wrestling matches. We had our fun with the fire extinguishers a few times, but our best work relied on Rick's uncanny knack for acquiring duplicate room keys. Once inside a room, we booby-trapped the place. Occasionally we got other players, but our main target was Tom Marr, one of the Orioles' broadcasters. I'd first gotten to know Tommy when he had come up to Rochester to broadcast the Red Wings game while the major league players were on strike in 1981. He knew that my grandmother in Aberdeen listened to Oriole broadcasts on the radio and rightly figured that she'd be listening to these games from Rochester as well, so when I hit a home run, Tommy shouted on the air, "Grandmother Ripken, it's gone!" When I joined the Orioles, that became his home run call for me, that or "Grandmother Ripken, that's outa here!"

Rick and I rigged a bucket of water above Tom's door—a structure too complicated to describe without providing schematic drawings— and waited inside for him to arrive after the ball game. The contraption worked to perfection. We used Super Glue to cement all his stuff to the counter in the bathroom. We stretched cellophane across his toilet bowl—an old trick, but always effective. We piled pine needles and pine cones under Tommy's sheets, soaked his pillow in bathtub water, knocked on his door at two a.m. When he cracked the door open— expecting something, of course—we fired away with the fire extinguisher and filled the room with foam. One time he held us out somehow, closed the door, and went back to bed, but the gap under the door was big enough for us to shoot the foam under it. I don't understand how Tommy was able to stay in there, because the chemicals in these extinguishers work by sucking out the oxygen, or so I understand. When Tommy woke up, he and everything else were covered with foam. When he got out of bed, there was a perfect outline of his body on the sheet. That's what he said.

We terrorized Tommy, but, obviously, he played along with us. In the hotels, Tommy could be an instigator himself, on occasion. He ordered seven cabs for Dempsey one time, and all of them wanted money. I was tougher to trap than Rick, but Tommy dreams that there's still time, even though he now works in Philadelphia, where he has a radio call-in show. Ask him if he ever got anything over on me and he'll say, "Not yet."

As the years passed and I began dating Kelly, then married and settled down and had children, the horseplay with my teammates faded out a little. Not enough time! Also, I was becoming more conscious of the relationship between Cal Ripken the baseball player and Cal Ripken the person. Like Charles Barkley, I don't really think professional athletes should be primary role models—*parents* and teaches and the other adults in the local community should be the primary role models—but after just a few years in the majors it became obvious that my actions could and did influence kids, whether I liked it or not. It dawned on me that just as I'd looked up to ballplayers when I was a kid, some kids were now looking up to me. Years later, I was watching when Mickey Mantle told the press conference held in Dallas while he was dying of liver disease, "I'm no role model." To me, Mickey seemed genuinely sad and embarrassed to have to say that. I admired his courage for doing so.

Why not be responsible in my actions? It's not that hard to do. As a young player, I'd always been impressed by the way the real pros like Eddie Murray and Frank Robinson and Brooks Robinson calmly returned the helmet and the bat to the bins after a bad at-bat. Maybe they got furious in private, as I've done occasionally, pounding away on a rubber tube hanging on a rope in a room off the dugout, but they didn't put on public tantrums. Maybe they yelled at the umpire from the little room off the dugout, but they didn't show him up at the plate. This is one of the areas that Frank Robinson talked about with Reggie Jackson in those conversations they had in winter ball that I've mentioned. Reggie had had a problem with his temper; he threw bats. Frank convinced him that all the good work Reggie had accomplished for twenty-nine days could be thrown away, literally, on the thirtieth. Frank taught him and a lot of other guys that a professional has to be in control of his emotions every day, every play.

Control (margin handwriting)

As a coach and manager, my father was such a fixture with the Orioles organization for so many years—almost four decades—that a certain mythology built up around him. His temper was part of that mythology. During one of the two years he managed the Aberdeen club, he was at the bottom of the pile in one of the worst fights anyone could remember. This happened in Winnipeg. If I know my father, he was trying to win that fight while breaking it up as well. The next day the two managers dressed in Indian robes and smoked a real peace pipe at home plate when they came out to exchange lineup cards for the game. My mother has the picture. All in all, Senior had his share of ejections in both the minors and the majors. I don't know who had more altogether, him or Earl Weaver. Earl was famous—and popular—for his colorful tantrums and ejections. I decided early that I wasn't going to do this *intentionally*. Baseball can be very frustrating, and there are times when you boil over, but a player also has a responsibility to his team. A manager or a coach can be doing a service for the team by getting tossed: stand up for your player, maybe fire up the team and the fans. But a player is of no use to anyone taking a shower in the clubhouse. It's one thing to have some fun at 2 a.m. in the hotel with Rick Dempsey and Tommy Marr, another to lose your cool and get out of control on the field in front of an audience.

After I came up to the majors, Ken Singleton pointed out one of my throwing incidents on videotape and asked if I thought that looked good. No, I didn't think it looked good, and I immediately remembered, and regretted, one such episode in particular. A day or two after I threw a batting helmet after striking out, a kid at a clinic I was coaching asked me about that incident. His Little League coach had probably been teaching the players not to throw their helmets, and this boy saw me on television doing just that. I told him I shouldn't have done it, and I haven't had many big displays of anger since then. The worst exception was probably in 1989, when I was thrown out in the first inning of a game against Minnesota for arguing a called strike. Drew Coble was the umpire. Starting off the game, Mike Devereaux and Phil Bradley had been called out on strikes that were on—or beyond—the outside corner, calls they questioned with long looks as they walked back to the dugout. I was thinking that Roy Smith, the pitcher, had good control on the outside edge. If he started getting the call on pitches three, four, maybe even five or six inches outside, we were in for a long game, because Roy could locate that pitch almost every time. Walking to the plate, I knew that if the zone was too big, I'd have to say something to Coble.

Sure enough, the first pitch was a called strike on the outside corner; close, but a reasonable called strike. But then the next pitch was a good distance outside, and Coble called it a strike. I stepped out of the box and said, "The first pitch was pretty good, but I thought that one was a little outside." That's what I said while smoothing the dirt with my cleats and looking down at the ground to avoid bringing the fans' attention. Umpires usually appreciate this courtesy. I was just about to settle back in for the next pitch when all of a sudden Coble stepped around to answer me and got really close to my face. I didn't think that was right, blew my stack, and of course he threw me out of the game.

That was the angriest I'd been on a baseball field in a long time. I lost it, didn't handle the situation well, and, sure enough, as I learned later, a boy had driven up with his father from Virginia mainly to watch me play. Instead, he spent the last eight innings in tears. That really bothered me, and stuck with me.

In 1983, parents really were telling their kids to drink their milk because Cal Ripken drank his milk. Parents confirmed this with me all the time, after I signed a small deal with a regional milk producers' cooperative. After my rookie season, quite a few companies approached Ron Shapiro, my agent, about endorsement deals. One of these was Esskay hot dogs, and that was an easy call because my family had eaten these hot dogs my entire life. I signed with Esskay. Two of the other offers were from the milk producers and Jockey shorts. The Jockey deal would have been a different kind of exposure altogether, to make the same pun that everybody else was making. My mother didn't like the Jockey idea at all. A T-shirt would be fine, she said, but not underwear. But the campaign was and is in good taste, and Jim Palmer, the guy I would have joined in the campaign, has a perfectly good image.

Ron felt that I could do one or the other campaign, but not both, and he pressed pretty hard with the idea that this would be a defining moment for me in the public eye. In hindsight, I guess it was. I tease Ron now about not being so certain which was the right choice, but the choice for me wasn't that tough, really. I couldn't see myself posing in my undershorts. I'm a milk person, both in substance and in how I want to be seen, and not a male model, in effect. I honestly believe that all the milk I drank as a kid—much more than Elly, Fred, or Billy—may be one reason I'm the biggest Ripken by far. So after a few weeks' consideration, I signed with milk. Five minutes after the first radio ad aired, the teasing began in the clubhouse.

"Drink your milk, Cal."

does milk do a body good?

Chapter Eight

With a full season under my belt, I was confident about my sophomore season in 1983, with no concerns at all about a sophomore slump.
I was intent on not digging a big hole for myself in April, like I'd done
the year before. Maybe that negative goal wasn't really the best way to
go about things, because I just plugged along for the first three months,
nothing great, but only one relatively modest slump, a definite improve-
ment over the previous year. The darkest moment of that year—and it
wasn't all that dark—was in spring training, when I showed up at camp
early to test out a sore ankle. A sprained ankle wasn't unusual—I was
always spraining both of them until I learned how to tape them—but
this time I ended up with a sore shoulder because of too much time in
the batting cage. I got a cortisone injection and, along with it, a warning
from Jim Palmer, who had received a shot in his pitching shoulder the
previous week. The shot masks pain, Jim reminded me. If you work out
after getting cortisone, you can tear up your body without knowing it.
He explained all the mechanics of the shoulder to me as well as the doctors had. But then, Jim's a pitcher; he knows shoulders. To reinforce his
warning, Jim also told me about a recent conversation he'd had with a
pitcher who had gotten an injection and then thrown nine innings over

the next several days. Not long after that he was selling insurance—a good way to make a living, but not what I had in mind for my life at the time.

I rested the shoulder, the ankle held up, the shoulder healed, and I made the All-Star team for the first time with good, solid numbers. Then, in the second half of 1983, I really caught fire, hitting about .340 for almost three months. I was waiting better on the ball and hitting line to line. The hits were coming in bunches. Life is tremendous fun in those circumstances. I don't remember exactly, but those months of good times on the field were probably when Rick Dempsey and I played our best pranks on Tommy Marr.

I'd never been on that sort of roll, not even in winter ball, but I didn't really dwell on it because the pennant race was shaping up. However, I did realize that I owed Eddie Murray a big thanks. Toward the end of the previous year, Earl Weaver had moved me from the fifth spot in the batting order to the third spot when we were facing a lefthander. Now, in 1983, Joe Altobelli moved me into the number three slot against everyone, and that meant that I had Eddie, one of the best hitters in baseball, and definitely the best clutch hitter, batting behind me every day. Eddie hit almost .400 with runners in scoring position; he hit .400 in September; he hit *over* .400 with the bases loaded.

Hitters tend not to want to admit this, and I might not have realized the impact at the time, but after Eddie was traded in 1988, I certainly realized that having a hitter of his caliber right behind you is a huge factor, and a switch-hitter of his caliber is beyond calculation. The opposing manager doesn't have many favorable options. He doesn't want to bring in a righthander to face me, knowing that Eddie would be batting lefthanded, his best side. But he didn't want to make two moves, a righthander for me, a lefthander for Eddie. The bottom line was that I benefited by getting to bat against quite a few lefties. I didn't receive one intentional walk the whole year.

For the last couple months of the season, it seemed as if the Orioles fell into the habit of losing the first game of a series, then winning the next two or three. True to form, after winning the American League East by a comfortable margin, we lost the first game of the playoffs against the White Sox before winning the next three, with the last two in Chicago. Then in the World Series, we lost the first game against Philadelphia before winning four in a row, the last three on the road. We were a confident, winning ball club. After all, that division title was the Orioles' seventh in the previous fifteen years, in a historically strong division. Even after getting down in each post-season series in 1983, we regrouped and came back, thanks in large part to our pitching. The staff gave up three runs to the White Sox in four games. The ERA for the season was 3.63.

Just a sophomore in the major leagues, I felt like a veteran as well. After the first ground ball, the World Series turned out to be just another series. The media scrutinizes every play in the post-season, but the players fall back on what they know and how they've been trained, and the hoopla recedes. Baseball becomes baseball, and you lose yourself in the game. I was surprised how relaxed I became after that first chance. I still remember clearly that I thought to myself, That was just like a grounder in July. On the other hand, I didn't have much to show at the plate for my relaxed frame of mind. In the playoffs, I'd been 6-for-15, but in the World Series, just 3-for-18. I hit a couple of balls hard that they caught, and, naturally enough, their pitchers focused on the middle of our lineup, just like our pitchers focused on the middle of their lineup. Mike Schmidt and Pete Rose were quiet for the Phillies. That Series was a tribute to our good pitching, which defeats good hitting almost every time.

Our hero was my roomie, Rick Dempsey, who had a great Series and was voted Most Valuable Player. For myself, I was trying too hard and I think Eddie Murray was, too. Partly to loosen up, I think, Eddie took his family and me and some others out for Mexican food and margaritas after the day game on Saturday, which we won, putting us up 3–1 in the Series. That was a great party, and we did loosen up—or at least Eddie did, because he busted loose on Sunday with two homers and Scottie

relax in World Series

McGregor shut out the Phillies on five hits, and without throwing one breaking ball: change-ups and fastballs only. That game was boringly good for us, just what you want to win the World Series. When I caught the humpbacked liner from Garry Maddox for the final out, the celebration began, although it was a little anticlimactic. I'd heard for years that getting to the Series is more exciting than winning it and found out there's some truth to the cliché. Still, T-Bone Shelby and I had a blast stalking everyone with our bottles of champagne.

The competition for MVP of the American League that year was between Eddie, Jim Rice, and me. Eddie's and my own stats were neck and neck (I lost the contest we had for least strikeouts, 97 to 90, with an expensive dinner at stake), and the MVP vote would be close, too. If one letter to the editor in Baltimore prior to the balloting considered my 25 errors in the field a negative of sorts, another responded with the fact that no one had complained the year before when the Brewers' Robin Yount was the almost unanimous choice, with 24 errors at shortstop. The local papers were full of stories and columns weighing the merits of the candidates. Eddie and I didn't talk about it once. He was home in California, I was home in my townhouse. I told the media that I'd be honored to win, of course, but I added that *every* player and coach on the Orioles understood that Eddie had been the club's most valuable player in 1983. Without a doubt. I'd be honored to finish second to anyone, but to him in particular.

When I joined the club in 1981, Eddie and I knew each other slightly from spring training, but mainly I think he recognized a guy with similarities. I was coming to the big leagues with a big buildup, just as he had. I'm a little reserved by nature, like he is. We were both single. Most important, maybe, he's a natural big brother, the opposite of a "big star" guy, always just as friendly with the people in the front office as he is with the biggest star on the team. Eddie was always giving crab feasts, and he opened his house to all the minor leaguers who were called up in September. If they needed a place to stay, they'd be welcome at Eddie's. If you can't be friends with this guy, you've got a problem.

He also had a close relationship with my father, which dated back to the 1973 Instructional League. Eddie has always had the habit of standing with his arms folded between pitches, and some in the organization were muttering that maybe Eddie Murray was a lazy ballplayer. Senior said, "Bull. That's just the way he stands. When you see this guy out of position on a play, you come talk to me. This kid knows who to play. Don't bury him." Maybe not those exact words, but something close. The funny thing here is that Eddie was scared to death of Senior. He misinterpreted all the gruff talk, like others have done, I'm sure.

Two years later, when Eddie was playing in Asheville, Dad again had an impact on his career. Eddie was taking some batting practice left-handed, as a way to shorten his stride when he batted righthanded, his natural side. He thought this maneuver helped correct his tendency to overstride. Jim Schaffer, who was managing the club that year, saw this and thought Eddie might be a good candidate for switch-hitting. Eddie liked the idea, too, but some people wondered whether he should be messing with the other side of the plate, because he had a great future batting righthanded. That season happened to be the one in which my father was doing advance and special assignment scouting, and when he came through Asheville he was asked about the Murray situation. He didn't see any problem, and he got on the phone to Frank Cashen, who was running the system at the time, and got permission for Eddie to switch-hit in the upcoming Instructional League. The rest is history. Sometimes Senior is given the credit for turning Eddie into a switch-hitter, but he only defended and encouraged the move when Eddie wanted to give it a try.

Six years later, when I came up to the majors, Eddie was already a star, and he had the habit during infield practice of hanging out at shortstop after he'd taken his own balls at first base. That's where we really started talking, standing out on the left side of the diamond. He couldn't adopt me at my position the way Lee May had adopted him, taking him down the first base line to work on pop-ups, but he helped me relax. He taught me how to think and behave like a big leaguer: keep it simple, stay within yourself, teammates come first, no false hustle, no complaints. A classic example of Eddie's approach to the game came in the World Series in '83. He was jammed in Game One by John Denny and hurt his wrist. He didn't have much of a series for the next three games, but he didn't say a word about the injury, and the tape was hidden by his wrist bands. But then the night before the fifth game he announced at the Mexican food restaurant that he was ready to go, and he was.

Sometimes we dueled each other playing catch. We were both pretty good. Eddie has a lot of natural movement, a hard sinker. In fact, this is one reason Earl Weaver's 1978 experiment of playing him at third base and Doug DeCinces at second base hadn't worked out. Eddie's throw on the double play tended to move into the runner with its sinking action. It was hard to handle on a close play, especially for DeCinces, who was new to his position. That particular infield combination gave up quite a few runs quickly, and Earl dropped it.

Since we were both single guys, Eddie and I had lots of solo lunches. He generally wanted to pick up the checks, but the funny thing is that the two of us had the same spending money for the month. He was making a lot more than I was at the time, but Ron Shapiro, who represents both of us, kept us on the same budget. I tried to get Eddie to wrestle but he only wanted to box, which I thought was too serious. If I did get him on the ground in a match, he'd just lie there, waiting for my energy to run down. That's what he said. Nor did he want anything to do with Rick Dempsey's and my hotel pranks. All in all, he thought I put too much energy into goofing off, and he made this point real clear at the post-season Topps banquet in 1983, I believe it was. Eddie presented me a candle with a wick on both ends.

In short, Eddie was the kind of friend ballplayers make in the minor leagues, but maybe not in the big leagues. You could even say that the downside of moving up to the big leagues is the loss of that special quality back in the minors, where the conditions aren't good, the bus rides can be grim, the food is often crummy (without intending to hurt the feelings of Mrs. Short, Will George, or Tim Norris), money is tight, and you're worried about making it to the big leagues—but still I think back to the minors and to winter ball as great times. A lot of guys will tell you that that's the most fun they had in baseball. We relied on each other for everything. Friendships established in the minors are often closer than those you have in the major league game. Camaraderie on the team is tight, with a sense of responsibility, even obligation, even though players are competing with each other for big league positions.

Consider my brother Billy's situation in 1995, when he found himself back in the minors after seven and a half years in the majors. He wasn't happy about that at all, and he chronicled the ridiculous conditions he found in the American Association with a hilarious series of snapshots. At the same time, my brother had a great group of friends, guys from the majors who found themselves in the same boat, and Billy will tell you that he had more fun playing the game that year than he'd ever had.

I was lucky. Eddie Murray was that kind of friend for me in the majors. He wants to be honest, he wants to be dealt with honestly, and when he feels he's not, he takes it to heart. Mainly, he wants to play baseball. On a barnstorming tour of Japan in 1984, we were sitting around looking at statistics and I said, "You know, Big Ed, you can hit five hundred home runs. You can get three thousand hits." I was surprised when he said those numbers didn't mean anything to him, that he was just going to do his best. He meant that, too, although when he was approaching the homer milestone in 1996, back with the Orioles after seven and a half years in Los Angeles, New York, and Cleveland, I know the numbers were important to him, as they should have been. It was difficult for him to talk about his "place in history," but to put up numbers like that, you have to be doing a lot right for a lot of seasons. I think he's the perfect teammate.

●   ●   ●

ABOVE The family home
in Aberdeen

ABOVE Senior in his
early days

RIGHT Born with a bat and
ball in my hands?

ABOVE Family day for the Tri-Cities Atoms. Senior, who managed this minor league team, is kneeling, with (l. to r.) me, Fred, Billy, and Elly.

ABOVE Spring training in Daytona Beach, Florida

LEFT Smiling away at age 7

RIGHT At the park with Mom.
From left, Cal, Jr., Elly, and Fred.

BELOW The Aberdeen Indians (1970).
I'm second from right, middle row.

LEFT In seventh grade. Still had my
hair and a comb in my pocket.

LEFT My freshman year of high school. Guess my growth spurt hadn't kicked in yet.

BELOW At Memorial Stadium with Senior before I was drafted. I'm 16 here.

BELOW Looking good for the prom (1978)

ABOVE My high school team my junior year. I'm third from right, middle row.

LEFT With the Bluefield Orioles in 1978

ABOVE Receiving the MVP for the second year in a row in the Caribbean League. Check out that trophy.

ABOVE In 1981, with the Rochester Red Wings.

RIGHT That's my rival at shortstop, Bobby Bonner, at a signing with me in 1981 for the Red Wings.

BELOW What's strange about this first-year card?

ABOVE Earl Weaver steps between Senior and an ump (1979).

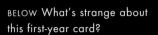

Cal Ripken, Jr.
ORIOLES • THIRD BASE

RIGHT Our first year together in spring training

BELOW 1983

BELOW Senior at an exhibition game in Nicaragua organized by Dennis Martinez

LEFT A father-son moment

BELOW 1987

The night the MVP winner was going to be announced, just about the same group of people gathered at my home as had gathered the previous fall for the Rookie of the Year announcement, and when I answered the phone I gave everyone another thumbs up. Then I called home and talked to Mom and Dad, who had called me half an hour earlier. That phone call was uncharacteristic, and it told me that Senior was nervous, too, and did care whether I won. Mom and Old Stone Face drove over immediately with the champagne.

I got 15 first-place votes, Eddie got 10. I got 322 total votes, Eddie got 290. For the second year in a row, Eddie was the runner-up. The factor that might have given me the edge was a certain value placed on shortstop and defense up the middle. I appreciate the votes for whatever reason, but regarding the value of shortstop versus first base, I could make a case for first base. First base is *vital* for infield defense. He handles everyone's throws and can make everyone in the infield better. It's also vital that the first baseman is a first-rate cutoff man on the throws to the plate from right field and center field. Those decisions are split-second and all-important, because they can make or break a big inning for the offense. Because of Eddie's power numbers, people forget he was a great first baseman, with terrific footwork around the bag. He won three Gold Gloves. Look what Don Mattingly, one of my favorite players, did for the Yankee infields in his era. He wasn't as big as some first basemen, so he didn't have quite the reach stretching for throws, but he more than made up for this with his footwork and his savvy. He instilled confidence in everyone. Sure, I could make a case for first base over shortstop—but a better one for shortstop. Anyway, I was thankful and very excited to win the vote. The following day Eddie called with congratulations, of course, and I told him he still had my ballot. He knew that anyway.

What a way to begin a career: in my first two years, the Orioles had gone to the last game of the regular season, then won the World Series. For myself, I'd won Rookie of the Year followed by Most Valuable Player. I take pride in my work, just as I hope everyone takes pride in his or her work. Awards are recognition for a job well done, a public pat on the back, but *not* winning an award can't take away the sense of accomplishment. Now I felt I had arrived as a big leaguer, and I would have felt that way even if I hadn't won. Nothing could take away from the fact that these had been two great years.

Coming off the World Series, expectations for the Orioles in 1984 were high, of course, but we were, for the most part, a veteran, maybe even an *aging* team in the key positions in the batting order, and we couldn't score the runs when we needed them. In 1983 we had scored 799 runs. In '84, just 681. That's a big drop-off, and it shows up in the standings as more one-run losses, because our pitching was giving us a chance. It was almost as good as the previous year, and Mike Boddicker finally emerged as a star. Earl Weaver hadn't really appreciated Mike as a pitcher. For one thing, he wasn't the kind of pitcher who was very impressive throwing on the side. You have to see him work from the mound game after game to appreciate his skills. Even though Mike put up good numbers every spring training, he stayed in Rochester in '81 and '82. "One more year in Rochester," he joked, but without much pleasure, "and I'm running for mayor." General manager Hank Peters would try to force the issue by bringing Mike up in September in each of those years, but Earl let him sit on the bench. In that incredible final series against Milwaukee in 1982, the fans were going crazy and Mike was, too, for a different reason. Earl wouldn't play him.

Mike finally got his chance under Joe Altobelli in 1983 and won 16 games. In 1984 he won 20 games—and later he gave me some of the credit. After a bad start, really frustrated, wondering why he'd bought a townhouse because he was convinced he'd be shipped back to the minors any day now, he was slumped on the bench after a loss and I sat down next to him and said, "I know what's wrong."

"What?"

"You're trying to be perfect."

"What do you mean?"

"Look, can you hold any team in this league to three runs?"

"Yeah."

"Well, do that. If you do that, we'll win a lot of games."

As it turned out, Mike and I had a similar exchange five years later, when the team was struggling and he was, too, trying to be perfect once again. I reminded him both times that his job was to keep us in games; it wasn't necessary to *win* the games himself. Although I wasn't a veteran like Reggie Jackson, somehow my simplistic encouragement hit the right note, like Reggie's had helped my hitting. In 1984, Mike immediately got on a roll, and his 2.79 ERA led the league. When Earl Weaver returned to the team the following year, he suddenly had the highest respect for Mike's ability on the mound.

About the '84 team, fans in Baltimore said, "Well, Murray and Ripken are having good years. What's the problem?" Ken Singleton was now thirty-seven years old, and his numbers fell off some. Ditto John Lowenstein, who was also thirty-seven. Gary Roenicke, the other half of the Lowenstein-Roenicke platoon in left field that had been so productive the previous two years—more productive than any other position, RBI-wise—*also* fell off. T-Bone Shelby had an off year. Rick Dempsey was hurt, as was Dan Ford. Batting behind me, Eddie Murray got off to a huge start, but when the league realized the lineup behind him was vulnerable, the pitchers started working around our cleanup man. Eddie led the league with 107 walks and set the American league record for intentional walks to a switch-hitter, with 25. That's a lot—although nothing like Willie McCovey's 45 intentional walks in 1969, which is remarkable. And Eddie played every inning of every game that season, which made two of us.

However, the Orioles' *biggest* problem that year might have been the incredible start of the Detroit Tigers, who won 12 of their first 13 games, 35 of their first 40. That kind of blitz is discouraging for the other teams. It's difficult, mentally, when you fall ten games behind after the first six weeks of the season—and not because you're playing badly. You need to make up significant ground fast, but if the other team plays merely .500 ball the rest of the way, which is what the Tigers did, the job is almost impossible. You need a 35-victory blitz of your own, and that's not likely. In the end, five teams in the A.L. East had winning records that season, but even with our 85 wins, the fifth-place Orioles finished 19 games out.

I had a good year, but my personal highlight in 1984 was playing in my second All-Star game with my father as the batting practice pitcher—the first father-son combo ever in an All-Star game. I was really proud of that, and Dad was, too. He wasn't going to say anything, of course, but I could tell. Mom flew out to San Francisco for the festivities, and she could tell, too.

The following year was a big transition and flip-flop in Baltimore. Kenny Singleton retired, John Lowenstein retired, and the Orioles went into the free agent market in a major way, signing Freddie Lynn, Don Aase, and Lee Lacy to big deals. The organization had previously signed a couple of free agents, including Steve Stone, who won 25 games in 1980, but multiple free agent signings in one year, each for millions of dollars apiece, was a first for Baltimore. It was an indication of changing times, within baseball and within the organization. Even the conservative Orioles—or at least our owner, Edward Bennett Williams—felt that some moves were necessary to encourage the fans about the future. I don't think it was coincidental that we acquired Steve Stone the season after Williams bought the ball club, and now five years later the Orioles were coming dangerously close to doing what our general manager, Hank Peters, had always said he didn't want to do: sign expensive players almost for the sake of signing them. Hank also said, "Signing a free agent isn't the greatest thing in the world, and losing a free agent isn't the worst thing in the world. You can survive either way." Hank had been the Orioles' GM since 1975, and he had ten winning seasons to show for his work. He had a knack for finding quality, "complementary" contributors to the team. These players may not have had much marquee value, but the team didn't need it on the playing field because we had Earl Weaver in the dugout. The Orioles featured solid ballplayers who were not necessarily stars and solid, sometimes great pitching. But now the minor league system wasn't stocked with quality, and suddenly Hank was having to do something he didn't want to do— go outside the farm system to try to build a winner.

The moves paid off, offensively. We led the league in home runs without having one guy among the top five, which seems unlikely, although Detroit did the same thing the following year. We were second in the league in runs scored. Fred Lynn, the only player to win the Rookie of the Year and the MVP awards in the same year (1975, with Boston), hit six ninth-inning home runs, three in sudden-death situations.

Unfortunately, and uncharacteristically for the Orioles, it was the pitchers' turn to struggle that year. Mike Boddicker went from 20-11 in '84 to 12-17. Mike Flanagan was hurt most of the time and only pitched 86 innings. Scott McGregor and Storm Davis slipped a little. And Jim Palmer was gone.

Overall, we just didn't match up with the league. All the player moves pegged us as a team in transition. That happens to every organization at some point, it's not necessarily a disaster, and when it does happen, the manager often changes as well. In our case the date was June 13, when Joe Altobelli was fired after 55 games, and with a winning record at the time: 29-26. According to the most colorful story I heard about the timing of that move, Joe's fate was sealed when he left Mike Boddicker in the final game of a series in Detroit to pitch to Lou Whitaker in the eighth inning, two on, two out. When Lou launched a shot to right, some say, Edward Bennett Williams was on the phone to Earl Weaver in Florida before the ball had landed in the upper deck.

An exaggeration, undoubtedly, but Joe did know the ax was coming. When the owner calls you a cementhead in the newpaper, that's a hint—and hard to excuse, in my opinion, and I say that even though I have a lot of respect for Williams. There had also been lots of media, lots of rumors in Detroit. In baseball, at least, I've learned over the years that where there's smoke, there probably is some fire somewhere. (And sometimes there's fire when there isn't any smoke. I've learned that, too.) Apparently Joe got an obligatory reassurance from Hank Peters in Detroit, but when we returned to Baltimore and went to the ballpark on Thursday morning for a game against the Brewers, Hank's secretary called and said that Hank and EBW wanted to meet with him at 3 p.m. Joe went to that meeting with his duffel bag already in the trunk of his car, ready to leave town.

One theory on that abrupt firing that gained credence over the years in Baltimore was that our owner panicked about season ticket sales for the following year and brought back the controversial but popular and proven Weaver, who had promised his boss when he retired that he'd come back if Williams asked him to. Altobelli wondered if there was a different explanation, or at least a second factor involved. He wondered whether his falling-out with the owner hadn't started the previous fall on the Orioles' post-season barnstorming tour of Japan. By that time, Jim Palmer, Benny Ayala, Ken Singleton, and Al Bumbry had been released by the club, but they were still invited to go on that trip because they'd been on the '83 World Series champions, and that was the Orioles team that had been invited to Japan.

Altobelli also brought some young players along, and Edward Bennett Williams was on the trip, too. In the first few games, Joe started Singleton and Bumbry for four or five innings, then put in the others. Hank Peters found Joe and said that EBW was asking why he was playing Singleton and Bumbry. Joe said that he thought it was the club's responsibility to give these guys a showcase in Japan, where maybe they might be able extend their careers. He thought it was the least the Orioles could do for them. After all, Joe said, Singleton had given the Orioles ten solid years, and Bumbry had given them twelve years, and neither player had ever said no when the club asked them to do something in the community. Then Joe asked Hank Peters, in effect, "If Mr. Williams doesn't understand that, what does he think of you and me? We haven't been here twenty-two years."

After he was fired seven months later, Joe wondered whether that episode was the beginning of the end for him and the Orioles. He still wonders. He also says he would do the same thing again with the veteran players. I respect Joe for that, I think he did the right thing, but ironically, as it turned out, none of those guys did extend their careers in Japan, while both Larry Sheets and Jim Traber, two of the younger guys on the Orioles, did.

Out of a job, Joe came through the clubhouse and wished us all well. My dad took over as interim manager while we waited for Weaver, and I had the second opportunity in three years to tell the press that I thought my father deserved his opportunity to manage the club, and that I hoped his time would come someday. I know that Rex Barney, the longtime PA announcer in Baltimore and before that a famously hard thrower for the Dodgers in the forties, wrote in his book about the ball club that Hank Peters wanted to name Senior to the job but then walked into Williams's office in Washington, D.C., to find Earl sitting there. That's not quite accurate, Hank says. He hadn't made any decision or recommendation. He did try to talk Williams out of bringing Earl back for an encore.

The press tried to get some hints of anger or bitterness out of Dad, but they were wasting their time. Freud himself would not have had much luck with my father, who doesn't believe in dreaming. Senior said, Look, I feel badly for Joe, I thought he was doing a good job, but in this business you're hired to be fired, Earl always provides a spark, one way or the other, I hope he does this time, I don't have a burning desire to be the manager, and even if I did, I'm still young. (He was forty-nine.) Williams was asked if he had been hesitant about hiring Dad because of the possibility of having to *fire* Dad with me on the team. Not a consideration, he said, and pointed out that the Yankees had fired Yogi Berra with Dale Berra on the team.

Frank Robinson might also have been disappointed that day. He'd been hired as a coach for us after being fired in the middle of the 1984 season in San Francisco, after three-plus years as manager and, before that, two-plus years in Cleveland. Some writers had immediately pronounced Robinson the heir apparent when Williams found an excuse for firing Altobelli. They were wrong. Ray Miller, who, along with Frank and Senior, had also been passed over, was mainly mad at the press, and he told them so eventually. He thought they had hung Altobelli out to dry over the weekend in Detroit.

All in all, the whole situation during that era in Baltimore was difficult and unusual, with four top coaches who had long histories with each other and the organization—Altobelli, Miller, Robinson, and Senior—all competing for the manager's job, in effect. Earl kept everyone when he returned in '85, and for a brief moment I thought his magic was going to work. We had a nice spell in July, closed some ground, but then we lost Mike Boddicker, Mike Flanagan, and Storm Davis with elbow, knee, and wrist injuries, respectively. And Freddie Lynn threw his back out—and, unfortunately, there was nothing unusual about that. On a per-at-bat basis, Freddie produced for the Orioles, but in the four years he was with us he missed a quarter of the games, the equivalent of an entire season. As he quipped at some point, "If I'd been a horse, they probably would have shot me." Eventually Fred got some flack for not playing through some of the problems, but Fred worked hard. I saw him practice making one-hop throws from different areas of center field to different bases, so he'd know what kind of bounce to expect from that infield. Most outfielders don't make that kind of assessment. All the games Fred missed were not because he didn't want to play. Take my word for it.

For myself, I suffered a power outage in the dog days: 3 homers over a six-week period in July and August, for a total of 18 on September 1. I thought the pitchers might be pitching me a little tougher because I now had something of a track record, and I found myself going to right field more often. All in all, though, I wasn't concerned—a good September would put me within range of my average of 27 home runs for my first three full years—but maybe for the first time in my career I got a taste of negative press. Day after day, there was always something about my lack of power. Even Earl Weaver got into the act, indirectly. At a banquet for Jim Palmer, Earl made some playful remark to my mother about "getting that boy of yours going." When Mom replied that I was fine, Earl said Mr. Williams didn't agree. That's when Mom said, "You've got some problems, Earl, but number eight isn't one of them." Then I hit eight dingers in September. I guess Mom got me going.

My mother was right. As a team and as an organization, the Orioles were headed in the wrong direction in this period. I didn't fully realize this at the time, and maybe no one else did, either, but the fact was apparent soon enough, because the following year, 1986, was the first losing season for the team since 1967, when I had been all of seven years old. Throughout the great years the Orioles had been tremendously lucky about injuries. The streak came to an end that year, when twelve guys went on the DL. Strange things happened all year, like the game against Texas in which we hit two grand slams—in one inning—and still lost. As the '86 slide picked up momentum, Edward Bennett Williams held a closed-door meeting with the team, a pep talk, in effect, but he soon undercut it with remarks to the press about Eddie Murray in which he made a veiled reference to Eddie's alleged off-season work habits and his poor clubhouse attitude, which was rubbing off on other players— Floyd Rayford, particularly, Williams said.

Eventually, I learned that the story was a mistake. The reporter who broke it had walked into this group interview late, and he didn't know that Williams had declared his remarks off the record. Naturally, the scoop was a big one in the sports page the next day—"above the fold," as they say in that business. Even given the hypothesis that Williams thought he was speaking off the record, I, like Eddie, failed to understand the logic of his thinking. After nine great years for the Orioles in which Eddie had played in almost every game, he had a series of injuries in 1986, including a sprained ankle and a pulled hamstring. For the *first* time in his career, he went on the DL. Murray hasn't given us a good year, Williams said, but actually Eddie ended up giving the Orioles a perfectly good year; not his best, but perfectly good: a .305 batting average, 17 home runs, and 84 RBIs in fewer than 500 at-bats.

I'd say the same for myself: a good year, not my best. Earl experimented with me in the fifth hole, and I'm not sure why. Maybe Fred was hot, or maybe Earl just wanted to shake things up, or maybe it was because I'd hit into a club-record 32 double plays the previous year. Double plays are a fact of life in baseball. If you hit your share of hard ground balls and don't have blazing speed, you'll have the DP beside your name fairly often. Anyway, for one or more of these reasons, I batted fifth some of the time, but batting fifth behind Eddie is no disaster because he gets on base forty percent of the time. But my RBIs were down some anyway, reflecting our overall offensive slump.

Earl has always maintained that the team would have been in the race in 1986 up to the end if it hadn't been for the injuries. We'll never know. We definitely would have been more competitive, but I'm not sure all the magic in the world would've kept that team in the pennant race. Our veteran nucleus from the early eighties was mostly history, and we missed those guys. However, we weren't a 14-and-42 team, either, which is how we ended the season. We ended up winning only 73 games, and the writers said we quit, gave up, folded. That's just sports talk. September wasn't our finest hour, no doubt about it, but I say we were a team now in transition that lost focus and concentration and found itself looking toward next year.

When Earl quit at the end of the season—and I'm guessing he did leave voluntarily; I don't believe he was forced out—one of the reasons might have been that he, too, saw a team in a rebuilding situation, and he just wasn't interested.

Chapter Nine

When Earl Weaver announced in September 1986 that he wasn't returning to the club next season, the players got into the act of choosing a successor; some campaigned openly for my father. Rick Dempsey said it wouldn't be fair to give the job to anyone else. Eddie Murray said that if Senior got the job he'd withdraw his request for a trade. (Eddie was under contract with the Orioles through 1991.) Jim Palmer, no longer even a player, said that Senior was the one candidate with "no negatives." He and some others also suggested that my eligibility for free agency the following year would be taken into account by Hank Peters and Edward Bennett Williams. That was pure speculation. And one player was quoted anonymously as saying there'd be a "mutiny" if someone other than my father were chosen.

Dad was gratified by the support, I'm sure, but still embarrassed. If you're looking for Earl Weaver's air of self-importance from Senior, you're wasting your time. I thought the choice of Dad was a foregone conclusion—but you never know. Frank Robinson was still with the team. Ray Miller was available. People were always looking for *angles* why Dad might get the job: the Orioles wanted to make sure I stayed, he had put in his time with the organization, the Orioles owed him, et cetera, et cetera. They seemed to consider everything except what was to me the most obvious reason: given his experience and the respect in which he was held by all the players, my father had certainly earned his shot as the big league manager.

And he got it that year, at the age of fifty. I don't remember how I found out—a phone call, probably. There might have been some tears shed by the notoriously unsentimental Ripken family that day. No one in the world ever deserved this opportunity more than my father deserved his. He had been loyal for years, and he was totally qualified, but when a reporter asked if he'd been "waiting" for the manager's job, Senior replied, "I haven't been *waiting* thirty years for this job. I enjoyed every day as a minor league manager and major league coach."

As we know, Dad doesn't dream, and he doesn't wait, either. The funny thing was that his job didn't really change that much. He had always had a lot of responsibility under Earl Weaver, then Joe Altobelli, then Weaver again. He was ready. Asked if the family relationship would have any bearing on decisions, Dad snapped, "No bearing whatsoever." That was true. Dad had always said they're my sons *off* the field, and he meant it. His attitude with us had been totally professional, even when we were little kids hanging around the fields in Elmira and Dallas and Rochester and Asheville. And I say "us" because Billy, in his sixth year as a professional, was on the Orioles' major league roster in spring training in 1987. The year before, Billy had traveled over from his minor league camp to fill out the roster one day when we had split squads, but 1987 was for real, although he wasn't expected to be with the club when we broke camp in April. Later, maybe. The tipoff of his chances of making the team—if Billy needed a tipoff, which he didn't—was the number he was issued: 56. A high number usually means high odds of making the team. Senior saw that number the first day and hollered, "Hey, Lawrence Taylor!" Another tipoff might have been Billy's first order of bats: the name was spelled "Ripkin." Of course, that kind of thing could happen to him after *fifteen* years in the majors. I know.

When someone asked if my brother and I had ever played baseball on the same field in any kind of organized league game, I was surprised to realize that the answer was no. We'd been in one organized soccer game—as described, when Billy, Fred, and I got into the big fight—and in a lot of pickup games, but never in the same league. In Florida, it was now fun seeing Billy the baseball player, the obviously improving second baseman. Maybe I was even a little surprised to realize that he could have played defense in the big leagues right then; hitting was going to be the issue for him.

My mother came down to camp that year in Miami, and, of course, there was a big media and marketing blitz for the three Ripkens. *Sports Illustrated* had us on the cover, and Edward Bennett Williams waved this issue at the state capitol when he was campaigning to get approval of the financing package for the proposed new stadium at Camden Yards. Dad, of course, wanted nothing to do with the Ripken angle. He wanted his sons looked at as professional ballplayers and himself as their manager. End of discussion. Generally Billy and I went along with the party line, although sometimes we called him "Bub" as a joke, because that's what he'd called us as kids.

Dad ran that camp at Bobby Maduro Stadium in Miami the way he had run all the previous ones—strictly—and he got the ball rolling with a forty-five-minute speech on the first day. That's a lot of talking, but with a ton of new players and a lot of bad memories left over from 1986, the Orioles needed it in '87. I think he wanted to set the stage for a fresh start for the team after a losing season. He summed up his baseball philosophy, in effect, while referring to his notes on a yellow legal pad. He repeated what I'd heard many times already: that baseball is fun when you're doing things correctly and winning ball games. He said that some of the Orioles seemed to have forgotten this in the last month of 1986. Overall that year we had committed 135 errors, a club record—but that number would come down, Senior said. (And it did, to 111.) If an infielder wasn't taking a drill seriously and laughed after bobbling a ball during a drill, this would not be appreciated or tolerated. Senior said he didn't want a lot of idle Final Four talk around the batting cage. He wasn't even in the Final Four pool. "No time," he said, correctly. On the field, he wanted you to think baseball and work on baseball. That's just the way he was.

I had heard the basics of his speech many times, but looking around the locker room, I could see that the players were paying attention. The older hands had respect for Senior; the new guys were trying to get a handle on him. This 1987 team that Dad inherited bore no resemblance to the team that had won the World Series four years earlier. Eddie Murray and I were the two main holdovers among the position players; Mike Boddicker, Mike Flanagan, and Scott McGregor among the pitchers. After campaigning for Senior to get the manager's job, Rick Dempsey hadn't been re-signed to play under him. Storm Davis had been traded for catcher Terry Kennedy. Rick Burleson had been signed to play second base, Ray Knight to play third. These three guys would add scrappy veteran leadership, but you had to wonder whether the overall flow of the Orioles' famous "complementary" talent coming up through the system was finally drying up.

At the start of the season nobody wanted to admit, at least not publicly, where the Orioles stood. Especially my dad. It was his job to be enthusiastic and optimistic, and he was great at that. But if you were listening and reading carefully, you noticed that he never said we had the talent to go all the way. What he said was we were going to work hard and play the game properly. As he had said at the press conference the previous fall when he was introduced as the new manager, "If there was one disappointment for me this year, it was that I could no longer say we had twenty-four guys coming through the door ready to put on the uniform and go to work." That would change. As Tom Boswell, one of the best baseball writers in the country, wrote in *The Washington Post* during spring training, "If the floundering S.S. *Baltimore* is to be saved, no man is more likely to do it. And if the ship is destined to go down, no one else would stand taller as the last man on the bridge."

After a miserable spring, I was on fire with the bat in April, but after a month Eddie Murray and Fred Lynn were hitting near or even below .200, and my friends John Shelby and Floyd Rayford had already been sent to Rochester for retooling. Then everyone came around, helped a great deal by a major league record for home runs in a month, 58 in May, but then we slumped again, losing 10 in a row. Just before and after the All-Star break, it was division-leading Boston's turn to lose a bunch of games while we won 11, and we closed the gap against them again. And it's my pleasure to give much of the credit for that 11-game winning streak to Billy Ripken. My brother was a big spark for us when he came up at the All-Star break. There's no doubt about that. As a brother and as a teammate, I was happy to have him on the Orioles. He had earned the opportunity.

While I made it to the majors in three and a half years, Billy's breakthrough hadn't come until his fifth year, in Double-A Charlotte in 1986. He had always been a terrific, smart infielder, but Charlotte was where Billy found himself as a hitter. Then in 1987 he was playing great in Rochester while Rick Burleson and Alan Wiggins were sharing second base duties in Baltimore. These two had taken over the position from Juan Bonilla, who had taken over from Lenn Sakata and Rich Dauer. Second base had been something of a revolving door for the Orioles (third base, too, for that matter), so I couldn't have been more excited to see Billy take up his position in the infield. He has great hands and knows how to play. He executes at a high, high level. Looking just at defense and baseball smarts and things that don't necessarily show up in the stats, he and Robbie Alomar are in the same league. Take a certain double play that must be turned in the big leagues. It *must* be—but failure to do so doesn't show up in the stats. Billy will turn that double play. As a steady performer on the other side of second base from me, he would bring stability. I believe stability is important. I like knowing who'll be playing alongside me tomorrow.

It was fun seeing Billy with the Orioles, period, because when he walks in the room, I smile. When he starts talking, I usually start laughing. One thing that ties us together is that we're much more alike than people realize. We're both very competitive; this quality, on his side especially, was the fuel for our feuds growing up, because he refused to accept the huge disadvantage he faced in size and age. While my brother Fred and I sometimes fought as kids, I just teased Billy unmercifully, and he always, invariably, finally blew his top. Someplace out on the road in the early years, I drove him berserk squirting him with a water pistol through the screened top half of a locked door, and he cut his arm pretty badly punching the glass panel underneath. I invented a neat game called "Sack the Quarterback" in which I was the defensive line, there was no offensive line, and Billy was the quarterback. When the two of us got together, things could "get simple," as Dad put it. Billy seems to have something of an inferiority complex, because he tells everyone that he's the Ripken without the piercing, sky-blue eyes. For this genetic deficiency, he blames the three-year gap between himself and Fred, the next youngest.

We're both cutups in private, although I'm reserved in public, while Billy is more of the class-clown type. He's the in-your-face, spontaneous one. He doesn't care about flaming out. I do. In spring training, with the three Ripkens posing for our hundredth photograph, I reached behind Dad's back to twist his cap sideways. Understandably, he looked accusingly at Billy before pulling the cap straight.

When someone asked our manager if he called his youngest son Bill or Billy, Senior replied deadpan, "I call him motormouth." Our mother liked to quip, "If he had been the first one, he'd have been the last one." Our father replied, "Don't you think he might be like this because he *is* the last one?" As our sister Elly revealed in one of her many interviews in 1995, Billy was one of those marital mistakes that sometimes happen. I don't remember this, but Elly said that Mom cried when she found out she was pregnant for the fourth time, while Dad said, "Don't worry. He'll be the joy." Our parents never denied the story. When Billy was at the center of some public episode in a restaurant many years ago, Dad scribbled on a napkin that he passed over to Mom, "Told you he'd be the joy." (Have I mentioned? My father has a very dry sense of humor.)

In neighborhood games, my little brother and I could be a potent combination. If I was picking one of the squads, and I usually was, I'd choose him first. I guess I was looking out for him, but I was also taking into account that the other team would often disregard him, because he was so much younger. We scored a lot of points with me at quarterback and him at wide receiver. In basketball, when I picked off an offensive rebound, I'd probably flip it back out to him for the open shot.

Billy was drafted by the Orioles in the eleventh round in 1982, and two weeks later he was on the road to Bluefield, West Virginia, the same Rookie League franchise I'd played for four years earlier. And he was on the road in my old LTD. By that time—1982—I'd bought a little BMW and had the idea of passing the Ford sedan along to Billy. I thought it would be worth more to him than it was to me as a trade-in, and Dad agreed it was a great idea. A couple of days before he left Baltimore I tossed him the keys and said, "It's your turn." Dad loaned him the same battered equipment bag he had loaned me, and he told Billy he wanted it back *again* when he made the big show. Fred helped with the drive to Bluefield, where Billy tried to get a bedroom in Mrs. Short's house on College Avenue, but she was already full. And soon enough, he, too, called home in frustration. Mom told him I'd made just about the same phone call shortly after I'd arrived on the same team.

If I caught some flack in Bluefield for being a coach's son, Billy caught even more heat. I had been tall and gangly and didn't look very good on the field; Billy weighed all of 160 pounds, and he struggled, too. The injuries came early and often in his career—broken middle finger of his glove hand, broken index finger on his right hand, assorted knee problems and shoulder problems—and they slowed his progress through the minors.

As I'd done, Billy made some off-season money as a substitute teacher in Aberdeen. In the off-season after 1983, his second year in the minors, he sponged off me at my condo. The idea was that in lieu of paying room and board he'd be in charge of fun and entertainment.

This would be a piece of cake for him—he's the life of the party in his sleep—but mainly he just looked up the movie times. We had a ball that winter, and I even cooked fairly often, using the same recipes Mom had sent off to Bluefield with me more than five years earlier. I cooked cafeteria portions: meat loaf the size of a small wedding cake. Plenty for everyone. But the highlight of that wild winter was up in the Catskills in New York, where I'd been named king of Winter Carnival. The queen turned out to be Miss Universe, from Down Under. Our parents joined Billy and me for the festivities, and we all had a great time. Billy, particularly, was in his element. When we left, the sponsors probably decided they'd picked the wrong Ripken to wear the crown.

Three and a half years later, he was in his baseball element with the Orioles, finally getting the chance to write that book he was always bragging he'd write, *One Day in the Big Leagues*. Historians reached for their record books and learned that we were not the first, not even the second, merely the third sibling keystone combination to play in the majors, following Granny and Garvin Hamner in Philadelphia in 1945 and Eddie and Johnny O'Brien in Pittsburgh in the early fifties. Dad greeted Billy with the same handshake and "Welcome aboard" that he greeted everyone with, and warned him that he might not play every day and that he might be pinch-hit for. But he wasn't pinch-hit for, because he hit .308. When he showed speed by beating out an infield hit or stealing a base, opposing players teased *me*. After recording no homers in Rochester in 238 at-bats (although he made sure everyone understood he'd been rooked out of one, when a drive that hit the foul pole was ruled a double), he nailed his first homer in just his first week with us. He was batting second, I was third, and he claimed he could hear me screaming from the on-deck circle in Kansas City as the ball left the field. Maybe he did hear me. I was excited, and so was Dad, but everyone else gave the newcomer the silent treatment.

Billy was the post–All-Star game spark in '87, but the team couldn't keep the blaze going. The year before, fans had thought Earl Weaver's magic and leadership were the key to our good position in early August.

In 1987, Senior must have been doing something right, but in both those years we just didn't have the ability to follow up over the closing months. Occasionally the best team will blitz the field early, like the Tigers had done in the AL East in 1984, but more often the good teams get better as the season rolls along. That had always been the Orioles' tradition. In fact, Earl Weaver used to get upset when his team was chastised for being around .500 at the All-Star break. Earl knew how it works: somewhere in late July or August, maybe early September, the best team wins nine, loses three, wins nine more, loses three, wins six more and the race is over. The Orioles didn't have that extra gear in either '86 or '87. We had burned our fuel getting to the point of even being in contention. In 1987, the pitching wasn't there, overall, with lots of injuries to just about all of them. Our closer Don Aase missed almost the entire season. We hit 211 homers but gave up 226, a large number that accounted for a team ERA of 5.01, the first team to post an ERA over 5 since the 1962 Mets. Billy's spark and a career performance from a rejuvenated Larry Sheets weren't nearly enough.

On the official highlight tape of the 1983 World Series you can hear our first base coach Jimmy Williams telling one of the National League umpires that I'd played every inning of every game that year. The umpire's reaction was "No Way!" as though playing every inning must have been a big ordeal. After our victory celebration that year, manager Joe Altobelli and I had a few minutes alone in his office and Joe said about the innings, "That was great, but I'm not going to let it happen again." I didn't know what to say, I was so surprised. Any number of times Joe had come up to me in a blowout and asked "Want to take these last innings off?" and I'd said something like, "Not really, Joe. I'm swinging well. I want to keep it going." To me, the issue couldn't have been simpler. I was learning the game, getting hits, exploring baseball. In my mind, when the game was out of hand one way or the other I had a good opportunity to use at-bats to experiment, if I wasn't hitting well, or to keep a good thing going, if I was. That was my approach. Playing the nine innings was no big deal. So Joe let me play, even though he said several times that he would "inevitably" have to sit me down sometime.

He's now the general manager in Rochester, and during the hoopla about the Gehrig record in 1995, we sat in his office when the Orioles were in town for the annual exhibition game and talked about old times. Joe asked if I remembered our earlier conversation. "Yeah," I said, and he laughed and said, "But I did let it happen again." And not just the next year. I played every inning under Joe again in 1984, then in '85 under him and Earl Weaver, then in '86 under Earl alone. When the same question came up Earl would say, "When we're winning, I want our best defensive player in there"—in '86 he cited an 11-run inning by Kansas City against Boston—"and when we're losing I want my best offensive player, who can get us back in the game with one swing of the bat."

There was some joking about the innings streak in the clubhouse a couple of times, maybe standing around the batting cage, maybe in a restaurant late at night, but, basically, playing every inning and every game was accepted, certainly in my mind. As I said in my remarks on September 6, 1995, I grew up with that old-school attitude that I learned from Senior growing up and then saw played out in front of my eyes by Eddie Murray, the definition of the everyday player for a decade until he got hurt in 1986. Eddie played every inning in 1984.

I had to be told that the streak extended back to June 5, 1982, the game after Jim Dwyer had pinch-hit for me in the ninth inning in Minnesota, and five games after the streak of consecutive *games* started. Still, in 1987, it seemed like these consecutive innings became a topic of interest. There wasn't a record as such, but researchers decided that I held it nevertheless. They found two players for the early Red Sox teams who'd played every inning for a streak of 424 game (Candy LaChance) and 534 games (Buck Freeman). As the subject gathered momentum, it seemed like reporters mainly wanted to ask me about my run of 7,000-, then 8,000-plus innings. I also think the fact that I was in a slump was a contributing factor to the attention, and also the fact that the Orioles had been touted as a contending team but weren't contending very well.

On May 16, I was hitting .326. A couple of months later, the average was down 40 or 50 points. I'd heard and read the normal rumbles during previous slumps, but this was the first time it had ever become fairly intense: Ripken is 1-for-this, 3-for-that over his last so-many games. The reporters had all the numbers, and therefore so did I. And they had all the questions as well, and my answers were sometimes short. I tried to be polite, but I was irritated and it probably showed. I didn't want an excuse for my slump, especially one as weak and *wrong* as needing an inning off. When you feel sluggish, you don't feel better sitting on the bench. At least I don't. I perk up when I trot onto the field. Sometimes my concentration flags and I find myself standing at the plate with two strikes and no idea what the pitches have been, but that happens to every player at times, maybe in September, maybe in *April*. The only streak that counts physically is *one season*. Then we rest all winter. And we have off days throughout the season. I didn't play all those innings without any breaks.

Anyway, in 1987, my manager—my father—thought he could do one thing to alleviate some of the pressure. On September 14 we were at the old Exhibition Stadium in Toronto, enduring a game which would have been remembered by O's fans anyway. That was the night we set the record by giving up ten home runs. Not surprisingly, Toronto won that laugher, 18–3. I was due up fourth in our half of the eighth inning, and while I was getting ready to step out to the on-deck circle, Dad called me over and said very quietly, "What do you think about coming out?"

"What do you think?"

"I think it's a good idea."

We never mentioned the streak. It was understood.

"Okay."

If I had said "I don't want to," if I had *insisted*, he would have left me in. But I wouldn't have insisted, because I had faith in his judgment. This one time, Senior was dealing with me as my manager *and* as my father. Old Stone Face would deny if, of course, but that's what I believe.

Batting in front of me in the eighth, Larry Sheets and Eddie Murray got hits, and then it looked like I had one, too, on a shot up the middle, but Manny Lee stabbed it and got the force out on Eddie, who was hobbling into second on the ankle that had been bothering him for a month. That left me on first base, and then Ray Knight made the third out on a comebacker. As I walked off the field, Jimmy Williams jogged over from his coaching box and said "I've got you," meaning that he'd take my batting helmet so I could head straight for shortstop. Standard procedure. When I said "I'm out of the game," he was caught totally off guard. My string of 8,243 consecutive innings was over.

Dad hadn't told Billy, so after the third out Billy reached for my glove before Senior whistled to him and shook his head. Billy was still in the dugout when I arrived, and he looked bewildered. He looked like he wanted an explanation from me personally. I thought he was going to cry, and seeing him made *me* feel like crying. It was so unbelievably strange to hear myself say, "No, I'm not in there."

I felt lost. I stood in the runway by myself for a minute, guys crowding around to shake my hand, my father among them. Rene Gonzales used the word "awesome." Jimmy Williams told me quietly how proud he was. I was surprised by the emotion, because I'd never much put stock in the streak *as a streak* to begin with. I just wanted to play. But now that it was over with, all of a sudden I could hardly breathe, and I had to get to the clubhouse to gather myself. I didn't want my emotions to get the best of me out there. Settled down and back on the bench for the final half innings, I sat next to Mike Boddicker, who asked if I was okay. My answer was, apparently, "Yeah." Mike said he'd had the feeling for a few days that "Bub" was going to make the move. At some point Larry Sheets tried to lighten the situation by quipping, "If you ever want to know what to do on the bench, let me know. I can help you." If I smiled, which I doubt, it was a weak one, although I usually appreciated Larry's wit and irony. He was having a great year; for the first time in his career, he'd been playing most of the games that season.

In the clubhouse after the game the press descended on me and Dad, wanting to know, "Why now?" Dad said it was his decision, I wasn't involved, he thought it was time, he didn't want me to have to deal with the hassles as I approached 10,000 innings the following year. That was old-school baseball in which the manager tries to protect his players and deflect criticism, no matter what. In the modern game, this doesn't always happen. Sometimes managers distance themselves from blame or responsibility. They might say, "It's not my fault. All I can do is put my best players out there. They have to perform. I'm not swinging the bats. I'm not throwing the balls." My father would never have said something like that. He never did that year, even when we were plummeting in September to a record of 67-95, 31 games behind Detroit.

Later, it was reported that management had pressured my father into breaking my innings streak. Not true, Dad said. In the clubhouse, I answered what seemed to me every imaginable post-game question, and then I answered them again, as wave after wave of reporters came up to my locker. Where were they coming from? Someone even wanted to know what my *mother* thought of all this.

Finally, hours after the game, I was able to talk alone with Dad. He told me that he knew how much I worried about the team and my hitting and that it wouldn't hurt me to take a seat in blowouts. He thought I should do it more often. I know the details of that conversation because I wrote them down later in my hotel room. For therapeutic reasons, I guess, I wrote nine pages of my thoughts and feelings on a legal pad. I've never kept a diary, but the fact that I wrote at such length that night indicates that sitting out just one inning had had a major impact on me. Years later, I had forgotten about those notes and their content until I found them when my wife and I were moving some stuff around in the closets. I don't think I mentioned them during the coverage of the Gehrig streak.

Those pages begin with a quick résumé of the preceding five years and with my idea that "I just wanted to play, period." That's the phrase I use. I note somewhat sarcastically that the only time the streak ever came up was when I was struggling, and that the attention had become even greater that September. I suggest that the reason Dad took me out was that he understood I would *never*—underlined—have taken myself out of a game. He understood better than anyone—because he had taught me—my belief that if I could play, I should play, and any criticism in this regard would only bring out the Ripken competitiveness and stubbornness. I note the time at the bottom of the ninth page: 3:36 a.m.

The very next day, my brother, still in a state of shock of his own, ripped ligaments in his ankle, and that was it for him for the year. That afternoon, at 4:10 p.m., I wrote two more pages in that legal pad, and at this point the consecutive *games* streak is also on my mind. Almost exactly eight years before I broke Lou Gehrig's record, this is what I wrote:

I have no feeling of anger or regret or disappointment. I also have no feeling of relief. I guess my feeling all along about the innings streak being "no big deal" was right. Although I take tremendous pride in my ability to play every day (& every inning), I don't perceive it to be a great accomplishment. The innings thing to me seemed to go hand in hand with the games streak. I always thought both would end at the same time. Now the question that lurks in my mind is will I feel the same way when the [games] streak has ended as I do about the ending of the innings streak. I do, however, have strong feelings about continuing the games streak & I probably would have objected to ending that if that were the case a couple of days ago.

Thinking back to the night when the innings streak was snapped, I do remember one feeling that I haven't recorded on paper. That feeling was one of giving up, giving in, or beaten down.

One paragraph later:

In a sense, because I don't believe all that bull about being tired from playing (mentally or physically), [I] was fighting back, refusing to give in to something I didn't believe in. So when the time came to come out of the lineup I felt I had lost the fight & at that moment I didn't feel good about myself. I almost felt I let myself down. Dad assured me that in no way did I give up or give in, and that that was not the right way to look at it. I believed him then and I believe him now. It's just that I played one way and thought one way for so long that I felt I was abandoning my ideals. . . . My approach is still going to be the same but I see my approach now in a different light. I feel better about it all.

If it had been just that streak, Dad knew I could have dealt with it. *Physically*, of course, the streak meant nothing. We both understood that. Sitting out one or two or ten innings was going to restore depleted energy? I don't think so. After stopping that streak, I would just punch the clock the next day and begin another streak, but at least the attention would be somewhere else.

Two weeks after sitting down in Toronto, I was ejected from a game for the first time in my six-plus-year career, for arguing a called strike with Tim Welke. Coincidental? Totally. After Tim punched me out, I walked away saying, "You missed two of the three pitches. The one you didn't miss I swung at." I wasn't particularly mad, just frustrated, but I guess my tone was pretty harsh and Welke took offense. He came out from behind the plate and when I stopped short while starting for the dugout, his mask bumped the bill of my batting helmet. With that, he tossed me. "Why did you throw me out?" I asked. His face went blank, and I took that to mean he didn't know. We exchanged some words I'm not proud of before I finally departed the scene. However, this argument had nothing to do with my missing an inning two weeks earlier.

Years later, during the Gehrig extravaganza, my brother Billy said that when he saw the look on my face in the dugout on September 14, 1987, he knew it would be a long time before I missed an entire game, if I had anything to do with the decision. I'm sure my father knew that, too, as well as anyone else who understood my competitiveness and desire to play. But breaking Gehrig's record for consecutive games was so far in the future it was unthinkable. The newspapers usually mentioned when I passed someone on the list—in September 1987, I was number six, behind Joe Sewell—but not a lot was made out of it. The most attention had come when I passed Brooks Robinson's Oriole record, 463 consecutive games, two years earlier.

"Is this a high point of your career?" a reporter asked at the time.

"I hope not," I answered.

Chapter Ten

On November 13, 1987, Kelly Geer and I finally got married. I say "finally" because there'd been a delay of a couple of years since we'd settled down as a serious couple while we tried to get a diagnosis for an illness that had first arisen two years earlier. I'll get to that.

Kelly and I met through the good offices of her parents. One night during the off-season following the '83 season, Joan and Robert Geer happened to see me in a restaurant in Cockeysville. I was there with Al Bumbry. From what I understand, it took a while for my future mother-in-law to get up the nerve to ask me for an autograph, but when she did she said something like, "Have I got a daughter for you!"

I wrote on the napkin, "To Kelly, if you look anything like your mother, I'm sorry I missed you. Cal Ripken."

That kind of forward statement is out of character for me. I don't know what came over me, but I'm glad it did. Kelly now has that napkin stored in a safe-deposit box, but at the time she was in fact under-whelmed by the gift from her mother. "Who's Cal Ripken?" she asked. Her parents were modest baseball fans—they'd never been to an Orioles game, but they followed the results on the sports pages—while Kelly was no fan at all. Still, a couple of weeks later she tapped me on the shoulder after I'd finished a promotional appearance in a different Cockeysville restaurant and thanked me for being nice to her mother. Before she had a chance to introduce herself, I said, "You must be Kelly."

The first thing I noticed was that she was so tall—six feet, or very close. Kelly jokes that I was attracted by her height because I wanted sons who'll be basketball players. That's not entirely true; she's also as pretty as her mother. But I do have to admit I was impressed when I was over at her place and saw her trophy for second place in the statewide "Dribble and Shoot" contest one year. I couldn't figure out why the trophy was so small, because that was a great achievement. I entered the competition one year, and didn't get past the second or third round. Kelly made it all the way to the finals, which were held at halftime at a Baltimore Bullets game. Kelly swears that her stock went way up that evening when I saw her trophy. Well, it didn't go down.

As it turned out, our first official date was more or less snowed out because it was hard to get around town, and since I had to leave the following day and needed to do some laundry and pack a bag, we ended up at my townhouse for dinner—salsa and chips, all I had on hand. That was the year my brother was around to handle the entertainment, so the three of us played cards and darts. Kelly wasn't much of a card player, and had never thrown darts in her life, so there was a lot of instruction. We didn't talk baseball, that I know. Kelly had played softball, but she didn't know major league baseball.

Nor did she know that it takes me at least an hour to get out of the clubhouse after the game, but she found out on our first baseball date at Memorial Stadium early in the 1984 season, when she waited alongside the fans who were hoping for autographs. Nor, unfortunately, did she know I was in the habit of then sitting in my car for another hour or so signing these autographs. All in all, I got the distinct impression she didn't find this part of dating a professional baseball player very appealing. In fact, it didn't take long before she quit waiting altogether. We started meeting at a certain time and place away from the park.

Eventually she became accustomed to a ballplayer's unusual schedule, and at the end of the '84 season she came with me on my first post-season barnstorming tour of Japan.

In the Tokyo airport, waiting to fly home, Kelly and I talked for the first time about getting engaged. Not a week later, back home in Balti-more, she began having headaches, then fainting spells and nausea. She worked in Piedmont Airlines' VIP lounge at BWI airport, and pretty soon her work and her whole life was in a shambles. And no doctor could figure out what was wrong. Or put it this way: each doctor she visited had a different explanation. In the beginning, I went with Kelly to the various specialists, but I quit. We couldn't get a definitive answer and I began wondering whether my presence as a ballplayer was getting in the way of the diagnosis, or creating extra pressure to find it. Maybe this would have been a good time *not* to be locally famous. Or maybe I was just paranoid.

Even when I wasn't with her, Kelly got the sense that the doctors weren't concentrating on the question at hand. Maybe the word had spread along with the referrals that Kelly Geer was Cal Ripken's girl-friend. She was tested for brain tumors, heart problems, cancer, Lyme disease, Hodgkin's disease, lupus. She was declared to have chronic fatigue syndrome and, at one point, a cervical vertebra injury. This injury probably stemmed from her fitness workout, she was told, and her therapy included one hour of neck traction once a week plus cortisone shots with huge needles.

Nothing worked, and eventually Kelly had to quit her job with Pied-mont, which she'd taken because she loves to travel. She lost twenty-five pounds. She got light-headed and almost blacked out once or twice while driving. Her health insurance was almost maxed-out. At some point, the word in the medical profession must have been that Kelly Geer is not only Cal Ripken's girlfriend, but she's got some kind of emotional problem as well. One doctor said, "Kelly, you're too stressed out from dating such a high-profile celebrity," and referred her to a psychiatrist.

She stared at him and her frustration boiled over when she said, "So you're saying Cal is making me sick? Going out with him is my whole problem? Is that what we're saying here? You know what stress is? Stress is not knowing what's wrong. Something is wrong with my body. Losing twenty-five pounds is significant."

She wasn't happy, but she went to see the psychiatrist because it wouldn't be an exaggeration to say that by this time she was desperate. This psychiatrist took one look at her and asked, "Have you ever been tested for Graves' disease?" Graves' is a thyroid disease. At the same time, she saw a headache specialist who began to suspect some form of migraine, and he also tested her for Graves'. Twelve other doctors had seen her over a two-year period, but none had ordered the complete thyroid profile, which is strange, in retrospect, because Kelly's mother has Graves' disease. It was right there in Kelly's history.

Within a couple of days we had the results. You can imagine the jumble of emotions for Kelly and her family, and for me: relief and frustration. Something must have gone wrong in this case. I'm a "Why?" person, and that's one "Why?" I've never figured out. Graves' disease is not an automatic diagnosis—it can even be hard to diagnose in some instances, and Kelly had "passed" the normal thyroid tests—but nobody had even ordered the complete set. Instead, Kelly had taken over twenty-five different prescription medications, all of which had given her allergic reactions.

With radiation treatments and daily medication, Graves' disease is controllable. There's no cure as such, but good control. Kelly is now a spokeswoman for the American Autoimmune Related Diseases Association, based in Detroit.

Not long after she got the proper diagnosis, I made the engagement official. All by myself, with no help from my much more mechanically inclined father and two brothers, I rigged up a sign made with old-fashioned Christmas tree lights borrowed from Dad and set it up in the backyard of my new house in Worthington Valley, in horse country (although I don't ride horses) north of Baltimore. During the 1986 season, Kelly had been practically a supervisor on that construction job. She hadn't had anything to do with the design—which she didn't really like, calling it a "bachelor pad"—but she was handling the punch lists—things to correct—while I was playing baseball. On New Year's Eve 1986, after a home-cooked dinner of filet mignon, lobster tails, and champagne, I took Kelly up to the balcony on the second floor and asked her what she saw in the yard. Nothing, she said. Look again, I suggested, and threw the switch. The bright lights spelled out WILL YOU MARRY ME?, and while she was looking at the lights I slipped a small box out of my pocket. When she turned around I was holding the diamond engagement ring.

I came up with that idea because I knew it would be hard for me to actually say the words in person, and I wanted to do something special. I thought these bright lights were pretty creative, and I guess Kelly did, too, because her answer was yes. She still wears that ring. Not quite a year later we were married in the Towson United Methodist Church on Friday the thirteenth. Kelly wore a Spanish lace dress by Oscar de la Renta, who, it turns out, is a big baseball fan. Maybe Rachel will wear that dress one day. My father was my best man, dressed in black tails, and he said later in his toast at the wedding party, "May the most that you desire be the least that you accomplish."

For our honeymoon we flew to London, where the weather lived up to expectations—a cold drizzle—and we saw the sights, drove out to Stonehenge, took in a couple of plays, and I was asked for an autograph in Westminster Abbey, of all places, by a tourist in town from Boston. Then we flew to Milan and took a trip by car south to Rome. We were concerned about driving ourselves, so we hired a car and driver, and as it turned out that was the smartest thing we did. The travel agency had prepared a list of restaurants, but our guy would always say "No, no," then lead us down some side street to a little place with six tables which had even better food than the previous little unknown place with six tables he'd taken us to the day before. I even found myself getting into the cuisine as it gradually changed—or so it seemed from our limited sampling—from the simpler sauces in the north to the heavier, tomato-based sauces farther south. It's true, I'll try to analyze almost anything. Anyway, it was all delicious and I felt like I gained twenty pounds.

Maybe I overanalyzed our experiences with the doctors, but I know that Kelly took them as a pretty clear sign that life as my wife would be a change for her. Now it was official, and it was a change. Out on the town in Baltimore, she was considered Mrs. Cal Ripken, first and foremost, as opposed to Kelly Ripken, and ten years later she still finds this situation . . . challenging. We both do. Who wouldn't? Everywhere she goes in Baltimore, someone will notice her because now she's just about as visible as I am. Her own life in the public eye in Baltimore has built steadily since the day we were married. When she meets people, they may want to talk about me or the Orioles or baseball. Or maybe they say, "I know a friend who knows Cal." It goes with the territory. At one of the first games she went to after we were married, a guy asked if he could kiss her on the cheek because his friends were watching. At that stage Kelly was sort of a soft touch and agreed. Then a couple of other guys had the same request. By the fifth inning, she had a new rule.

When I went into professional baseball, I pretty much knew what to expect. Kelly didn't bargain for this, and raising kids with a husband who's more or less gone for over seven months every year isn't easy. We try to talk about situations and be sure that we're at least working toward solutions, or as much of a solution as there can be. All in all, she's handled the situation amazingly well. She's strong; she deals with it. And really, I hesitate to even bring up this subject because it sounds like I'm complaining or looking for sympathy, and I'm not. We have a great, enjoyable, wonderful life. We're very fortunate. But there are these challenges, and this is a book about my life in baseball—and away from it.

My situation is what makes our life different. Other families have their different challenges. I figure there's enough baseball in our lives as it is, so I try to leave the game at the park. I stay in the clubhouse a long time after the game, reflecting on it and on myself professionally, maybe getting rid of bad feelings. If Kelly and the kids have come to the park, they've gone home long before I'm ready to leave. I could do my post-game evaluation sitting in the den while everyone is asleep, but I try to do it *solely* at the ballpark. Nevertheless, Kelly doesn't have to hear from me or read the newspaper or watch TV to know how the Orioles are doing, how I'm doing, if I went out to a basketball game in spring training.

In our daily lives away from the park, where are our quiet places? Anyone who has small children knows it's not at home. Most couples can get out of the house to a movie or a dinner, but around town in Baltimore, it's a little harder for us. I feel that privacy is very important, and we have to work for it. In the off-season we have one "date night" every week—a dinner and a movie, usually—after almost none at all for eight months, thanks to my job. Or sometimes it's "date afternoon" at the 2 o'clock movie. She gets the tickets and the popcorn, gives me the sign, and I hurry in. It's a great escape, and then we—or at least I—can spend hours trying to figure out a doubtful plot line. (For instance, the coincidence in *Silence of the Lambs* that has Clarice—Jodie Foster—turn up at the killer's house at the same time the other FBI agents are busting down the door of the wrong house. When these agents realize their mistake, how does the Scott Glenn character instantly know that Clarice is in trouble? I've probably watched that movie half a dozen times trying to figure it out. Brady Anderson wants to know, too.)

On date night, I'm just the husband, and on the whole nearly everyone understands this. When I take my daughter Rachel to an activity, I want to be there just as her father, not as Cal Ripken, Jr. But the other kids may crowd around giggling because I'm horsing around with them, and their parents may crowd around, too, and maybe a few want autographs. I say, "I'm just Rachel's dad right now. I hope you understand." I don't take that attitude to protect myself from signing, but because this needs to be *her* activity, not an extension of my life as a ballplayer. Most of the time people understand; occasionally they don't.

If our first child had been a boy, we would have named him Calvin

Ripken III. By the time we did have a boy, Kelly and I had changed our minds about that. We want our children to have every opportunity to establish their own identities, and the name is the first aspect of the identity. By 1993, when Ryan was born, we realized that his having my name would have made this more difficult. And what about teaching our children about strangers? We want them to feel that the world is a good, safe place, but that we also have to be careful regarding strangers. Yet a lot of "strangers" in Baltimore say hi to me. Rachel invariably asks, "Is *he* a stranger?" and we have to answer, "Well, yes." It's confusing for her, and it will be for Ryan. They see everyone as a friend, which would be a wonderful way to look at the world if this were a perfect world.

Forget 1988. I know I have, large chunks of it. Literally blocked them out. It was great to be married and settled into our new house, and it was a lot of fun to be in the starting lineup on Opening Day with my brother on the other side of second base and with our father as the manager—a baseball first—but just a week later, on the afternoon of Tuesday, April 12, I was driving to Memorial Stadium, and heard on the radio that Senior had been fired just six games into the regular season. All losses, but . . . six games. I was in my car, about a mile from the park, and my first thought was that this was some radio guy fooling around. But this was a music station, not talk radio, and listening to his tone I realized he wasn't fooling around. Reporters had already determined that this was the earliest firing in a season of a manager in the history of the major leagues. My father.

I don't remember what happened when I came into the clubhouse. Dad had already left, I know that. When Billy arrived a little later, our trainer, Ralph Salvon, a wonderful guy both of us had grown up with, took him into the little hideout off the clubhouse that we called the "embassy"—the ceiling was so low I had to duck down when I slipped in there—and said that Dad had asked Ralph to tell Billy not to worry about this, to do his job to the best of his ability, the way he always had. Typical Ripken behavior. Ralph may have passed on the same message to me, but I just don't remember, and I can't ask Ralph, because he died later that year. I don't remember what I said to Billy. Something. I don't remember my first conversation with Dad, or whether I called him right away or waited. Ask Freud why, but I remember very little from that day.

I do remember that our new manager, Frank Robinson, called Billy and me into the embassy and said he wanted us to know that he hadn't lobbied for the job. Frank said he had the greatest respect for Dad, but that Senior was going to be fired no matter what. He said he hadn't even wanted the job, that he had been happy where he was, that he had made the decision very reluctantly. I don't think Frank got into the details at the time, but he told me later that he had gotten a phone call from Edward Bennett Williams on Monday in Cleveland, before the last game of the road trip. Over the phone Williams asked him to take over the club. Frank told me that he was stunned by the question, that he had told the Orioles' owner that Senior was a good manager who deserved a real opportunity, not just one season and six games in the next one. Williams replied that if Frank didn't take the job, he'd get someone else, but he wanted Frank to do him this favor. Frank asked for a little time to think about it and to talk with his family, which he did before calling Williams back less than an hour later and repeating what he'd said earlier, that Senior deserved more time. But Williams wasn't going to change his mind: Frank or someone else would be the new manager of the Orioles. Frank then said, "Well, I don't want someone else to come in to manage the team, so I'll take the job."

Therefore, Dad was already a lame-duck manager during the game Monday night, which the Orioles lost 7–2, our sixth loss in a row, with about five thousand fans in the stands in Cleveland. It wasn't until he came to the park on Tuesday and was called upstairs by Roland Hemond that he finally knew. Roland had taken over for Hank Peters as general manager the previous fall in a front office shake-up. Tom

Giordano, the scouting director when I'd been drafted in 1978, then the director of minor league operations, was also shown the door.

Dad thought he'd been called to meet with Roland to talk about player moves. He was fired instead. Roland has said he didn't know about Edward Bennett Williams's phone call to Frank Robinson in Cleveland, setting up the change. He learned of that decision after the fact on Monday when he was summoned to Williams's office in Washington, D.C.

Maybe I should have realized the previous fall that Dad's days as manager were numbered. He hadn't been rehired until after the shake-up, and at the press conference introducing the new front office people Williams said, "This is neither the beginning nor the end of our reorganization. It's the end of the beginning." In retrospect, it's not hard to figure out what he had in the back of his mind. Frank Robinson said that Williams had wanted to let Senior go in the fall but was talked out of it by his front office team, including Frank. Then Williams had wanted to make the move in spring training but was talked out of it again. That's what I've been told, and maybe so. There was plenty of speculation around.

One widespread explanation was that our owner was a "big splash" kind of baseball man who'd hired Joe Altobelli though his heart wasn't in it. Joe would take the team to the World Series and win it, and he would have a winning record after that, but this wasn't enough. Williams wanted flamboyance, so he brought back Earl Weaver. Then, the theory goes, when Earl left and EBW hired Senior out of some sense of obligation, his heart wasn't in that move, either, because Senior was, if anything, an anti-splash kind of guy, despite his confrontations with umpires à la Earl. At the first opportunity EBW wanted to bring in another strong personality from the Orioles' glory days—Frank Robinson.

This was the analysis of some people in spring training camp. I guess Dad was supposed to feel lucky he had the six-game trial in '88. One intrepid reporter even asked him in camp if he had thought about the possibility of getting fired. I'd liked to have seen the look he gave that guy, but all Senior said was, "Not for one second."

The "flamboyance" explanation seems like bull to me. I don't work in the front office, and I don't know all the politics of the organization, I just think it's more likely that EBW was frustrated with the direction of the team after years of excellence, and he wanted someone to blame. Maybe he also felt an urgency because of his poor health. All I *know* is that I felt deeply for my father. I couldn't imagine how painful this must have been for him, who had been so loyal to the franchise for thirty-one years. He must have been angry and hurt beyond words, but, so far as I know, the harshest thing he said publicly following the firing was, "I wasn't happy about the thing." He said he was going to take a couple of weeks to decide whether to accept the club's offer of another job. Boston was reportedly interested in his services as manager, but nothing came of that.

For myself, I knew the organization had been changing subtly, but now all of a sudden I didn't recognize it at all. That firing—not the firing itself, but the way it happened—made it clear to me that this organization wasn't the Orioles anymore, not as I'd known them. Rather than doing the hard work of rebuilding an organization over the long haul, the decision was made to try to get there with a quick fix. I was especially angry because anyone who had been watching the six games we lost would have known that we might just as easily have won two or three of them. We weren't going to the World Series that year, but those first six games weren't indicative. I was off to a slow start. So were Eddie Murray and Fred Lynn. We scored seven runs in the six games, were shut out twice, and all of us had had opportunities to drive in key runs. The only guys who could hit the ball were my brother and Joe Orsulak. As a team we had one home run, by Rick Schu in Cleveland.

But even with a record of 0–6, the firing was absurd. At some point in this long story Roland Hemond acknowledged that my father had been "dealing from a short deck." That remark didn't lift my spirits, because everyone should have known *and acknowledged* in the beginning that we were a little short on talent. We had good players, but we had some holes, too. In fact, we were in a rebuilding mode. Everybody is optimistic in the spring, but it was very unlikely that Senior or any other manager was taking this Orioles team to a championship. In spring training, you could tell that the high level of execution just wasn't there. With the influx of different players and young players I was thinking, This is a problem. Patience and more teaching were going to be required; more talent, too.

Then, after Senior was fired, we kept losing ball games. Players were confused and disappointed. I was confused and disappointed and *angry*. Senior was more than just my manager. He was my father. At some point, Frank Robinson asked Billy if he wanted to take the lineup card to home plate. A couple of other guys had already done so, but maybe Billy could be the lucky messenger. Billy said okay and then mentioned the plan in passing to me. I asked him if this was Frank's request, and he said yes. I didn't like it and convinced Billy to change his mind, for several reasons. First, Dad hadn't liked for others to take the card out, with the rarest of exceptions. He thought it was the responsibility of the manager. Second, why *Billy*? Whatever the answer, I thought it was in bad taste. If not *manager* Ripken, why *player* Ripken?

One thing I want to make clear: over the next three years, whenever the consecutive games streak came up in relationship to any slump I might be having, Frank Robinson was totally supportive. He handled the streak business better than any manager I had. His response was consistently, "The easiest part of my job is knowing who I'm going to pencil in for shortstop every day. I wish I had eight other players like him." He kept it simple, he didn't give the media anything to run with, and given his baseball experience and Hall of Fame record, the media couldn't debate the point; given his stature in the game, they couldn't debate him on a lot of things. So Frank and I got along fine, and I have no reason not to accept his assurance that he hadn't in any way maneuvered my father out of his job. I think Frank really wanted to be a general manager as his next challenge in the game. He'd already done everything on the field.

I could also readily understand Frank's point about Williams's persuasiveness, because I'd encountered it myself over four years earlier, after the 1983 World Series. I was overwhelmed at the time with post-season invitations, and when I turned down one of the Orioles' caravans to Washington, D.C., EBW called me directly and introduced himself as "Ed," which surprised me right off. He went on to say that he understood I was out of gas, and maybe the club had asked me to do too much, but he'd consider it a personal favor if I'd attend this reception in Washington. What could I say? In addition to being the owner, he was a dynamic, persuasive man. It wasn't hard to see why he was a winner in the courtroom. And when I arrived at the affair in Washington, "Ed" was there to greet me, introduce me around the room, and make me totally comfortable. I really appreciated that.

Immediately after the firing, however, because I was so disappointed with the Orioles and probably overanalyzing the evidence, I wanted to blame someone, anyone. But at least I kept the emotions inside while trying to sort everything out. The media were keeping close tabs on us that April—meeting us at the airport, at the hotel, at the ballpark—but I wasn't going to gratify everyone by lashing out at our owner or general manager or field manager or anyone else. What would that have accomplished? So for the most part I shut up. Billy didn't say much, either, even after he made that cover of *Sports Illustrated* for all the wrong reasons, slumped on his bat, a national symbol of the Orioles' decline. For both of us, there was lots of resentment, and it wasn't our responsibility to go public with our feelings. I did say, "As a player, I have no opinion. As a son, I'll keep my opinions to myself." That was fair enough, I thought. Later I went as far as to say that Dad had been "wronged." "Raw deal" was the phrase more than one player around the league used to describe what had happened to Senior. Dozens of guys told me this while standing at second base.

One or two days after my father's firing, EBW walked through the clubhouse, and we shook hands and he said something like, "These are tough times." I didn't say much, obviously, and I'm sorry we never had the opportunity to sit down and really talk things over. The following spring, after Dad had been rehired as third base coach and Roland Hemond said the firing had been *his* decision, I said I still didn't think I had the whole story. I'll say the same thing today.

As it turned out, of course, we lost 15 more in a row under new manager Frank Robinson, for a grand total of 21 losses to start the season. We finally won 9–0 in Chicago and I broke out of my own slump with four hits, including a homer. Then we lost two more and returned home with a 1–23 record. So how many fans came out to that next game against Texas? 50,402. Talk about the glory days in Baltimore: our fans were the last vestige of the Oriole Way. Still, that was a bittersweet game. The support was great, but it was too bad we *needed* that kind of support. That game was also when the official announcement was made regarding the new park to be erected at Camden Yards.

I finally got red-hot with the bat, maybe inspired by Morganna the Kissing Bandit, who nailed me that night as I was stepping into the batter's box. Then I settled into an average season for me, not my greatest but productive enough. A tough year for all of us. But I have to say, losing can be a learning experience. Maybe we come out the other side better people, better able to handle all of life's experiences, winning and losing. I know that close friendships are made when baseball times are tough, almost like in the minors. You rely on teammates more. We had a good bunch of guys in Baltimore in what I think of as the dark years. On the other hand, bad times also usually mean turmoil in the organization, and careers can be affected, because new managers and front office people have different estimations and different plans for the players. My friend Larry Sheets could have been a guy whose career was hampered by what was going on with the Orioles.

For Larry, 1988 was pivotal. As I've described, he had quit the game in the minors, then come back, then left again, then returned again in 1982 with a more dedicated outlook and with a wife who supported him. Three years later he found himself in the starting lineup on Opening Day after Lee Lacy tore his thumb diving for a ball in the outfield right at the end of spring training. Larry hit well in 1985 in a platoon situation, and he was even starting to get some respect from Joe Altobelli against left-handers. But then Joe was fired, and Earl Weaver immediately returned to a platoon. When Earl retired and my dad took over the club, he played Larry almost every day and Larry responded with his best season, hitting .316 with 31 homers. When Larry was pushing for 100 RBIs, I told him, "I'll be out there for you. I wouldn't mind scoring a hundred runs." We both came up just a little shy, Larry with 94 RBIs, myself with 97 runs. But then Senior was fired in '88 and Larry came up with the theory that he couldn't get a manager to stay around long enough to support him. This is not a novel theory; lots of players share it regarding their own careers.

In any event, Larry slumped in 1988 under Frank Robinson, the next year he'd see diminished playing time, in 1990 he'd be traded to Detroit, in '91 he'd play in Japan, and then he was out of the game. Today Larry runs baseball camps around the Baltimore area, and he's developed a mean golf game. In fact, he's thinking of getting into some golf course development work.

Was the turmoil in the Baltimore organization going to affect my own career? Certainly the future with the Orioles and the stability of the organization had been called into question. Did I want to play here any longer? This question also crossed my mind. I had only a one-year contract for that season, because the Orioles and my agent Ron Shapiro hadn't been able to come to a long-term contract after the '87 season.

For the previous four years—'84 through '87—I had played under a four-year contract for a lot of money—the first third-year player to sign a multiyear, multimillion-dollar contract. The money in that contract had been great (although I never saw it because Ron put me on a $1,000 allowance every two-week pay period), but the key for me had been the long-term commitment from the Orioles. A long-term contract is a commitment from the club to you as a player, and nothing, nothing, is more important. Any young player wants to make some money, of course, but his first priority is job security and knowing that he fits into the club's plans for years to come. I would have been eligible for arbitration after the '84 season, but I chose security and the club's commitment. I thought the four-year contract for '84–'87 was a classic win-win deal. And the *four* years in the contract were the perfect number, too. I probably could have gotten a fifth year, but I didn't want it, because four took me right up to that first year of eligibility for free agency.

But at the end of that contract, in 1987, I wasn't interested in free agency, and I guess the club knew this. On the day before I had to file for free agency, I instead signed for just that one year, 1988. It was immediately suggested that I had signed for the one year in order to see how things went with Dad's new job as manager. Well, there is some element of truth to that, but I also had a lot of other questions at the time, including the direction of the Baltimore organization. And those were the collusion years, which weren't a good time to be negotiating, to say the least. Taking everything into account, the one-year deal seemed the way to go.

So now in 1988 I was playing out my contract, my father had been fired, and, to top it all off, rumors of a trade were everywhere. I asked our media relations people to advise all the reporters that I wouldn't discuss the subject, but I couldn't get away from it. It was just in the air. The most prevalent theory called for some kind of blockbuster deal with Boston, four or five of the Red Sox prospects for me. Other teams came up in the news reports, too. I was astonished. *Trade?* Somebody else telling me where I would play, like it or not? I couldn't have imagined a more unsettling situation. That was the first time in my baseball career that I might have turned up at the ball park to play shortstop for the Orioles and been given an airplane ticket instead. I determined right then that a no-trade clause would be in my next contract, if at all possible.

The front office understood that I was naturally angry about my father, they knew I had strong doubts about where the organization as a whole was headed, and they assumed I wanted out. Therefore, they wanted to get something for me in a trade. In fact, if I had had to make the decision in April or May, right after Senior had been fired, I might have left Baltimore. I *probably* would have. But then I settled down, on the field and otherwise, and a cooler head prevailed. I had just gotten married, too, and I was thinking not only about control of my career but also about stability for my family. I wanted to be in Baltimore, the town. My only doubts were about Baltimore, the baseball organization. What was happening with it?

On the negative side, Edward Bennett Williams was now dying of cancer. We all knew this. Who would the new owner or owners be, and what would they have in mind for the future? I had no idea, but in all honesty, I didn't think the situation looked too promising. Like my father, I took pride in the Baltimore organization, and in the late eighties a lot of the little things and some big things that had been part of the organization for decades were increasingly missing. That's the way I saw the situation, and it gnawed at me.

Since it played an important part in my own internal deliberations in 1988, I'd like to explain briefly what I mean when I refer to the Oriole Way. Understand that these are my perceptions; other "old-timers" in the organization might well put a different slant on things, although I'd think they'd all agree that, simply put, the Oriole Way is the knowledge learned over a long period of time of the best way to teach and play baseball—or, if not the best way, as good as any. With a lot of hard work, sweat, and trial-and-error experimentation, these baseball men separated the methods that worked for us from those that didn't. The Oriole Way is the carefully thought out teaching of cutoffs, relays, positioning of players—every one of the dozens of stratagems on the baseball field. The game hasn't changed in its essentials in a hundred years, and the strategies haven't changed, either. The Oriole Way tried every possible variation on these strategies, picked certain ones, and rejected the rest.

It's not guesswork. Veterans of the organization could tell you exactly why the Orioles played a certain situation a certain way. It didn't mean they were smarter than everyone else in the game. They had a system that worked, that's all. The organization then built on the proven methods. It was simple and logical. Teaching baseball got to be more of a science. The coaches didn't have to reinvent the wheel every season, with every group of new players. Everyone had a proven system that was taught consistently at all levels. Managers in Double-A knew that players coming to them from A-ball knew the system. Earl Weaver in Baltimore didn't have to worry whether players coming to him from Triple-A Rochester knew the system.

Of course, a lot of organizations teach similar fundamentals on the hit-and-run, pickoffs, and so on. I think a key with the Orioles was the *consistency* of their instruction and pride in execution. "Do two million little things right and the big things take care of themselves": that was one of Dad's favorite sayings. The Oriole Way is fundamentals; pride in the fundamentals was almost a code of conduct.

Let's look quickly at one situation—the rundown—in which Oriole teaching differs from that of some, maybe many, organizations. The idea in the Oriole Way is to get the runner running too fast to change direction quickly, and then to get the out with one throw and one only. Say the pitcher and the shortstop have the runner at second base picked off, so he has to take off for third. In order for the shortstop to get the runner running hard, he wants the *maximum* distance in which to do it, so the third baseman goes straight to third base. Some organizations teach that the third baseman jumps into the base line, *cutting down* the distance between himself and the shortstop. The logic behind that strategy is to keep the throw as short as possible, but the problem is that cutting down the distance between the two fielders as a way to achieve shorter throws makes it *less likely* the runner will be at full speed when the ball is thrown. If the runner's not running almost full speed, he can change direction and you end up throwing the ball back and forth. The Oriole system teaches its method as the best way to assure *one* throw. The third baseman catches the ball, takes a step or two, and applies the tag on the runner who can't turn around.

Fielding errors and throwing errors will happen, but strategic and mental errors can be minimized. That's what the Oriole Way accomplished, mainly with simplification and dedication to execution. For Earl Weaver, losing "mentally" was not acceptable. Earl would eat you up for a mental lapse, because he understood that if you make the other team *earn* every base it gets and if you're alert and *take* every base the other team gives you as a gift, you'll win more games than you lose because the game can be decided in any one of the nine innings, and in most games every run counts. Don't beat yourselves; make the other team beat you.

However, if you're short on talent, the best instruction can't make you a good major leaguer. Good instruction makes winners out of *talented* ballplayers. The Baltimore organization identified, drafted, and developed their baseball talent and kept it flowing up through the ranks. As a kid hanging around my dad while he did his paperwork in the mornings before going to the park, I was always asking him, "Why did you send this guy to Double-A? Why did this guy get traded?" And he had a specific answer every time, not just, "He was ready." When Senior joined the club in Baltimore in 1976, twenty-three of the twenty-five players on that roster had played for him in the minor leagues. During that entire era, just one player released by the Orioles got to the major leagues with another organization. That's my father's recollection, though he doesn't remember who that player was, and neither does anyone else I've asked. Maybe there was more than one guy, but there weren't many. On the other hand, a lot of guys *developed* by the Orioles ended up with other major league teams. Senior used to say every year in spring training, "If you get all the way through our system, you *will play* in the big leagues. Maybe not with the Orioles, but with someone."

Other organizations were looking to the Orioles not only for players, but for managers as well. Billy Hunter, Joe Altobelli, George Bamberger, Jim Frey, and Ray Miller all left the Orioles in a short period of time around 1980 to manage other major league clubs.

I'm not suggesting that the Orioles were the only good organization in the sixties and seventies. During that period, the Dodgers also developed a productive organization: Dodger Blue. The Yankees had a strong minor league and scouting system, and won and lost the World Series twice each between 1976 and '81. The fact remains, however, that people throughout the game would agree that shortly after Bill Veeck sold the St. Louis Browns franchise to a group in Baltimore in 1954, Paul Richards and his team of scouts and coaches, some of whom I probably have never heard about, began to set up one of the very best organizations in the business. (Richards also made the key suggestion to shift minor leaguer Brooks Robinson from second base to third base.) The Orioles had just one losing season, 1967, in the twenty-three seasons between 1963 and 1985. To accomplish that, the engine had to be hitting on all cylinders in the front office and on the playing field, all the way from rookie ball to the major league club.

As I surveyed the scene in 1988, the engine had been sputtering for a number of years. I have a lot of pride in the way I was brought up in baseball, and I was concerned. Another factor that concerned me in '88 was the impending departure of Eddie Murray at the end of the year. He had asked to be traded after '87, Roland Hemond's first year as the general manager. Hemond said, "One reason I'm here is you, Eddie!" Eddie had destroyed the White Sox, Hemond's former team. But now the bad blood between Eddie and the media and the front office was too much to overcome, and that whole situation was one of the saddest I've witnessed in baseball.

According to Murray mythology in Baltimore, his problems with the papers began during the 1979 World Series, the one in which the Orioles took a 3–1 lead in games over Pittsburgh before losing in seven. On the day of Game Two, a Dick Young column about Eddie's family appeared in the *New York Daily News*. The piece was flattering regarding Eddie but unkind about the way his family had treated the scout who signed him. Eddie couldn't understand how someone would write a story like this *without* talking to him about it. Of course, I wasn't on that team. When I did join the O's, I knew about the Young piece, but not the details. Eddie and I never talked about it, that I recall.

The piece scarred Eddie, but it didn't keep him from talking to the press. When I came up a couple of years later, he talked if the situation warranted it, but there's no doubt that he had a way of keeping the media at a distance. A dirty look or short answer would do the trick. Often, though, Eddie was just frustrated that attention directed his way should have been directed elsewhere. Say Eddie has hit a homer in the first inning and those two runs hold up as the difference in the game, and say Mike Boddicker has pitched seven shutout innings for the victory. The reporters file into the locker room and immediately take a right turn (this is in old Memorial Stadium), heading for Eddie's locker. Eddie says "The story's over there," points to Mike's locker, and walks away. If you know Eddie, he's trying to give credit where credit is due, paying tribute to a teammate by saying, in not quite so many words, "It's no big deal that I hit a homer in the first inning on a mistake pitch. The pitcher deserves the credit for this game."

If Eddie did get the big hit in the ninth or made the error to cost the game, he'd usually be available to the press for a brief interview. Get Eddie going in a restaurant or over the telephone and he can talk for hours—he loves to talk on the phone—but the man is basically very reserved, and I don't think people understand this. He rags on himself about being so quiet. He tells the story about when he made the Orioles in 1977, and he and Earl Weaver didn't exchange a word for months. One day in June, they happened to pass each other in the tunnel and Earl said "Hi" and Eddie said "Hi." Eddie then overheard Earl stop Doug DeCinces and ask, "What about this kid?" Doug replied, "What makes you think he talks to me?" (Doug and Eddie knew each other from playing together on a winter ball team in Los Angeles.)

I don't think a player should be penalized for being a short interview. Usually there's not that much to say anyway. Reporters, however, can take brevity personally. This attitude might have been part of Eddie's problem with them. He might also say something like, "I'll talk to you today, I may talk to you tomorrow, but I might *not* next week. I'm here to concentrate on baseball." He just wanted to do his job to the best of his ability. He's so honest and direct it's scary, and, as he puts it, media coverage was something he did *not* dream about when he dreamed about playing baseball while growing up in Los Angeles. Eddie said with some bitterness before he left Baltimore, "The only thing that counts is what the media does," but here's a guy who nevertheless does *not* care what the media does. He just wanted to be one of the *team*, not a vocal standout. He wasn't impressed by huge books of clippings on himself. In his large family—eleven brothers and sisters— there had never been a lot of "I and me," as he put it, while interviews are nothing but "I and me," and he wasn't comfortable with them. He didn't mean to be rude with anyone, he meant to be good-hearted, but his attitude didn't come off that way, and I guess it was inevitable that he'd feel his answers and the context for those answers were sometimes distorted.

The serious deterioration started in 1986, I think. He was upset when the club publicized his purchase of seats for kids, after he'd asked that the program be anonymous. He thought a conversation he had with Hank Peters, our general manager, about wearing glasses or contacts was private and off the record, but within a week the story was out that Eddie Murray might need glasses. Maybe Eddie blamed the messenger of this message. Then came the killer, the interview with Edward Bennett Williams I've mentioned, in which our owner questioned Eddie's desire and work ethic. Eddie prided himself on playing every day. That year was the first time he'd even been on the disabled list, so he was upset with the story and everybody knew it. What everybody didn't know was that the interview was supposedly off the record, as I've explained, and the story never should have come out.

Mistake or otherwise, the damage was done. Eddie wondered how the owner of the team could even think something so off base. Eddie Murray a bad influence? He was a tremendous presence on the team! He was a leader of the Orioles almost from day one. When he was on the DL in 1986, he drove the guys on the bench crazy with his cheerleading. I thought the situation could have been defused if Williams had said he wasn't criticizing Eddie, but trying to motivate the team by challenging Eddie, because Eddie was the leader. But nothing like that was said.

Larry Lucchino, the president of the club, asked Eddie how Williams and he could get back together. Eddie asked for an apology. Williams did call him one night to apologize, and Eddie said, Thank you, but I want a public apology, the same way the story was put out. Over the off-season, Williams did apologize publicly and Eddie said, Fine, we're straight.

He may have been straight with Williams, but now the criticism was picking up all over town. To put it bluntly, in my opinion Eddie became the scapegoat for the team's declining fortunes. Being the proud and stubborn man he is, he pulled back. Now he wasn't talking to the press at all. I've been told that the writers covering the game in the press box were silently hoping that Eddie wouldn't get the big hit so they wouldn't have to try to interview him after the game and be rejected. A sad situation with misunderstandings all around, and I urged Eddie to go public with his feelings about being a proud Oriole, about wanting to play in Baltimore, where the fans are special. Eddie did give one television interview, I think, but his words didn't come out the way he wanted them to. It sounded as if he was knocking the fans, which was the opposite of what he intended. When I say this, I'm not just covering for Eddie. I know what he felt because we had talked about it, and I know what the fans felt, too, because I'd heard them roar "ED-DIE! ED-DIE!" a thousand times since the day I'd joined the team.

I look back over Eddie's last couple of years with the Orioles in 1987 and '88 and think maybe *I* could have done more to shift the momentum. I worry that I came up short here. Maybe I could have said in the strongest terms, "Wait a minute! We're about to drum out of town the greatest teammate ever, and one of the greatest Orioles ever."

But that kind of outspokenness isn't really in my nature, either.

On the positive side regarding the Baltimore organization, work was scheduled to begin in 1989 on the new downtown park at Camden Yards, although this wasn't much of a factor for me because I loved old Memorial Stadium anyway; everyone who played there did. What was most important to me was the fact that the Orioles were no longer pretending to have all the pieces of the puzzle. Too late to help my father, we had admitted we were rebuilding and had already made one good trade, getting Brady Anderson from the Red Sox. Brady had been one of the names mentioned in the Ripken blockbuster that never happened. After he arrived at the end of July he struggled statistically, but I saw a lot of talent and potential. My brother was struggling, too, but he was still the steady fielder, and I liked knowing that he should be at second base for years to come. Billy just couldn't shake his feelings about the firing, but he would. (A day or two after the event, he traded in his number 3 for Dad's suddenly unused number 7. He and clubhouseman Jimmy Tyler did this without consulting the front office. "Minimal paperwork," Billy said. We all had to figure out how to deal with the situation; this was one of Billy's ways.)

I thought about all these pros and cons and then thought about them some more. By August, my anger had modulated. In the end I made the decision to stick with the rebuilding, thinking it might take a few years for us to be a contending team again. I thought that I was young enough to withstand the rebuilding process, and I wanted to help bring the Orioles back. But my agent didn't tell the Orioles this. They'd been trying to set up a trade under the assumption I was angry enough to leave. In their minds, there was always the chance I'd leave. For the sake of the negotiations, Ron Shapiro let them continue to think this. He told them I'd been hurt by the way they handled Dad's firing, which was true. Negotiations moved along, and in August we signed a three-year deal with an option for a fourth year. That's the way the deal was advertised, but the fine print said that the option had to be exercised at the end of the *first* year. What kind of option for the club was that? None at all, really, unless all of a sudden I just couldn't field or hit the ball at all. For all practical purposes that was a four-year deal, but the club wanted "three-and-one" because those were collusion years, when no contracts were being written for longer than three years. So we came up with this wrinkle to get the four when only three could be official. That was also the contract with the all-important no-trade clause and the provision that I would not violate the contract if I got hurt playing basketball in the off-season. Some of the commentators said the Orioles got a steal, that I could have made much more on the open market. Maybe I could have, but my priorities were to wipe 1988 out of my mind, get the no-trade clause, settle down, and forget "the business side."

Then that tough season was over. Not a great one for the Ripken family, although Dad did come back. In June, he agreed to be a special assignment scout for the remainder of the year. After the shock of the firing had worn off, and when he got some feelers that Frank Robinson might want him back in the coaching ranks the following year, he and I had several long conversations about what he should do. These weren't so much father to son as baseball man to baseball man. My view was that the negative reaction around Baltimore when he'd been fired gave him a pretty good opportunity careerwise, and maybe even financially. If I were in his shoes, I said, I'd ask for the opportunity and the *power* to revamp the whole minor league system, while getting paid well for the job. The Oriole Way as I've just introduced it in the simplest terms was one of the subjects of our conversations, and we agreed that the system had only one way to go: up. He could make a huge impact and, frankly, get the credit I thought he already deserved—he and a lot of other people, because the sustained achievement of the big league club for a couple of decades was due to the talent drafted and then developed by the minor league system over all those years.

But could any one person reenergize the tradition? If anyone could, it would be my dad. Think about it. He's a great teacher of the game, he understood how to implement the Oriole Way in every way. But did he still have the enthusiasm to give it a try? No. He didn't feel he had the time or maybe even the energy for a huge undertaking like that. He had given sixteen- and eighteen-hour days for fourteen years in the minors, and the idea of going back and almost starting over, in effect, was too much. And there wasn't any way to do it while sitting behind a desk. I thought there might be some way requiring less time but still having a huge impact, but Dad thought he'd have to be absolutely hands on, like he'd always been. Delegation is not one of his strong suits.

When he talked with the club about returning in some capacity, he didn't even broach the idea of running the minor league system. However, returning as third base coach was feasible. He said in so many words, "I'm coming back for Billy. You're developed. You don't need my help anymore." He wasn't thinking in terms of a protective capacity, but of a teaching capacity, being a presence with the team. After the firing, Billy's emotions had gotten the better of him, there's no denying it. He hit .207 in 1988, which is a sophomore slump and then some. Just as Senior had acted as a father as well as a manager in putting an end to my consecutive innings streak, now the father in him was coming out again.

Following a brief, secret meeting in a hotel in Pikesville late in 1988, Senior agreed to return to the field the following year as Frank Robinson's third base coach. He would also run spring training camp for Frank, just as he had for Earl Weaver, Joe Altobelli, and himself. Back to the future, I guess. By way of explanation for this decision to come back, Dad said with his usual dry understatement, "I guess you know I'm an Oriole."

Chapter Eleven

Sixth inning, Memorial Stadium, Opening Day 1989. Joan Jett, a big Orioles fan, has brought down the full house with a rocking rendition of the national anthem. Roger Clemens is pitching for the defending AL East champions, the Red Sox. Roger has already fanned me in the second inning on hundred-mile-per-hour fastballs (pitches like those you remember, and maybe even have nightmares about). My team is trailing 3–1, with two on and one out, and I'm fortunate enough to work the count to 2–2. I foul off a couple of pitches before Roger tries a high fastball that tails just a bit over the plate, and I'm able to get on top of it and drive the ball over the wall. The fans go wild and my heart is pounding as I circle the bases. Really pounding. That was the kind of tough at-bat against the best that makes the game so challenging for the pitcher and the hitter, and it was such an exciting way to start the new season.

The whole game was that way. Our rookie right fielder Steve Finley had already made an amazing catch earlier to kill a Boston rally, robbing Nick Esasky with a desperate lunge the instant before he hit the wall on a dead run. The play sent Steve to the hospital with a separated shoulder, and he came back to the stadium later with his arm in a sling.

After my homer gave us a one-run lead, the Red Sox tied the game, but then we won it in the eleventh, and you could feel a big relief in the clubhouse: with the first game, we'd already gotten the monkey off our back. There would be no repeat of 1988's losing streak to start things off. Nor did the reporters have to inform me after the game that this was the first time I'd ever gone "yard" (lingo for hitting a homer) off the Rocket.

What's more, the whole *season* went the way of Opening Day. It seemed to set the tone for a surprising 1989 for the Orioles, as we posted a winning record for the first time in four years and had a great pennant run under Frank Robinson, and with my father back in the third base coaching box, as peppy and loyal as ever. That team was unlike any I'd ever played on. We had thirteen rookies, nine sophomores, and only three players over thirty years old. Eddie Murray, my closest friend on the team, was gone, traded to the Dodgers. His number 33 was retired, an honor previously granted only Brooks Robinson, Frank Robinson, Earl Weaver, and Jim Palmer. His 333 homers were the club record at the time. Eddie's departure was sad, and I still missed him sorely as a friend and on the field, but maybe it was all for the best.

We actually led the AL East by seven games in July, when "Why Not?" became the new and unexpected marketing slogan for the front office. Then we lost a host of games and slipped back, but we rebounded and traveled to Toronto only one behind the Blue Jays with three to play. Sweep and we win. But we didn't. We lost the first two games in agonizing fashion, after leading each in the eighth inning. We were *one pitch* away from winning the first game before the Blue Jays tied it and went on to win in the eleventh. After enjoying 116 days in first place, that fairy-tale year was over. True to form, thousands of our fans waited at the airport in the rain to welcome us home, and then toasted us again the following day with a rainy parade through downtown Baltimore.

How did the Orioles compete in '89? We had pretty good years from a bunch of guys, we were steady fielders in the infield, terrific in the outfield, and we had good pitching as well. Jeff Ballard was our improbable ace, winning 18 games. Two rookie pitchers, Bob Milacki and Gregg Olson, really came through and were the main reason the '89 Orioles were the first team in history to get 25 wins and 25 saves from rookies (that statistic compliments of George Will, who worked on his book about baseball, *Men at Work*, during the season). Olson moved from setup man to closer shortly after April 26, when he struck out Dave Parker, Dave Henderson, and Mark McGwire in the ninth inning of a 2–1 victory in Oakland. Those curveballs were unhittable. He was our MVP, and that curve was his pitch. As it turned out, it was one of Gregg's curves that broke in the dirt in the eighth inning of the first game of the big Toronto series, allowing the tying run to score. Hey, live by the sword, die by the sword. Gregg was incredible that year. On my twentieth home run, Cleveland center fielder Brad Komminsk caught the ball but dropped it while falling over the wall. Four bases for me. (Honest Brad told me later that he'd thought about retrieving the ball and pretending he'd held on.) Joe Orsulak hit cleanup against the Yankees in New York and responded with two home runs. That's the kind of year it was for us. We made the plays and the ball seemed to bounce our way. All in all, you'd have to say we overachieved. We were also fortunate that the eastern division had no really dominant team. That was the first year of the Blue Jays' great stretch of seasons, but they won only 89 games. We won 87.

Given recent history, that was an exciting, great season for the Orioles. For me, it was exciting and strange. I'd always known what Eddie Murray meant to me as a friend, mentor, and teammate. In 1989, I fully realized what he had meant to my career. It was humbling, I have to tell you, as I got the full impact of life at the plate without Eddie Murray waiting ominously in the on-deck circle. As I've said, his presence in the lineup carries so much weight it's unbelievable—as powerful a presence as anyone's in this era. Maybe that's slightly exaggerated, when you think of Belle and Griffey and Thomas and McGwire and a few others, but not much, because unlike all those guys, unlike almost all the other great power hitters of this era, Eddie's a switch-hitter. As I've said, many times managers had been forced to leave in a lefthander to face me because Eddie was coming up, and they preferred seeing him bat from the right side.

The year before, when the Orioles had lost so many games, pitchers on pennant-contending teams told Eddie and me that they'd be fined if either of us beat them. With Eddie gone in '89, maybe they got fined double if I did the job. I've never claimed to be the greatest hitter in the world, or a big-impact number four hitter of Eddie's caliber, but in those rebuilding years for the Orioles I was the only player with any kind of track record. I'd been used to a lineup in which Eddie Murray was feared as the main man because he *was* the main man. When Eddie departed, so did my clutch, switch-hitting protection in the lineup. This was new, and it was frustrating. I was used to contributing at a certain level, putting up certain numbers. Now I was getting fewer real opportunities. In previous years, the pitcher might have had to challenge my strength rather than risk walking me and facing Eddie. On a 3–1 count, for example, I could pretty much count on a fastball from certain pitchers. Not anymore.

When Eddie went on the DL for the first time in his career, in 1986, it was quickly apparent we were a different team without him. Even if he was slumping he contributed because of his reputation; the slump wouldn't last forever. In my first five or six years in the league, I anticipated a time when I might be thought of in the same way. In 1989, I began to wonder about that ambition. Certain players have the ability to get hot and carry a team, not only on the scoreboard but *emotionally* somehow. Eddie could do that. I couldn't. Like a lot of other hitters, when I get really hot I can affect a bunch of games in a row, but this is still different from Eddie's impact.

As I've explained, Eddie didn't have the appetite or the personality to be the center of attention. He just wanted to be a cog in the wheel, but he was so good as a player that he became the *ultimate* cog in the wheel with the Orioles, and therefore the center of attention. With him gone,

I realized I wasn't cut out to be the ultimate cog in the wheel, either. Initially in '89, Frank Robinson moved me to the cleanup position, then switched me back to the third spot when Mickey Tettleton showed off his power in a breakout season (and gave the credit to Froot Loops, thus acquiring an unusual nickname). Mickey hit 26 homers for us, most of them before he went down with an injury in August.

Wherever I batted that year, I was never completely comfortable with my new role. I tried to deny any extra pressure, but I finally accepted the fact that I had gone from being a small part of a great team to a bigger part of a rebuilding team. That's an adjustment. It put me in more of a teaching role, a mentoring role. At the plate, it meant I was going to have to acquire real patience, and that was a battle for me. I'd always been patient, but I could also count on probably getting a pitch I could get a good swing at. Let's face it, I'd been spoiled. Now I was in a situation where I might not get that pitch *at all*. This requires an even greater patience, and I didn't always have it. My strikeouts didn't go up that year, but my walks went way down, only 57 compared with 102 the previous year.

I had my highlights, like that Opening Day homer and then one off Nolan Ryan in late May, when I turned around a curveball after being blown away in my first at-bat, and when I was down 1–2 in the count as well. I was fortunate; against Nolan, you counted your blessings—usually on one hand, because the cliché was true, his fastball exploded in the strike zone. I guess another highlight, and just as unexpected as the homers against Clemens and Ryan, was on August 17 when I passed Steve Garvey on the consecutive games list, at 1,208. The Orioles surprised me with a sixth-inning tribute on Diamondvision, and I was caught off guard again when forty thousand fans gave me a standing "O." Larry Sheets told me I couldn't just hide on the bench, like I was trying to do, so I waved from the steps. The fans appreciated that, but they were even happier that I had snapped a slump with three hits and my sixteenth homer of the year.

Even with my sense of uneasiness at the plate for much of the season, my power numbers were pretty good, at 21 and 93, and a good September would have given me more homers and RBIs than Robin Yount, who won the MVP Award, and more of an MVP-sounding batting average, instead of my .257, which dropped about twenty points in September. In fact, some commentators suggested that my serious September slump was all that kept me from a second trophy. I didn't buy that at all, but I did take notice when one writer more or less blamed my September slump for the Orioles' failure to win the pennant. When I saw this reporter the following spring training I asked if he thought the Orioles would have been fighting for the pennant in the first place without my homers and RBIs and my presence in the middle of the infield.

He said no.

But he'd written as if I or any other player, even an Eddie Murray or an Albert Belle or a Frank Thomas, can just *will* himself to a higher level of play in September: "Okay, boys, hop on my shoulders, I'll carry you to the Promised Land." If you can will yourself to play better, wouldn't you will yourself to play better all the time? I sure would. Unfortunately, baseball doesn't work that way. In the fourth quarter, the opposing team can double-team Michael Jordan, but it can't intentionally walk him and it can't pitch around him. He *will* get his hands on the ball, and he will get his shots. In baseball, pitchers and strategy control the game and control your opportunities at the plate. When confronted by an Albert Belle or Ken Griffey, Jr., or Frank Thomas or Mark McGwire, the opposing manager and pitcher can decide that someone else on that team is going to have to win the baseball game. They can make sure that McGwire will see nothing worthwhile to hit in this at-bat in the eighth inning.

That's the situation I felt I was in for the last six weeks or so in 1989. My dilemma wasn't *that* bad, of course, because I'm not McGwire or one of those other guys, but in my imagination, it was. The big mistake I made was not accepting the situation, exaggerated though it might have been in my mind. I wanted to contribute so much I contributed not nearly enough. When I did get a good pitch to hit, I was surprised, but most of the time I didn't even wait for something decent. I played right into the opposing team's hands and expanded the strike zone rather than accept the walk and leave the rally for the next man up. With the kind of magic we had going all year, he probably would have come through.

Patience would have been much more helpful to the team, but patience can be hard for all of us. Frank Thomas's patience under these circumstances is unbelievable, but even Frank, as smart as they come, a hitter who stays within himself with the best of them, must have a threshold for frustration, high though it might be (and a lot higher than mine). It would be interesting to see what would happen if August 15 rolled around and Frank was walking at a pace of 175 times a year as opposed to his normal (but still very high) 120 or so, and if his offensive numbers therefore weren't quite in line with his standards. The Big Hurt would have to be almost superhuman not to start swinging more. It's called human nature.

For a twist on this phenomenon, let's skip ahead to 1996, when the Orioles had Brady Anderson, Rafael Palmeiro, and Bobby Bonilla with 100 RBIs apiece guaranteed in September. Todd Zeile, who joined us during the season from the Phillies, and I were on schedule to become the fourth and fifth Orioles to reach the century mark. For the first couple of weeks in September, I was distracted by that nice round number, before I was able to say to heck with it and settle down, ending up with 102 RBIs. Todd Zeile ended up one short of the target, and he admitted he'd been pressing to reach it. This has nothing to do with our being overly stats-oriented. It's impossible for ballplayers not to think like this, even in a pennant race, even when we know it's counterproductive.

In 1989, the bottom line was a disappointing September for me, but the team sure had a great run.

Rarely have I approached a reporter to say that I thought a story was truly unfair, and most of those have been regarding another player. But I didn't believe I should've been blamed for losing the pennant in 1989. I'll admit it. Maybe you're now saying, "Oh, boy, this guy turns out to be thin-skinned." No, I don't think so. I'm secure enough in my abilities not to be threatened by what's written in the papers, and I'm not threatened by the possibility that readers may believe the stories. But I also realize that as television—and now Internet—coverage of baseball has grown exponentially, the newspapers are left without a new story to tell the following morning. Fans already know the score and the details, so newspapers have to find other angles. Opinion and criticism are much in evidence. In the big picture, all this "extra" coverage is great. It increases interest in baseball, gets fans to thinking and examining every aspect of the game, and enhances their enjoyment. I don't think there's any doubt about it. Does it bother me that someone might read something I think is unfair? Yes, a little, but it's a small price to pay. I keep in mind that opinion is only opinion, which can be based on a little fact or a lot of fact, or none at all. I apply the same skepticism while reading the rest of the newspaper.

Flash forward to 1995, when Phil Regan was fired as our manager after just that one season. Stories immediately came out to the effect that one problem had been his failure to get me on board. Supposedly, Phil had alienated me because I didn't like much of anything he'd wanted to accomplish during the abbreviated, post-strike spring training and had torpedoed his whole program and tenure. These stories were also helped along by the post-season comments of some of my own teammates, it's true. Let me tell you what really happened here.

According to the stories, one of the big problems between Phil and me was his bunt plays. After the first workout when the plays were laid out for us, I asked Phil to explain some points. I won't go into the details, which are complicated. In fact, *because* the plays were complicated I asked Phil if I could make a suggestion. He said sure, and I said, more or less, "We only have three weeks to cover a lot and we have a new guy [Bret Barberie] in the infield. Why don't we try running the plays we had last year and incorporate him? Why not have one guy learning the plays that three of us already know, rather than have four guys learning plays that none of us knows? If you're unhappy with the execution when you have the twenty-five guys selected, we'll have time early in the season to change the plays."

Phil said he'd think about it. We had been standing out on the field after the workout for about forty-five minutes. Maybe I did get a little argumentative. I probably did, because Phil's idea for positioning the shortstop (me) on one or two of the plays was problematic, in my mind. But the next day Phil approached me first thing in the morning with a big grin and said, "I've thought about what you said, Cal. We'll stay with what we have for spring training."

That was that on the bunt plays. Phil Regan did not "lose" me in spring training. We didn't have a long, drawn-out battle that tainted the whole season. You could have read one article after the season and thought I didn't like or respect Phil Regan and had set out to bury him. That's absolutely wrong. I like Phil and have a lot of respect for him as a baseball man. Throughout the season, we had many conversations about situational baseball that both of us enjoyed and learned from. The big issue with Phil that year was the fact that his first big league assignment was a highly pressurized situation in which his every move was going to be dissected: a tough, tough job.

As I've explained to different reporters, my primary loyalty is to the team, not to the press corps. Maybe that sounds harsh when stated so directly, but I don't intend it that way. It's just that trust and credibility with the team is the main thing for me. I wasn't going to violate various confidences in order to assure that the press knew everything that was going on in 1995 or any other time.

I've always had a natural reserve, and although I'm comfortable with the press now, I'm not an open book, and never will be. To a considerable extent, my relations with the press were modeled on Eddie Murray's, before his completely fell apart. I learned from Eddie about getting prepared. He taught me to take care of business, to let nothing interrupt my preparation for the game. When I first came up to the big leagues, I'd talk to reporters during batting practice. Eddie advised against it. Focus on the game, kid, he suggested.

My reference to Eddie in my thank-you speech on September 6 after breaking Gehrig's record raised some eyebrows. When I saw him later in Cleveland, where we flew for our next series, he teased me hard about an ulterior motive. As we stretched in the outfield before the first game, Eddie said, "You're slick. You're so tired of all the coverage you decided to come up with a way to get them to lay off for a while. You figured, 'Hey, I know, I'll give a lot of credit to the guy they love to hate. That'll do it.' You're slick."

I can honestly say that motive never crossed my mind while I was working on my speech.

Eddie and I also exchanged the lineup cards at home plate before that game in Cleveland. Unless I'm seriously mistaken, this was the only time I've done that, but the Indians had planned to replay my remarks about his influence on me and they asked if I'd take the card out for the occasion, and I said I'd be glad to if Eddie said yes. Eddie agreed, and when I saw that he was really appreciative of the moment, I took it a bit further and started to play to the crowd.

Eddie teased me again by asking, "Are we now playing the public relations game?"

I replied, "One of us has to."

He laughed. I love the guy. Eddie's heart is huge, *huge*, but if you don't understand this, if you don't understand him, you might mistakenly believe he really is one of the ten biggest jerks in baseball, as he was labeled by *Sports Illustrated* in 1996. There might not be a player in either league who's held in higher regard by his teammates while being held in such low regard by the media.

Eddie's situation isn't the normal one, but, overall, it's not much of an exaggeration to say that the relationship between the media and the players in major league baseball has evolved into something of a standoff, for the simple reason that *they* want everything they can get, and sometimes *we* don't want to, or cannot, provide it. For example, when a player is going badly he certainly doesn't want to talk about that, and a player hitting really well may not want to talk much about *that*, either, because he might be a little superstitious or just doesn't want to overanalyze. To make this point, I can't do better than relate the story I told George Will for *Men at Work*.

In 1987, I was on a really hot streak when we arrived in California. One night Ruppert Jones, standing at second base after a double, complimented me on how great I was swinging the bat. "You haven't taken a bad swing since you've been here," Ruppert said. "Swinging really good, with your hands away from your body like that." Was he playing a mind game with me, mentioning my hands? That's what I suggested to George, or maybe Ruppert was just being genuinely positive. Anyway, the net effect was that in my next at-bat I was thinking about where my hands were, keeping them away from my body. I immediately went into a little slump.

I've always tinkered obsessively with my stance—the list of changes tried and discarded would be too long to print—but I've always felt that working hard and trying things was good for my mental health, even if the results are not immediate, and they usually aren't. At least I feel that I'm doing everything possible. Reporters see me try these stances in BP, sometimes in the game, and they want to talk about them. I don't. I have enough light bulbs flashing on and off—although when the bulb finally does go on in my brain, it usually stays on for a while. And as Billy put it one day, "You see six different guys with six different stances, so why not *one* guy with six different stances? What's the big deal?"

So there's stuff I don't want to talk about. I know it would hurt my game to talk about it. Maybe this is why I have a reputation for sometimes being guarded and "safe" during interviews. Remember, I think before I speak. I don't spout off a lot. I'm available to the media when I feel I should be, but I don't feel obligated to make myself available at all times, because that would be impossible. To fully understand this, you have to appreciate the special relationship that the press has always had with the players in baseball: daily access on the trains—in the old days—on the field, in the clubhouse. Always much more access, I understand, than in the NFL, the NBA, and the NHL. Like the players, the beat writers covering baseball live and breathe the game for seven months, and this is necessary. There's no other way to report this daily game, and all this up-close reporting is a big part of what makes baseball special. We players do understand this—at least most of us do. However, now that this coverage has expanded, all the attention and requests for interviews can be a bit overwhelming. I try to be as fair as possible, but I have to look out for myself as well. I've sought refuge in the training room and the weight room, not out of disrespect, but out of a need to stay focused on the task at hand, which is baseball.

Two months after the '89 season ended, nothing the media or anyone else said or did mattered all that much when Kelly's and my daughter Rachel was born on November 22. That was the happiest Thanksgiving holiday of my life. I may have been in something like a dream state six years later when I took the lap around Camden Yards on September 6, but that was actually the third, maybe even the fourth time I'd had such an incredible sensation. The first time was my wedding night, although that feeling wasn't quite as bizarre. The second night was when I saw tiny Rachel and she let out her first big cry, and the third time was when Ryan was born.

Before Rachel was born, Kelly and I didn't know whether we had a boy or a girl on the way, and we didn't want to know, and we didn't care. I hear about parents who want one or the other, maybe a girl after a couple of boys, or vice versa, but I have a hard time believing that it really makes any difference when the time comes. I think all any parent wants is to hear that first cry, because crying is breathing, a sign of good health. That's what I remember most about that day, wanting to hear a healthy cry.

Chapter Twelve

Frank Robinson said that for the Orioles the 1989 season had been like catching lightning in a bottle. That was the good news; the bad news was that the Orioles couldn't store the lightning in the bottle. All the magic in 1989 had hidden the fact that we were a rebuilding organization. "Why Not" once again in 1990? Because rebuilding is usually a three-, four-, even five-year process. You're letting people develop to reap the benefits of their physical talent and their experience, assuming that you've scouted well in the first place and have talented people throughout the system, and assuming that you have some money for the occasional "complementary" free agent. The expectations for the O's were high going into 1990, but the magical moments that had seemed common the year before were now rare. Our pitchers had about the same ERA and our hitters produced almost as many runs, but we won 11 fewer games and were never a factor in the race. We couldn't store last season's lightning, nor did it strike in the same place.

For the first half of the season, I was not much help offensively. On June 11, I was booed when I struck out in the fifth inning with a guy on first. I remember the exact date only because it was my 1,307th consecutive game, tying me with Everett Scott for second place on the all-time list. First I was booed, then politely applauded when that news was flashed on the Diamondvision screen. I was hitting .217 at the time—not good, even for a shortstop—and I was well under .200 with runners in scoring position—not good for anybody. The next game, Frank Robinson tried to take some pressure off by dropping me to sixth in the lineup, the first time I'd batted that low since my rookie year, and I missed a grand slam down the left field line in the fourth inning, with the ball turning just foul. Then I grounded into an inning-ending double play.

More boos—but now I was prepared. Two years earlier I'd come to an understanding on this subject. I'd been promoting milk for almost my entire career, and in 1988 the milk cooperative's campaign ran a short spot on the Diamondvision at Memorial Stadium before the second inning. Almost like clockwork, it seemed, I'd make the third out in the first inning, and immediately the picture of me enjoying a glass of milk would appear along with the announcement. And equally close to clock-work, the fans booed. This went on for about a month, and as usual with me, I needed to come up with an approach to handle a new situation. I had a long conversation with someone—my agent Ron Shapiro, perhaps—who led me to the understanding that the fan reaction isn't personal. A boo is a reaction of displeasure. It doesn't mean the fans dis-like *me*. The same logic applies to a cheer. They're not really cheering me, they're cheering my home run. That's why fans can boo a strikeout in the fourth and demand a curtain call for a homer in the eighth, and it's easy for an athlete to forget that there *is* a difference between him and his performance on the field. To put myself in the place of the base-ball fan I only have to think about myself watching basketball on televi-sion. I'm a fan there, too, and when somebody throws the ball away in a key situation, I might shout at the screen. I wouldn't actually boo sitting courtside, but I'd still react with some strong body language.

After the milk-ad episodes, I matured. I quit worrying about the boos and the radio talk shows. When the team loses, everyone wants a reason and probably someone to blame. Because of Eddie's problems with the Orioles for the last several years he was with us, he took most of the heat when our long slide began in 1986, while I was more or less insulated from that criticism. Once Eddie was gone, it was my turn, but I was determined that what had happened with Eddie wasn't going to happen with me. I kept my mouth shut, I didn't lash out, I kept plugging, I kept reminding myself this wasn't personal. I knew our fans just missed the good ol' days and were impatient for their return. Who wasn't? My goal was just to play as well as I could and try to help the team turn it around. When Frank Robinson sensed one day that I was down nevertheless, he reminded me that he'd been booed plenty of times, too.

Frank also defended putting me in the lineup every day, because this was when those questions first cropped up with some regularity. In fact, a few days before I passed Everett Scott and assumed second place on the consecutive games list, one of the authors of the Elias Baseball Analyst was asked if Gehrig's record was important, and he said he thought it was overrated as a great baseball record, because it's not a record of skill, but of will.

I respectfully disagree on two counts. First, doesn't it take skill and talent to earn the right to be in the lineup night after night, year after year? I think so. Or, as I said in 1990 while standing by the monument to Lou Gehrig at the base of the flagpole beyond the left–center field wall at Yankee Stadium: "A team is really just a group of individual accomplishments meshed together. You have to count on the person to your right and the person to your left, the person hitting in front of you and the person hitting behind you. I'm proud I can be counted on."

Second, "will" implies intention, which I didn't have. I intended to play *this* game. I've always looked at every game as a one-game season. I don't relate this game to the previous one or to the following one. There's no "will," there's no carryover. "If we've got to beat Roger Clemens tonight, am I one of the nine best guys we can put on the field to try to do that?" That's my approach, and that's the approach of every manager regarding every guy in the lineup.

Beginning in 1990, questions about the streak became prominent when I was in a slump, usually with the assumption that I was slumping because I was tired from playing all these games. Sixty games into the season in 1990 I was supposed to be tired? Come on. I wasn't even tired the previous September, when some observers decided that streak fatigue had caused my slump during the pennant race. I felt like Superman that month! We were really in the hunt. My adrenaline was pumping. My problem was mainly a lack of patience, as I've just explained.

Still, the assumption seemed to be in some quarters that if I didn't feel one hundred percent, I shouldn't have played. Well, we have to get a couple of things straight: first, come July and August, after we've played 100 games, very few ballplayers feel one hundred percent for many days in a row. Impossible. You wouldn't feel one hundred percent if you played only 100 games for the entire season. Certainly playing 150 games is the same as playing 162 games. No difference. Everyone's traveling the same, sleeping the same, eating at the same odd hours. The scheduling demands are the same, and the resulting daily grind—the fact that you have to do it every single day whether you're in the ball games or not—is the fatiguing factor in a baseball season. I think you can get so tired playing pro basketball or hockey that you almost fall off your stool after the game, but the nature of baseball is different. Playing nine innings is no sweat, in comparison.

One year, Brooks Robinson was in a slump and Earl Weaver called him in and said he was going to rest his third baseman for a couple of days. And that's what Earl did. After the rest, Brooks went 0-and-12 or something. Now Brooks went looking for his manager and said, "I respect what you did, Earl, but to me, it doesn't make sense. I can't get out of a slump sitting on the bench. I don't get tired playing baseball." He wasn't tired of playing; he was tired of being in a slump. The assumption that the guy who hasn't played in a few games is "well rested" is false. In fact, this guy might be up to speed physically but now he's a little rusty because he hasn't been playing. Some guys do respond to a day off; others, like Brooks Robinson, don't. And if fatigue really is the problem, is one day going to solve it? Or even two? I don't think so.

Say you work in an office and you're *really* tired. Does the long Memorial Day weekend help? No. You need a vacation. With ballplayers, that doesn't come until October.

You could argue that the advantage of the day off or the Memorial Day weekend is *mental*, not physical. Some players feel this way, but some of the worst-feeling days can turn out well and trigger hot streaks. That's been my experience. Sitting in my rocking chair fifty years after my career is over, I might look back and decide that a three-day blow here and there might have stabilized my performance and cut down on some of the slumps. I might decide that I could have been a career .290 hitter instead of a .275–280 hitter. But I don't think so. Slumps are part of the game—a given. Year in and year out, Eddie Murray hit .400 for a week, maybe two, and .200 for a week, maybe two, hot and cool, back and forth, for an average of .300, 30 homers, and 100 RBIs. The same holds for *every* everyday player. The slumps and hot streaks average out.

If I had really wanted to move my career stats up a notch or two—if I wanted to get selfish about it—the way to accomplish that would have been to take my days off against Roger Clemens, Randy Johnson, and a couple of the other toughest pitchers in the game. If you told me I *had* to take ten days off, my choice of games, I guarantee they'd be against guys I have a hard time hitting. Physically, you can bat against these guys, no problem, but mentally it *is* hard not to think, I'm not sharp, it can't get much worse than this—oh, yes, it can, Randy Johnson's pitching. It can be mentally uplifting to take the day off and ask somebody else to battle this guy. And if I "rested" those games and took the 40-plus at-bats and, say, eight hits off my stats at the end of the year, my batting average would go up about seven points and I'd have a more productive season *on paper*.

But would that higher average have helped the team on those days I was on the bench against the best pitchers? I don't see how. This is the big question: do the Orioles have a replacement who will do better than me—day in, day out—against Clemens, Johnson, and the other top players? If so, then he should be already playing, day in, day out. You can platoon players, you can give people days off, you can try to make player-for-player matchups, but to me, it's more important to have your top-of-the-line guys in against these guys because of their experience, their presence in the order, their contributions that can help you beat one of these pitchers *if* you can keep the game close. They can be beaten. Maybe my walk is key. On the other hand, maybe the replacement does match up well lifetime against Clemens. If that were the case, you could make a good case for giving me the day off. Manager's decision, not the player's. When the Orioles faced Nolan Ryan when he was with the Angels, Earl Weaver concocted all sorts of strange lineups. One of the stars always seemed to be Tommy Shopay, a part-time player or, as Earl put it, a base-on-balls man who filled in for Paul Blair.

During the slump in '90 I tried to avoid looking at my batting average flashed on the scoreboard. I knew what it was, but I couldn't bear to see it up in lights. At times like these you wish you were back in the minors where, at least in my era, the batting averages weren't posted. But there it was, even if I didn't look, almost like a nightmare: .209 . . . .209 . . . .209.

At this point, Frank Robinson decided that he'd had enough. He called me into his office one afternoon at Memorial Stadium and said, "Let's talk, Cal." The first thing he did was address my state of mind. He told me about 1965, when he was 0-for-22, with nothing but lazy fly balls and easy ground balls, totally convinced he'd never get another hit, much less two in the same game. But he did. He told me about how he'd been described in Cincinnati as an "old thirty" when he'd been traded from Cincinnati to Baltimore the following year. He told me how he'd used that remark to motivate himself (with great success: he hit a homer in each of his first three games with the Orioles, hit one completely out of Memorial Stadium on Mother's Day—a pennant reading HERE was thereafter flown at the location—and never let up. Frank won the Triple Crown that year, and only one other player subsequently has done that—Carl Yastrzemski the following year).

Twenty-four years later, Frank gave me a new perspective on the highs and lows not just of a season, but of a *career*. Slumps are an accepted part of every season, but many players don't understand the equivalent highs and lows—the slumps—that are inevitable in any lengthy career.

During my rookie slump in 1982, it had been Reggie Jackson pulling me over to third base for the words of encouragement that worked to perfection. In 1990, it was Frank sharing his big league experience with me. My father hadn't had a long major league career—this was one aspect of the game he couldn't tutor me in—but Frank had the career and the authority, putting everything in perspective, saying the right thing at the right time. He also pumped up my ego by saying I was the only guy he'd ever seen who could hit home runs off the "T." (I've never seen anyone else do it, either. I'm good off the "T," for some reason. Too bad real life means pitchers!)

Once I believed that I wasn't necessarily finished as a hitter, Frank and I began working on some technical matters underneath the stands at Memorial Stadium, where the pitchers and catchers worked in the off-season. Frank knew that I'd been getting a lot of flack for listening only to my father, not to Tom McCraw, our batting instructor, and not to Frank, either. But he also understood I had vivid memories of that bad slump at the start of my career when I was listening to everyone and getting more and more confused. Eight years later I was leery of listening to lots of different advice. In theory I agreed with Senior's thinking that you have to ride these things out—like I just said, slumps are part of the game. Now, however, I agreed with Frank: something had to give.

In the best of times, I don't have the prettiest swing in the game. I don't have a pretty swing at all. When I'm struggling with my buggy-whipping style, I can either get so far out in front of the pitch that all I can do is pull up my left shoulder and flick my hands at the ball or—the opposite problem—wrap the bat so far behind my head while waiting for the pitch that it takes too long to get through the zone. One way for me to prevent this last problem is to lay the bat back, toward the screen, while waiting for the delivery. However, I can overdo this. On the tour of Japan in 1986, I was struggling when Koji Yamamoto, former third baseman for the Hiroshima Carp, told me that compared with two years earlier I was laying the bat so far back it was parallel to the ground. Mickey Tettleton hits that way all the time, but I realized immediately that such a drastic position might have been causing my problem at the time. I altered my bat angle on the spot and hit two home runs in the next game. I really heated up for the rest of the tour, and I stayed hot for the first part of the next season, too, but then cooled off and started tinkering again.

Frank Robinson spent a lot of time watching me, and the way he explains it, sometimes I'm too fast with my body, other times too slow. To me, there are different parts to the problem: I'd either rush out too fast with my body, making it near impossible to recognize the pitch, or with my head, or I'd pull the bat around too late to do much good at all. These were all different symptoms of some kind of batting disease. Over the past couple of years, I had also brought my feet closer together so that I was standing almost straight up. In an effort to "trigger" back to my natural position, I wound up lunging at the ball. The problem here is, when you go at it that way, you've already spent all your money on the swing before the ball comes by and you've got nothing left but your wrists with which to flip the bat at the ball. It's true that hitting requires quick hands, but not quick hands alone. Anyhow, no matter what strategy I tried, it was all pretty ugly on videotape.

I went to work with Frank on assuming a slight crouch and widening my stance three or four inches as a way to slow down my body and to wait, wait, *wait* before swinging *through* the ball. This was about as radical a change of stance as I'd ever made over a short period of time, and I wouldn't have done it without a lot of confidence in Frank. A good teacher has to be able to apply experience and knowledge of fundamentals to specific players; he has to know his hitter and tailor the ideas to the skills. I had confidence in Frank, but concerns as well, which he tried to ease by telling me about the radical change he'd made to break out of his slump in 1965. Overnight, literally, he changed from a deep crouch with the bat laid over his shoulder and choked up a couple of inches to standing almost straight up, holding the bat straight in front of his body, and not choking up at all. A complete makeover from one game to the next, but Frank was desperate, and it worked. He hit about .300 for the year, with his usual power.

I got good results, too, in June 1990, at least in the short run. Late that month I had four consecutive three-hit games using my revised stance, although the problem had been mainly mental. Looking back, I think Frank's wisdom about the ups and downs of a career was probably more important than the altered stance. But the stance didn't hurt, obviously. Even against a couple of very hard throwers, Greg Swindell and Roger Clemens, I was able to wait patiently and see the ball clearly. By the time I went to the All-Star game, my .209 average was history. With the slump and the Everett Scott mark behind me, I was rolling so smoothly in July I took time out to lay down a perfect sacrifice bunt, my first bunt of any sort in eight years. Dad couldn't resist a little dig at everyone who'd been prodding me to take a day off: "If Cal was so tired at 1,307 games," he asked, "how come he's so rested at 1,327 games?"

But then I stalled again late in the season, and the doubters came back in force. When I endured another weak September, they had the numbers: after compiling a .287 average for the last month of play from 1982 to '87, I had now posted three Septembers in a row down around .200.

You never know for sure, but my best guess, looking back, is that I had a tough time shifting gears from playing for the team to playing for myself. The whole first half of the season, you're hoping and playing for a pennant race, and even when things are going badly, you keep thinking, Well, we've got the second half still to come. You keep your head in for the team's sake, but then when the second half starts to go sour, you think, Well, we've got another two months . . . one month . . .

and then there's just nothing left but you and your own performance, over which you figure you do have some control.

Growing up with the Orioles, I'd been spoiled; I was now going to have to learn an attitude that worked in the bad times for the team as well as the good times. When the focus is where it should be, on winning, you don't even see your stats; you couldn't care less, you just want to do your part for the good times. But when you're losing, the statistics take on a bigger role. For one thing, you can use them for motivation and goals. When you're coming up on September hitting .277 with 20 home runs and 73 RBIs, you're thinking that a good month can move you to .290, maybe 28 home runs, maybe 95 RBIs. That kind of self-motivation can work or it can be fatal, but it's impossible not to think like this when the team is playing out the string.

For myself, this motivation was fatal in 1990. When I actually try to achieve certain stats, I usually come up short. If I deliberately try to hit a home run, I don't. If I try to drive in a run, I can't. And there's also the fact you're probably playing some teams that are still in the pennant race. These guys are pitching really tough. So you have the other team working you carefully to begin with, and you're trying to do too much and pressing, and all of a sudden it's mid-September and you're slumping.

After the '90 season there were also other numbers, not just the September stats, that I didn't care for. I'd slipped from averaging 26.6 homers for the first six seasons to 21.6 homers for the next three; I'd slipped from averaging 95 RBIs to 86 RBIs. My batting average had slipped, too. In the off-season I thought about those numbers and felt I had to do something. At my age—I had turned thirty in August—and after the year I'd had, you start to have questions, or at least I did. If my physical skills had begun to deteriorate, there wasn't much I could do about it—when they go, they go—but I wasn't ready to accept that diagnosis. I had another explanation. Dad had always said to prospects, "You have to be in the best shape of your life on the first day of spring training, because it's downhill from there, no matter what you do. The game will wear and tear on you, so be in the best shape you can possibly be when you report for duty." I reasoned that this must be even more true the older you get, so in that off-season after 1990 I dedicated myself to conditioning. Mentally, with Frank Robinson's help, I was in a positive frame of mind about my career. Now I decided to add to that a focus on physical conditioning. Always dedicated in past seasons, I moved it up another notch: *total* dedication, one hundred and ten percent, spurred on by the fact that my career-long—lifelong—dream, a gymnasium of my own next to my house in the suburbs north of Baltimore, was finally ready for business.

In previous winters I'd played on the Orioles basketball team, stocked with guys who lived in the area, including, at various times, myself, my brother, Mike Boddicker, Storm Davis, Tim Stoddard, Al Bumbry, Rich Dauer, John Habyan, Pete Harnisch, Joe Orsulak, Craig Worthington, Gary Roenicke. Other guys suited up off and on as they came through town for whatever reason. Orioles trainer Ralph Salvon was our trainer, too. We practiced at a local girls' school, Bryn Mawr, and traveled around playing in charity tournaments and assorted pickup games. It was great promotion for the Orioles. We played against Sugar Ray Leonard's team a few times, and won. We almost always won, and if things got really tight, Stoddard, six-foot-seven, 250 pounds, maybe more, would clear house under the boards.

Then Larry Lucchino, the president of the Orioles, nixed the official off-season team after the '87 season on the grounds that the games were too rough and posed too much risk. He had a point: the injuries had begun to mount up, most notably Mike Flanagan's torn Achilles tendon two years earlier. On occasion the opposing players looked on this game as their chance to show us baseball players a thing or two. Sometimes the game got pretty rough, which could lead to trouble.

When the Orioles team disbanded, I had set up my own games for Monday, Wednesday, and Friday nights at the Bryn Mawr gym for the following two off-seasons, and that setup worked well. I selected the players in the games. But in 1990 I had my own gym, which I'd wanted as far back as I can remember, even as a kid, when I'd come in from shooting baskets in the winter with my hands frozen. Mom would say, "When you grow up and become a major league baseball player, you can buy a farm and convert the barn into a gym." And that's exactly what I tried to do. For a year and a half I checked out real estate, looking for a farm with an old barn with a decent roof. I wasn't all that interested in the farmhouse itself. I figured I could make do with a bedroom and a simple kitchen in the converted barn. The house was not my priority; I wanted the gym. Family and friends humored me; my agent Ron Shapiro and soon-to-be wife Kelly humored me. Finally I ended up buying some property and building both a house *and* eventually a gym—a complete facility: almost-full-sized basketball court, batting cage, weight room with just about every machine and device there is, locker room with nice wood lockers. And, thanks to my wife, a score-board. I hadn't thought about this feature, but when I opened the big Christmas present in 1990, I realized it was a necessity. Extra players rotate as scorekeeper.

The gym was a splurge, but I rationalize it on the grounds that if it extends my career just one year, and I believe it will, it will have paid for itself many times over. And it saves me time, too, because I don't have to drive an hour or so a day to work out. Now that Kelly and I have young Rachel and Ryan, I'd rather stay home.

Opening Day for the second season in 1990 was November 1. On six days and/or nights each week, every week for the rest of the off-season, we played either street hockey or basketball or both. Sometimes we'd play one game in the morning, another in the afternoon. We had traffic jams in the driveway, with guys coming and going. Thursday night became exclusively basketball night, and a real event, with the ex-college players and semi-pros and the occasional ex-pro. The quality of these games gets better and better. In fact, depending on the caliber of the teams, the intensity of all these games was—and is—either NBA semifinals or NBA finals. We play hard for at least two and a half hours, each game to 25, ball out on fouls. Post-streak, we have actual NBA team basketballs compliments of Spalding and the NBA. I used to provide "pennies"—mesh pullovers—but now we have full uniforms from Starter.

If anything, the street hockey games in my gym were more physical than the basketball. A group of us had discovered the pleasures of street hockey while we were just messing around in the Orioles clubhouse, using unorthodox equipment—bats and balls and sneakers. We realized what terrific exercise it is, and several times a week in the off-season we'd set up a rink in the visiting clubhouse at Memorial Stadium, turning tables on their sides for the boards. I was always looking for fun ways to get my exercise. We'd tear the place up and then put everything back in place before we left, and all this took a lot of time. My gym solved that problem. The main hockey players were myself, Billy, Habyan, Traber, and Harnisch, as I recall, and whoever else showed up. Harnisch had played real hockey as a kid and had an awesome slap shot. Still no skates in these games—just basketball sneakers—and all of us got more injuries and bruises from hockey than from basketball. One year just a few weeks before spring training Traber smashed me into the wall and dislocated my finger. Time was called while I pulled it back into place.

The only problem with the hockey program was that a lot of the players were also the basketball players, and as families grew and bodies got older, they couldn't commit to six days a week, year after year. Basketball is still going strong at my place, but I haven't been able to reassemble the hockey teams the past couple of winters. That first year in the new gym, however, all of us were going strong. For the first couple of weeks we were exhausted, then we wound up in great shape.

I also hit more balls off my "T" and off the batting machine, I threw more baseballs against the wall, and I lifted heavier weights—and this was dicey for me, because I'd inherited Dad's old-school mentality in this area, too, which holds that weights and baseball don't mix. I say that about Senior, but after the '87 season Dad had gone along with Richie Bancells, the Orioles' new trainer after Ralph Salvon died, and lobbied the front office for some new equipment, which the team bought. Richie also developed an off-season program to build strength and stay in shape, for anyone on the team who wanted one. This would be a *maintenance* program, Senior emphasized, and he probably rationalized his change of heart on the grounds that in the old days players had worked in the off-season, usually at manual labor jobs, while these modern guys don't lift a finger and have to do *something* in order to stay in shape. I can hear him now.

With weights, it took me a long time to get over my inherent cautiousness, because there's no question they can be risky to your baseball skills. For example, too much shoulder work can definitely restrict fluidity of the throwing motion. Little by little, however, I blended weight work into my skills work, listening to my body, being certain in my mind, where it also counts, that I wasn't hurting myself in any way. I've now developed a program carefully planned for every day of the week, Sundays off, using machines to focus on sport-specific muscles and free weights for overall strength, emphasizing different muscle groups on different days. I'm still not as aggressive as, say, Brady Anderson, but I am catching up. For example, I squat well over three hundred pounds, which is plenty.

As the off-season progresses through and beyond the holidays and into the new year, I slowly taper down my strength program and slowly incorporate more and more skill work. By the time I report for spring training, I'm into a maintenance phase on my strength work and building into serious skills work. In spring training, I keep the same careful, cautious approach. Camp is six weeks long. I want to build up so that I'll peak when the season starts. There are certain tests and indications along the way: get some hits, yes, but popping the ball is the main thing. Stats don't necessarily mean a thing. There's a tendency in the first week to overdo things, even if you come into camp in great shape. You come in feeling giddy and happy and you go out and hit and throw for too long, and suddenly you're sore. I've thrown in the off-season, but it's not the same. Running and legwork in the off-season is definitely not the same. Nothing prepares you for running, stopping, and turning in cleats on a sandy field. I have a schedule every day. The first week I'll start with twenty minutes of easy ground balls, no more, no less, and work up from there. Senior: "Don't try to build Rome in a day." Then again, the young player in a position to make the team comes with different goals. He might not feel he has the luxury of pacing.

When the season gets rolling, the maintenance program tends to get shorter and shorter shrift, especially if I feel I need to save energy. I listen to my body. The focus is the game. I'll curb my practice, if necessary, and save my strength for the game. And I watch my weight, which has a tendency to go up, mainly, I think, because of the irregularity of our meals, although everyone has irregular meals and some guys lose weight.

Almost every ball player has, at some point, a terrible spring training followed by a great start followed by an average season, and vice versa. In 1991, the first year after I began working consciously and conscientiously on matching my physical fitness with my mental preparation— in other words, totally motivated—I arrived in Florida in great shape and had a great spring, a great start, and a great season. Using the new stance Frank Robinson and I had developed the previous year, this was the best I've ever hit, consistently, for an entire six months with barely a break. I carried a laptop computer around the country with me, and as a way to learn the database program I used baseball statistics for my raw numbers, plotting how I did against various pitchers almost in as much detail as I'd done in the minor leagues. It was fun, helped me learn about computers, and maybe it helped a little with the bat, too. It didn't hurt, anyway—and my black bats didn't hurt, either.

Before the season, I'd been on the phone with our traveling secretary, Phil Itzoe. (On most other clubs, the clubhouseman handles the bat orders, but Phil has always handled this duty with the Orioles.) I put in my standard order for the P-72, the thirty-five-inch, thirty-three-ounce model I'd been using most of my career. As much as I experiment with my stance, I don't change bats very often. However, I do change the *finish* on the bat, almost every year. In fact, I can identify by year a picture of myself holding a bat. In 1990 I was swinging an "unfinished" Louisville Slugger, but just before Phil and I rang off, I added without giving it any thought at all, "Let's make them black this year. Let's see what kind of luck that brings."

Of course, I don't really believe the finish brings luck. If I did, I wouldn't have been so cavalier in my request. I would have weighed the options. Some players believe the black bat is harder to pick up coming through the zone, especially if the batter has a short, really quick, really late swing, like Paul Molitor's, which can definitely surprise you. If the bat's harder to pick up, so is the ball coming off the bat. The question comes up: does Molitor swing a black bat? Sometimes.

Anyway, if the black bat *was* good luck for me in 1991, it wasn't for the Orioles. We didn't even come close, and we probably weren't going to after Glenn Davis went down with a strange nerve injury in his neck after just a dozen games. Glenn had averaged 27 homers for the past six years in Houston, and with a lot of missed playing time. Without both Glenn and the good young players we'd traded to get him—Steve Finley, Pete Harnisch, and Curt Schilling—it was going to be tough in 1991. Once again, the Orioles resorted to patching things up with new players; it's hard to win that way, even with guys the caliber of Dwight Evans, who came to us that year after a great career in Boston. Actually, his presence made for an interesting sidebar in '91. I liked "Dewey" a lot, everybody did, but the relationship with the team didn't necessarily start out that way. After being a major star in Boston for almost twenty years, he showed up in our camp as a new face in new surroundings. An adjustment was required. On our team, everybody rags everybody else—young guys, old guys, it doesn't matter. Everyone is fair game. In the beginning, when one of the younger guys ragged on Dewey in the standard clubhouse way, he might have said, "Don't make me go to the media guide." That was a veiled way of challenging players to compare their lifetime statistics to his. Of course I knew about his lifetime stats—he hit 379 homers for the Red Sox—but some of our guys didn't. (No surprise. When Robin Yount won his second MVP Award playing center field in 1989, I heard guys who didn't know he'd played shortstop when he won his first one seven years earlier.)

One day in camp Dewey called in sick. I'd never seen or heard of that before. Nothing wrong with it, I guess, but generally you don't call in sick. You show up, look awful, and the trainer sends you home. When Dewey came to the park the next day, feeling better, we teased him by wearing black armbands with his number 24. I don't think he was amused. Soon enough, though, Dewey was one of the gang and became one of the most popular guys on the team. He contributed on the field, too, in a part-time role. Generally, though, we didn't have all the horses, and that was that. From the beginning of the season, I accepted this fact. In fact, we were as bad as we'd been in 1987, ended up with 67 wins and 95 losses, and changed managers yet again, with Johnny Oates taking over for Frank Robinson in May.

I tried not to let any of that bother me. I needed that year for my own sanity. I had to confirm in my mind that I could still play the game at a high level, that I wasn't an "old thirty."

At the All-Star game in Toronto, everything came together for me in a way that I would never have dreamed of. I was hitting .348 going into the game, leading the league, but I was going so great I even became a little miffed at that number. In my last at-bat at Yankee Stadium before the break, Randy Velarde made a great play behind the bag. If the ball had gotten through the infield I would have had a nice, neat .350 to carry to the All-Star game. I wanted that hit, I admit it, but Randy played me up the middle and that's where I hit a bullet.

In my eight previous All-Star games, I was 3-for-17, with 1 double, no RBIs. We were facing great pitching, of course, but I was tentative, even in the field, playing not to make the big error that lost the game. But in order to succeed, you have to risk failure. That's what baseball is all about, basically. You have to *want* to be at the plate in the ninth inning. In 1991, my confidence was so high, I had so much momentum, I honestly felt that I was going to do something big in that game. I had never felt that way before. I was going to be totally aggressive.

First, however, came the home run hitting contest. I had been in one other contest, in Minnesota in 1985, and hadn't done well. No surprise, really. I'm not a slugger like Reggie Jackson or Cecil Fielder, but in '91 I was fifth in the league in home runs at the break, with 18, so I qualified. I was excited but also a little concerned, thinking to myself, I'm hitting so well, I don't want to mess up my swing. Don't get too excited, don't change a thing. It doesn't matter if you hit no home runs. The main thing is don't mess up your swing.

For BP before the contest we faced Hector Torres, a pitcher from the Toronto coaching staff, and I could not hit one out. Not one, as I recall. I'm not sure why; maybe I was trying to hit some out to impress the fans. I'd gotten away from the swing that had brought me there, exactly what I had sworn I wasn't going to do. When I was told that Hector was the pitcher for the contest, too, I thought, Oh, man. But I am *not* going to let this affect me. I am *not* going to try to match Cecil Fielder. If I don't hit any out, fine.

Because we hit in reverse order of our standings in home runs for the year, I was first up for the American League. Each of the five hitters on each team would be allowed ten "outs." If we swung, anything but a homer was an out. By the way, swinging for the fences fifteen or twenty times in rapid succession is more tiring than you might think. That's why BP rotates so often and you never take more than ten swings. Extra BP, where you're trying different things, requires more consecutive swings, but five minutes of hitting is a *lot* of hitting. You get arm weary, have to use the body more, and tend to get a longer swing because you can't snap the bat. Eventually you reach a point where you're not getting anything positive out of the session, maybe even something negative if the body remembers the long swing and your mechanics get totally out of whack. I was thinking about all this in the dugout before the contest. I told the othe guys I wasn't going to mess up my swing no matter what.

As I stepped into the box, the big crowd in the Skydome was buzzing and cheering. I took a few pitches, swung at the next one, and hit a screaming line drive into the camera stand in dead center field. That got my attention. That proved a lot to me right there. I usually pull the ball if I'm trying to hit homers; the fact that I didn't pull that one told me that I was in the good groove I'd enjoyed all season, waiting on the pitch, not anxious, not overswinging. I turned to our dugout on the third base side and signaled, That's one. Then came two, then three, then four. At one point I hit seven in a row. I was in this incredible groove. If you saw the videotape, you'd agree: my swing is effortless; no effort whatsoever. It looks like I'm trying to hit easy fungoes to Little Leaguers in the outfield, but I was hitting balls as far as I'd ever hit them. Teammates were on the top step of the dugout, yelling and screaming. Catcher Rene Lachemann looked up at me and said, "Cool off, buddy."

I, Cal Ripken, Jr., won the contest with 12 homers on 22 swings, the first shortstop in history to do so, and I had only one question: how'd I do it? Well, I kidded with someone, the balls must've been juiced. The contest hadn't been a big fan favorite in recent years, and the organizers—Gatorade—had asked all of the participants beforehand how to create more excitement. I suggested they make sure we had warmed up and had hit at least some BP off the same pitcher who'd be throwing the contest. They took that suggestion, and it helped me, at least. I hadn't homered off Torres in practice, but at least I'd seen his pitches. Then Cecil Fielder hit a couple of balls *over* the bleachers in center field, up against the Jumbotron. I'd never hit *one* ball in my career as far as I hit a series of them that afternoon in Toronto, and Cecil's shots were just incredible. But the conclusive argument against the theory of the juiced ball was the final score, 20–7, American League. If the balls were hot, why weren't the other guys cashing in? No, I was just in one sweet groove that day, that year.

The following night we played the All-Star game and I came up in the third inning against Dennis Martinez of the Montreal Expos, with Rickey Henderson and Wade Boggs on base, and I connected for one last time in Toronto on a 2-1 count, and the ball sailed over the center field fence. That was a great swing around the bases, and nothing changed for the rest of the season. I even closed with a rush that September, after tailing off just a bit in August, a mini-slump that revived memories of the weak final month the previous three years. I decided without a lot of back-and-forth that I'd go about things differently this time. I shagged flies, I played touch football in the outfield with Brady Anderson and Gregg Olson, I didn't take batting practice the whole month—the longest layoff by far in my career—and I therefore avoided Senior, because I knew the Great Practitioner would hassle me about this. Best of all, I didn't hear a word about how the streak was wearing me down. As some witty guy put it—my brother, probably—the critics of the streak were the ones who seemed worn out in 1991. I don't know whether it was the computer, the black bats, the touch football, the friendly media, or what, but something worked that September. I drove in 11 runs in four games in Detroit over the next-to-last weekend. I was smokin'.

I suppose my biggest, just about my only, personal disappointment that entire season came on my final at-bat, which was also my final at-bat in Memorial Stadium, and, as it turned out, the final at-bat in Memorial Stadium, period, because we were moving to the new park at Camden

Yards in 1992. The atmosphere was electric that Sunday afternoon. This was where the Orioles had dominated the American League for so many years—not recently, and definitely not that year, but within memory. The pile of bricks on 33rd Street certainly wasn't the prettiest park in the league, it was no Fenway or Wrigley, but everyone loved it and now it would be history. The best fans in the game had come out for the farewell moment.

First, however, the ninth inning, Tigers ahead 7–1. With Gregg Olson on the mound, one out, Johnny Oates came to the mound, hesitated a moment, then raised his left arm for Mike Flanagan in relief. After three and a half years with Toronto, Mike had returned to the Orioles in '91 as a reliever, and pitched well, too, in his seventeenth year in a major league uniform. He had first played in this stadium in 1975. Now on the mound for the last time ever, Mike had a hard time keeping his emotions under control. You could tell. When he struck out first Dave Bergman and then Travis Fryman with his sweeping curve on 3-2 counts, the crowd erupted. Then came the bottom of the ninth, with Frank Tanana pitching for Detroit in the long shadows of late afternoon. Difficult hitting conditions, but I wanted badly to go out with a bang, a parting shot from one of the last links. I had wanted a big weekend, period, but had pressed and gone 2-for-14. This final time up, I got ahead in the count, looked for and got the fastball, but then wasn't able to track it real well. I think my swing was longer than normal, too, for some reason. Anyway, I hit an easy one-hopper right to Skeeter Barnes at third base, who whipped it to second, around to first, double play. Just like that, it was all over at Memorial Stadium.

Ten years earlier, in my first Opening Day at-bat, a three-run homer; now in my last at-bat, a 5-4-3 double play. As Billy said, a crying shame.

But then came the incredible scene. There was more emotion in Memorial Stadium that weekend than there had been for the World Series in 1983. Much more, and we were a bad team. It goes to show the power of nostalgia and memories; it goes to show the depth of loyalty of the Baltimore fans. On Friday, all the team's great broadcasters had returned for their introduction. On Saturday, the players had met the fans at the gates and handed out calendars, the All-Time Orioles team voted by the fans had been introduced, and various memorabilia items, including the HERE pennant for Frank Robinson's stadium-clearing homer, were given away. On Sunday, *something* was scheduled, but exactly what was a well-kept secret. I didn't know and hadn't tried to find out beforehand. Even I wanted to be surprised.

After I'd grounded into the double play, the 1991 Orioles hailed the crowd and took a curtain call. Then a strange silence hung in the air before a white stretch limo drove onto the field and the grounds crew emerged in tuxedos to dig up home plate to deliver to Camden Yards. After they had driven off, there was more anxious silence before the theme music from *Field of Dreams* filled the stadium along with James Earl Jones's famous "Build it and they will come" speech from the movie. Then, with just the melody from the movie playing, no introductions, no words at all over the PA system, Brooks Robinson, glove in hand, trotted out of the dugout to tap third base for the last time and stand silently. Then Frank Robinson emerged in his Orioles uniform, ran down the third base line to touch home plate for the last time, and jogged out to right field, where he belonged. Boog Powell came out next, then Jim Palmer . . . Don Baylor . . . Rick Dempsey. No introductions were necessary as dozens of former Orioles streamed out of the dugout, one by one, to take up their old positions on the field. I waited my turn in the clubhouse, where all these players had suited up in secret. Covered with goose bumps, I was the next-to-last Oriole to take the field, followed by Earl Weaver, and who deserved that honor more?

The 118 former and current players gathered for the ceremonies formed a huge circle around the infield to honor the fans. I think the only guys missing were Eddie Murray, Mike Boddicker, and Storm Davis. Eddie was with the Dodgers, whose pennant race with the Braves had come down to this last day of the season, with the Braves winning. Mike and Storm were with the Kansas City Royals, who had been out of the race in the West for months. Nevertheless, the Royals management wouldn't give the two former Orioles permission to be in Baltimore for this once-in-a-lifetime event. They both resent that refusal to this day. It is pretty amazing.

Rick Dempsey led one final O-R-I-O-L-E-S cheer, we all threw base-balls from the field into the stands, Diamondvision showed the arrival of home plate at the new field across town, Rex Barney, propped up in a hospital bed, pronounced for the last time in this stadium his signature line, "THANK Youuuu," and everyone sang "Auld Lang Syne."

This is a memory to last a lifetime.

Chapter Thirteen

I'd been a David Letterman fan for years, so I was really looking forward to going on his late-night show after the '91 season. I was a little concerned, too, because the man's unpredictable, and you—the guest— are pretty much at his mercy. After mulling my options, I decided I wouldn't engage him if he started to rib me. I'd sit there and take it like a good sport and not even try to fire back. Other than by sneaking brother Billy on in my place, wearing a mask, I wouldn't stand a chance. Repartee is Dave's area of expertise. On the other hand, Mary Connelly, the woman who conducted what they call the pre-interview on the telephone, told me not to worry. "He really likes athletes," Mary said, "and the chances of his doing that to you are minimal."

Mary and I had talked for an hour and a half, going over possible subjects for the interview. When I arrived at the studio in Manhattan, we sat down again for forty-five minutes and she said Dave likes this, this, and this, so he'll probably ask you about them, and he might also decide to take you out into the hallway to field some grounders. How would I feel about that? "Sure," I answered, but I was thinking, It's only a seven-minute segment. You mean all this pre-interviewing might have been a waste of time?

Super Dave Osborne was on the show before me, the guy with all the stunts on ESPN (at that time), but he was putting on his game face, so I didn't have much of a chance to talk to him in the "greenroom," which is what they call the waiting room. When I finally walked out into the bright lights—I was the last guest on the show—and sat down on the couch, I was totally surprised by the setup, which seemed entirely different in person than it appeared on television. (This was before they changed the set a couple of years later.) For one thing, the couch I sat on wasn't facing Dave. I more or less had to look across my left shoulder to talk to him. A little uncomfortable and, I thought, a little strange, but this is television. And when we began talking, Dave seemed to be looking *behind* me instead of at me. I didn't know if he was getting directions from back there or looking at a monitor or if this was just another one of his many mannerisms. My curiosity about all this made me miss his first question. I wasn't paying attention because I was wondering what was going on *behind me.* Uh-oh! I thought, but then I caught the last few phrases and figured out what he'd been talking about, based on the pre-interview stuff. My answer was more or less to the point, and things rolled along to the break.

If you've noticed, before every break Dave usually leans forward and appears to whisper something privately to his guest. I'd always wondered what kind of remark he was making, and now I had my opportunity to find out. When we got to the commercial, Dave told the audience we'd be right back and, as expected, leaned over to say something to me—a baseball question, as it turned out—but before I could answer, the director or someone on the set said "You're clear," and Dave abruptly sat back in his chair. He wasn't interested in my answer; we sat in silence for the entire break. This really intrigued me, and I decided he was regrouping, preparing for what he'd do or say when we came back on the air for the next segment. I related this to my getting ready to step into the box before fifty thousand fans. You tune everything out, or try to.

Then all of a sudden someone started counting down, "Five . . . four . . . three . . . . two . . ." and *whooosh!* Dave turned his famous personality back on. I was fascinated. We talked some more and then, as his assistant had predicted, he asked me out to the hallway to play some baseball. He'd hit, I'd field, so he presented me with this glove, if that's what you want to call it. Even in Little League I'd had a better glove than this one, and it didn't quite fit, either. But what the heck: I had other problems to cope with as well. I couldn't have been more than thirty or forty feet from Dave—for sure, less than the distance from the mound to home plate. On the tape of the show I watched later, it looked much farther, but believe me, it was close. I suddenly realized these would be tough chances in my brand-new dress shoes with the slick soles and no traction. Plus I was standing on carpet right in front of the elevators, while the floor of the hallway was tile, with a narrow rubber strip at the junction. Some bad-hop action right there, I thought. *Plus* they'd set up this huge bank of bright lights directly behind Dave, directly in my eyes. Now the degree-of-difficulty factor went way up in my mind; it was going to be hard to see the ball, much less catch it. Still, I expected Dave to hit something of a tapper, given the conditions. When he swung hard, I knew I was in trouble.

He lined the first ball into the low ceiling, so that was a fairly easy catch off the carom. His next effort was better contact, a sharp grounder I never really picked up off the bat. It hit my glove wrist and knocked loose the clasp on my watch. So now my watch was dangling from my wrist. I tried for a one-liner—"Guess that's why I've never won a Gold Glove"—and looked up to see Dave ready to hit another one. By now I was concentrating harder, and it was a good thing, because the ball was right at me and skipped toward the part of me that would be protected, so to speak, if I had my uniform on. But I didn't have my uniform on. I got my hands up and caught the ball before it could do any damage, and I made some crack and Dave did, too. Maybe I caught the next shot, too; then the next one, maybe the last, hit that rubber strip between the carpet and the tile and bad-hopped over my head and banged against the elevator door.

Five or six balls altogether, as tough a set of chances as I'd ever had on any field. Then the credits started rolling, Dave walked up quickly to shake hands, and *poof!* he was gone. Disappeared. Outta there. So much for introducing my wife. Better luck next time.

A couple of weeks later, things finally changed vis-à-vis the Gold Glove. I picked up my first fielding award in 1991, and I was happy to get it. I'd been told that one reason I'd also won the MVP Award over Cecil Fielder that year while playing for a losing team was my defense. If true, that was fine with me, because defense deserves the recognition. Still, both awards were a surprise, and the MVP nod, very surprising. The crowd's chant of "M-V-P—M-V-P" when I came to the plate in the final series hadn't convinced me in the least. Cecil had now led the league in homers and RBIs two years in a row—huge numbers, too: 51 homers, 132 RBIs in 1990, followed by 44 homers, 133 RBIs this year. In 1990 the standard explanation for Cecil's second-place finish to Rickey Henderson had been that he played for a second-division team while Rickey had one of his great years leading off for the team that went to the World Series. But here in '91, Detroit had a good year and finished second to Toronto, while the Orioles had finished sixth. But they gave the award to me, the first winner ever who had played on a team with a losing record.

I was surprised. Cecil was angry. "What do I have to do?" he asked, and that was a tough question to answer. What more could he do? Not much. I could understand his frustration, and I had to comment quite a bit about the situation after the award was announced. As I've said, all of us want to be recognized for our work, and it's nice to get the award and to be proud of it, but you can't base your happiness on winning, just as you can't be all that unhappy about not winning. Look at Ted Williams, the most famous example in this regard. Williams didn't win the award in 1941, when he hit .406 (DiMaggio and his 56-game hitting streak won). Williams didn't win it the next year, either, when he won the Triple Crown (Joe Gordon won), and he didn't win in '47, *either,* when he won the Triple Crown again (DiMaggio beat him by one point in the balloting). But at least the Splendid Splinter did win the award in 1946 and 1949.

The first time the Orioles played Detroit following his disappointment, Cecil and I talked about the situation. I like the big man a lot, and we'd become good friends. He wanted me to understand that he wasn't upset with me personally. I'd known that, but I felt better when he said it. The vote went my way, not his, but 1991 had been a great year for both of us. For me, it had been a year in which I could do no wrong, my highest marks for homers (34) and RBIs (114), but the statistic that leaps out at me, that shows more than any how locked in I was that year, was the strikeout total: 46. That's low for anyone, but it was only the tenth time in history a player had hit over 30 home runs with fewer than 50 strikeouts.

The Orioles held a press conference in Camden Yards, still a work in progress, and we toasted for the cameras drinking milk from plastic champagne glasses. A little corny, but I am the local spokesman. Under the circumstances, I was more than willing to play along with almost anything.

The Gold Glove for '91 was the icing on the cake, because I've always taken a lot of pride in my fielding, and then, as the seasons went by, I had to overcome the idea that I was too big to play shortstop. Today, size is almost a dead issue—Seattle's Alex Rodriguez, one of the next great shortstops, will end up very close to my size. Right now he's six-three, at least 200 pounds, and, judging by his baby face, still growing. Athletes at every position in every sport are getting bigger and stronger, and size in the infield is now considered almost a bonus, but I'd been hearing about my supposedly detrimental size for ten years.

The year *before* I won the Gold Glove, I set four major league records for shortstops—consecutive errorless games (95), consecutive errorless chances (431), fewest errors in a full season (3), and highest fielding percentage (.996)—but still didn't win the Glove. Ozzie Guillen picked it up. I didn't feel snubbed, exactly, but I didn't feel recognized for my work, either, and the Gold Gloves are voted by the managers and coaches. Rangers manager Bobby Valentine said he was embarrassed by the vote. I didn't know what to make of it, but in any event it didn't take away my sense of accomplishment. One year later, I was very happy to accept the honor. It had taken a while to get credibility for being anything other than an offensive-minded shortstop. Maybe the 3-error season in '90 had turned the tide. I didn't need the pat on the back a year later, and I try to avoid worrying about things completely out of my control, but I appreciated the award. I really did.

The only downside in the field that year was that I had to replace my favorite glove, which I had started using almost by accident in Minneapolis in 1989. Kirby Puckett had rifled a couple of his patented top-spin smashes into and out of my old glove—one for an error, one for a force out instead of the double play. So what? you ask. Well, in my experience, nobody, but nobody, got as much action on the ball as Kirby did, especially on artificial turf. You'd have to stand out there to believe it. I'm not sure even minor leaguers could relate to it. I understood the difficulty of those chances, but I was still miffed about the miscues and immediately switched to my practice glove, the same model as my other one—Rawlings Pro-6HF—but fractionally bigger and looser, more like a third baseman's glove, or an outfielder's. If a glove can have a sweet spot, this glove had a huge one. It held the spinning shots a lot better, and it was flat enough in the pocket to allow me to get the ball out quickly on the double play. The change paid off immediately, and I might never have tried it in a game without Kirby's help, so to speak. Maybe I owe him one.

I used that glove for the rest of 1989, all of 1990, and into '91 until part of the webbing ripped halfway through the season. At the All-Star game the Rawlings representative sewed in some new leather. A simple procedure, I thought without concern, but the operation changed everything. It was no longer the same glove. In fact, it had a totally different feeling, and I had to retire it.

• • • •

Basically, here's the "problem" with my play at shortstop: I'm not flashy. My style is considered normal, efficient, maybe even boring—anything but flashy. If I had stayed at third base for my career, I would have been considered flashier, because of the nature of the position. It requires more diving, throwing on the run, bare-hand plays. You have no choice. At shortstop, you have fewer of these plays. While the third baseman has to field bunts bare-handed almost regularly, the equivalent play for the shortstop, a topper, happens only a few times a season. When it does, the bare-hand pick-up is required. Otherwise, I follow this maxim: if the ball's moving, catch it with your glove. Even at third, catch it with your glove if you have the time. Bare-handing is a risk. Omar Vizquel for the Indians does it on two-hoppers with topspin on artificial turf. You would think that sometime the ball is going to carom off Omar's hand for a very preventable error, but I haven't seen it happen; guys who follow the Indians have told me they haven't seen it, either. That's amazing. Still, it's a risk in the eyes of us old-school types.

At third base, you have plenty of time to dive and get back on your feet and throw out the fastest runner. I did a lot of diving while playing third base in the minor leagues and for a couple of months in 1982. It's the nature of the position, in which you cover a smaller area with a goalie-type mentality. But at short, very few guys are quick enough to dive flat out and pop up and throw in one motion. Ozzie Guillen happens to be one of them. He's like a gymnast. I never had that ability.

Mark Belanger taught me that it's one thing to make the *stop*, another entirely to *complete* the play. Why dive if you can't make the throw for the out? On a lot of balls, I know I can dive and make the stop, but then I won't be able to throw the guy out. It looks good but that's all, while on this same ground ball I *might* be able to catch, set, and throw in one motion. If I make the play this way, it doesn't seem like the great play it would have appeared to be if I'd dived.

The biggest compliment you could pay my fielding is that I make difficult plays look easy rather than make easy plays look difficult. I take pride in the statement—I don't know who said it first—that I make the plays *appear* routine. I know the pitchers, I know the hitters, I'm usually in the right position, I read the ball well. If I do my job, I don't get the attention.

I play this way because I have no choice in the matter. I'd love to be as quick and fast as Ozzie Smith. But I'm not, so I play the position another way, with an emphasis on efficiency in the setup. I've learned certain techniques to get my body in position for the throw more quickly. One of these is to take the backhand off my right foot rather than the left foot, which is the fundamental play. If I plant my sliding right foot and reach across my body to make the backhand stop, I'm already in position for the throw. It comes down to this: instead of catching, planting, and throwing, in that order, I'm often planting *first*, then catching and throwing. Belanger tried to teach me this play when I was a teenager hanging around Memorial Stadium, but I didn't understand what he was driving at. Not too long after Earl Weaver moved me to shortstop in 1982, I happened to make a play in the hole this way, without really thinking about it. I immediately remembered Belanger's teaching from seven or eight years earlier, and started working hard on the details.

I may need a lot of arm strength on that throw, and I have it, although a lot of people would say I have an average arm because all they see is my almost sidearm or three-quarters throw on the routine plays. But this saves the arm, and it's accurate for me. Playing shortstop in the low minors, I had made too many throwing errors. The shift to third base in Miami was important because I started to understand control, and I came up with that Graig Nettles–style three-quarters flip. I realized I could get the ball to first base quickly enough without throwing a thousand miles per hour, and I'd save my arm and have more control.

When Earl Weaver shifted me from third to shortstop in 1982, I carried the flip with me. Umpires have asked me if I *intentionally* throw out runners by half a step. No, but after a while a fielder has an automatic internal clock that calculates how much time he has against a given runner. I'm not the only infielder who records a lot of close plays at first. My intention is a successful play, not necessarily a close one.

I'm convinced the three-quarters flip has reduced the mileage on my arm, but some players disagree with my thinking here. Mark Belanger, for one, threw hard over the top all the time. He thought it was *better* for his arm, a theory I believe he picked up from Luis Aparicio, who played the same way. I've mentioned how I ease into my spring training regimen, taking extra care not to overthrow and come up sore. Luis's solution to the almost inevitable dead-arm period in spring training was to "throw it out," stretch it out. He knew his arm wasn't hurt but just needed strength, so he threw hard every few days. Instead of playing catch at 50 or 75 feet, he played catch at 120 feet and threw fifteen or twenty balls hard. It worked for Aparicio, it worked for Belanger, but what about Rick Burleson with the Red Sox, Angels and, for one year, the Orioles? He was another guy who threw hard every time, and Rick blew out his arm. Was it all the hard throws?

One year I didn't have the luxury of easing into my throwing regimen in the spring. This was 1995, when spring training was only three weeks long following the settlement of the strike, so I had to change my approach. I pushed my arm harder than I normally would—and it worked. My arm felt great all year, and it seemed to reach peak strength and efficiency earlier in the season than it ever had. Naturally, I was impressed. Maybe Belanger and Aparicio had the secret after all, so I decided to follow the accelerated regimen in 1996. And I hurt my shoulder. It wasn't serious, and I'd played with other arm injuries at various times, but this one kept me from developing arm strength. After the season started, it was almost impossible to rehabilitate this injury quickly or completely. Maybe taking a week or two off would have helped, but I couldn't do that. I played through the injury, which was okay until I had to make a really hard throw from an incomplete setup. I need my arm, and it wasn't until the last month of the season that the

LEFT With Kirby Puckett at Memorial Stadium around 1990

ABOVE With Ryan in the pool

ABOVE Teaching Rachel the finer aspects of the game at Camden Yards

RIGHT Family reunion at Camden Yards

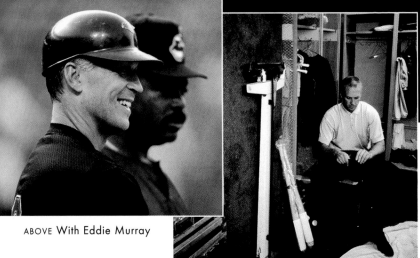

ABOVE With Eddie Murray

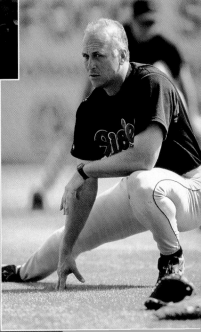

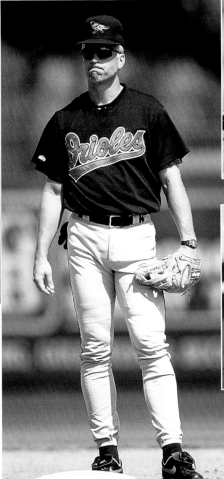

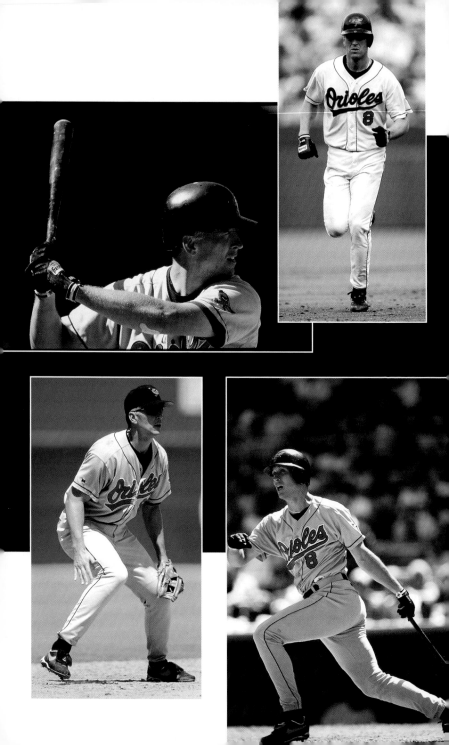

STREAK NIGHT 2131

LEFT AND BELOW
My home run in the
Streak Game

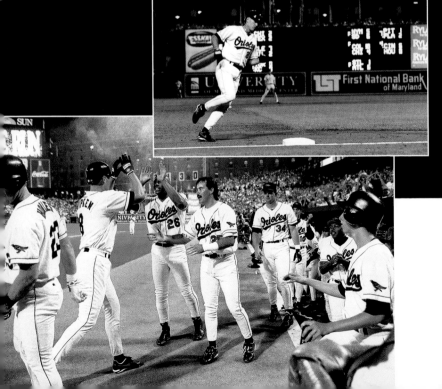

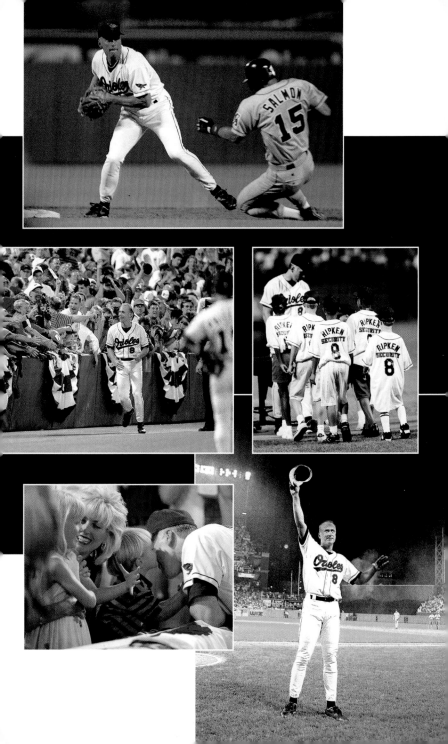

strength in it was almost all the way back. I'm not sure why the speeded-up program worked in 1995 but not a year later. There were a lot of variables. I do know that from now on I'll stick with my old way, slow but sure, utilizing the full six weeks of spring training.

Ozzie Smith is—or was, because he retired at the end of 1996—another shortstop who gets a lot of half-step outs at first base. I'd seen Ozzie play in All-Star games and on television, and of course I'd seen replays of The Play—one of the most famous fielding plays of the last many years. This was back around 1980, when Ozzie played for San Diego, before the questionable trade to St. Louis for Garry Templeton. Running full speed behind second base, he dived flat out with his glove extended for Jeff Burroughs's hard ground ball. While he was in the air, horizontal to the ground, the ball caught a pebble, skipped left—and Ozzie reached back quicker than the eye can see and speared the ball with his bare throwing hand. That was amazing, but I was even more impressed by how quickly Ozzie was able to hop up—like a spring, almost—and make the throw to first base. Unbelievable athleticism on that play. I don't have that ability, never did, and I wonder who else does.

In 1986, I got my first extended view of Ozzie's style and ability in a post-season barnstorming tour of Japan. This was an All-Star squad from both leagues, and we stopped off first in Los Angeles to assemble everyone and have a workout at Chavez Ravine. Since we didn't have our coaches yet, the squad was pretty much on its own, and I suggested to Ozzie that we take turns hitting fungoes for each other. I'm systematic, and I wanted to give Ozzie a chance to get loose, so I moved him left, right . . . left, right . . . left, right. Then I had a sneaky idea. After establishing the pattern I took the opportunity to *break* it, just to see for myself how quickly he could react. He was anticipating the ball to his left, but I hit it to his right—and he reacted so smoothly I was amazed. He shifted direction *effortlessly*. I had now seen for myself the skill behind The Play. Boy, was I envious. I mumbled "Sorry" and used the fact that I wasn't adept with the fungo bat as an excuse for hitting the ball to the wrong side. I never told Ozzie what I was up to.

Did Ozzie Smith at his best get to balls I don't get to, and never did get to? Yes. Ozzie's pure range afforded him the luxury of playing more people straight up. I think he played every hitter about the same way, pretty much in the middle of his range, which was so superior he could stay there and reach everything anyway. There was also the turf factor in St. Louis (until they switched back to grass) and in most of the National League parks: artificial turf allowed Ozzie to play deeper. But did Ozzie therefore *complete* more plays behind the bag or in the hole than I do? Probably not, because I've learned to position myself. I'm required to be adept at positioning myself initially and then anticipating the ball with my first step. In short, I have to use my knowledge of positioning to cut down the territory to cover. I get a kick when a guy says to me after a play, "How the heck did you get to that ball?" I like it when I read something like, "Ripken seems to play everyone up the middle and deep, but every time you hit the ball, he's standing there."

Still, I can be wrong in my positioning. With his quickness and speed and ability to recover, Ozzie seemed never to be out of position. From what I understand, he was also as smart a player as there was. He invented his own version of the plant-catch-throw play with a sliding maneuver on artificial turf, and he was one of the first to perfect the intentional one-hopper off the turf to first base. The guy was the complete package: positioning, anticipation, the best physical and mental skills.

I love being absorbed in the situations of the game. I had been a good third baseman in the minors and then early in 1982, my rookie season, but playing third base you can't see the catcher's sign. If the ball isn't hit to you, often the play is finished as far as you're concerned. There can be a feeling of standing and watching; you almost become a spectator. You're not involved in as many steals, hit-and-runs, coverages, relays at short or second. Meanwhile, the middle infielders have a responsibility on almost every play. With a runner on first base, every random thoughts

pitch requires a decision on who covers second base on a steal. I love learning the batters and pitchers, information I need for this decision and for my own positioning. Is the hitter in a slump, and therefore more likely to try to take the pitch to the opposite field? Does he pull the first pitch? How about late in the count? Is this a hit-and-run count? Is this a good hit-and-run batter? What's the history of the opposing manager with the hit-and-run? If the catcher sets up outside, is the pitcher likely to hit this target? Is his control good enough? Does he change speed on his fastball on certain counts?

Every pitch is a new world. Situational baseball is a constant adaptation that requires thinking along with the pitcher, the catcher, the hitter, and both managers. The shortstop is right in the middle of it. For me, this is the real fun and challenge of the game, more so than my four or five at-bats. I guess there's an analogy between this preference and my desire back as a high school kid to be drafted as a position player rather than as a pitcher. As I said, pitching is great when you're pitching, but what about the rest of the time?

At shortstop, you can apply what you know about baseball on almost every pitch. A good example is this situation: fast runner at first base, fast man at the plate, single to right field. With a possible play at third base, the shortstop's job is to get in position for the cutoff on the throw from the right fielder to the third baseman. On this play, I play "deeper" than most, if not all, American League shortstops. I'm so deep I'm almost *at* third base; sometimes I can reach out and touch the third baseman, whereas most shortstops would be thirty feet in front of him. This deep position is not officially part of the Oriole Way. I guess it's a modification based on experience.

For teaching purposes, by all means you want to position the cutoff man toward the middle of the infield to help the right fielder line up his throw, and then teach the right fielder to throw the ball "through the chest" of the cutoff man. But with big league outfielders who know where to throw the ball, I can see the situation better from the deeper post. If there's a play at third, let the ball through, of course. If there's not a play, I can see whether the runner has made a wide turn at first base. My feeling is that the manager and the coaches can have all the charts and defensive alignments in the world, but circumstances change according to who's pitching, who's hitting, who's running, and who's in right field. I know the arm of the fielder, the speed of the batter, the speed of the runner. It's my job as the cutoff man to absorb these variables and make the decision. On the Orioles, we got a lot of outs with Joe Orsulak playing in right field, mainly because Joe could really "sell" the play by charging the ball hard and coming up firing toward third.

Actually, I first started cutting off from a deep position while playing third base. On the throw from the left fielder to the plate, I realized that the deeper I was—the closer to the catcher—the better position I had to see what was happening with a runner at third. Often he's held up by his coach very late, puts on the brakes a third of the way down the line, and slips on the grass. Happens *all the time*, the cutoff man sees the slip only if he's playing deep. That's why if I was cutting off the throw from left field, I stationed myself directly right in front of the catcher.

When Earl Weaver moved me to shortstop in 1982, I took with me the strategy of playing deep for cutoffs, and Earl understood it and approved. One year at the All-Star game, Alan Trammell asked me why I was so deep, and we had a long, long conversation. The next time we played Detroit, there was Trammel, playing a little deeper. On a barnstorming tour of Japan after the '96 season, I talked about it with Alex Rodriguez, the unbelievably talented shortstop for Seattle. He'd never thought about this play and was really intrigued by the possibilities. Senior's line for this kind of teaching is "trying to put a forty-year-old head on a twenty-year-old body." In this case, I was trying to put a thirty-six-year-old head on a twenty-one-year-old body.

This is the stuff I love about baseball, and there's no better place for it than shortstop. Almost from the beginning, however, there were rumbles about Earl Weaver's gamble when he moved me over, because I was bigger than the other shortstops. These rumbles never stopped, despite the trend in the past decade toward bigger and bigger players. I guess I just don't *look* quick enough for the job. Forget all the statistics which show that I get to just as many balls and get just as many outs and turn just as many double plays as everyone else in the league. There's always been talk about when I'd return to third base. Here are a few "highlights"—some of which I only discovered while writing this book. Maybe it's a good thing I didn't know about them. Otherwise, I might've gotten discouraged.

•   In 1985, our owner Edward Bennett Williams said I wasn't playing the position as well as I had the previous two years and wanted to consider a different man for the job. "He just keeps growing," EBW said about me over a decade ago. "He put on a few more pounds this past year. That's not because he's fat, it's because he's so big. And the bigger he gets, the less his range." Others more or less agreed, but they were willing to give me a few more years. My own grandmother, a big fan, started asking me what my problem was.

This little dust-up from our owner happened to be the year after I'd set the American League record for assists with 583, and the same year I'd finish a few assists behind Tony Fernandez, while leading the league in putouts and double plays. That same year, in his *Baseball Abstract*, Bill James came up with an assessment for shortstops that took into account factors like innings played, pitchers' ERAs, and pitchers' strikeout ratios, and his calculation confirmed that I fielded my position perfectly well. With hitting, you see the batting average, the power numbers, and that's that. Who cares what the guy looks like swinging? With fielding, you have the errors, the assists, the double plays turned, the total chances, the putouts. Shouldn't these numbers be the criteria, not some judgment based on style or lack of style? James asked this question. It's a good point. If an infielder can no longer play his position, the numbers will bear this out, believe me, just like they'll bear out a decline in hitting.

• When Earl Weaver announced his retirement in 1986, some observers suggested that one good reason to hire my father as manager for '87 would be that he could convince me to move to third base. There had been some speculation about letting Jackie Gutierrez play shortstop. These observers forgot one thing: Senior would have to be convinced first, and Senior knows baseball. Earl Weaver, attending to his last month as manager, came to my defense as a fielder, although he did add that if he had a Mark Belanger around, he'd put him in for me as a defensive replacement in the late innings. I could see Earl saying that, but when push came to shove, would he have done it?

After my father did get the managing job, there were reports that moving me to third was stipulated in the deal. I guess those reports were wrong.

• In June 1988, a headline in the *Baltimore Evening News* read "Has Cal Jr. Lost a Step?" The question was triggered by the fact that I had led the league in assists and total chances for shortstops in 1987, while I was in eighth place for the first two months of '88. What could I say in reply? I thought I was doing the job, and two months seemed like a small sampling. The piece did point out that with eight pitchers who had been with the club less than two years, I wasn't as able to take risks on positioning. (Actually, when you know the pitcher and the hitter, positioning really isn't a risk at all.) Another factor was the ten righthanders on the Orioles staff, inducing the other clubs to produce as many lefthanded batters as possible, which should cut down on chances on the left side of the infield.

At the '88 All-Star game, one popular question was "Ozzie or Cal?" Regarding me, Joe Morgan said, "He's played too many games, and it's beginning to hurt him. . . . He'd extend his career if he moved to third." Giants manager Roger Craig said, "I think he's a third baseman." The Cardinals' (and Ozzie's) manager Whitey Herzog said, "He wouldn't play shortstop for me."

• In 1989, I played a couple of weeks at third base at the beginning of spring training. The organization wanted to look at Juan Bell, who had come to us in the Eddie Murray trade and had played a good shortstop in Triple-A the previous season. They wanted to get something out of the Murray trade. After about two weeks Frank Robinson called me in and said, "I think we'll go with experience."

• In 1992, this from the *Sporting News*: "Scouts and opposing managers say his range in the field has significantly deteriorated this season. Even some Orioles baseball people quietly speculate that a year from now, the club's best defensive lineup might have Ripken at third, prospect Manny Alexander at shortstop. . . ." This was the year the managers and coaches voted me a second Gold Glove.

• And in 1996, it finally happened. The front-page headline in *The Baltimore Sun* read, "At Third, Cal Ripken." By that time in the season—I made the move on July 15, and it lasted for six days—the story had gotten completely out of hand anyway. But that's for later in this book. Then after the '96 season the Orioles signed free agent Mike Bordick to play shortstop. This made it official: I was moving to third base. My attitude had always been that if they want to move me back to third base, fine; it's management's decision, not mine, just like it had been Earl Weaver's decision to move me to shortstop in the first place.

Chapter Fourteen

Oriole Park at Camden Yards? The Birds' new venue was everything they said it was going to be and more. In my opinion, it's the epitome of the modern game of baseball, with its sky boxes, better sight lines, big screen, and blasting music. The designers wanted—and achieved—a stadium with modern amenities but also an old-time feeling of coziness, with loads of character. The Bromo-Seltzer clock tower beyond left field and the B&O warehouse beyond right field are great. The whole place is great—the best of the new parks.

Initially, however, I have to admit that I missed Memorial Stadium. For one thing, everyone who was there the last weekend of the previous year carried away a tremendous feeling of nostalgia. It wasn't a great facility, technically speaking, and down in the guts beneath the stands it was dank and smelly, but for me, at least, Memorial Stadium *was* baseball. It had been the scene for the entire history of the Orioles to that point, and it was sad to leave that history behind. The atmosphere at Camden Yards seemed a little different. The standard distinction that people drew was between blue-collar Memorial Stadium and a more corporate Camden Yards. I don't know about that. The distinction I drew was between a much more appealing place—who wouldn't want to go to Camden Yards?—and a place like Memorial Stadium that maybe only diehard fans would enjoy coming to. The Orioles draw much larger crowds now than we ever did at Memorial Stadium. It didn't sell out, but it was more boisterous. Maybe you heard more from individual fans because it *wasn't* filled, I don't know, but at first in Camden Yards I missed the old camaraderie. Or maybe I just missed the old days, period. I do think you can say with some validity that Camden Yards represents the modern game of baseball as *entertainment*, while Memorial Stadium represented the game of baseball as just that—the game of baseball, take it or leave it.

Would I rather the Orioles were back at Memorial Stadium? No way. We're building a new tradition and history at Camden Yards, which is the way it should be. Just don't ask me to forget the old pile of red bricks on 33rd Street. I can't do that.

We had a great new park in 1992 in Baltimore, and we had a new spirit as a team as well. As a team, we *had* to be better than we were in '91, when we finished in sixth place, 14 games under .500. Johnny Oates had taken over for Frank Robinson the previous May, and although there hadn't been much Johnny could do to save that season (not that managers save seasons), he thought and I thought that we had some more horses in '92. The rebuilding program that had started in 1988, overachieved in '89, then fallen back in '90 and '91, might be ready to put something together. Glenn Davis was healthy again, Brady Anderson and Mike Devereaux were looking to make big contributions, Sam Horn was coming off a season in which he hit 23 homers in only 300-plus at-bats, and Rick Sutcliffe was on hand to lead the pitching staff. There was real confidence in spring training; you could feel it.

Of the new personnel that year, Rick was the most important addition, and for that good fortune we could thank Johnny Oates. In the eighties, Rick had been a good, solid pitcher with the Cubs, except when he was hurt, and at thirty-six years old, he thought he had a few good years left. But as a free agent he also wanted to be on a winner, and the Orioles had had losing seasons the previous two years. Over the telephone in the off-season, Johnny campaigned with Rick on behalf of Baltimore. These two guys went way back to the Dodgers in 1979, Rick's first great season. Twelve years later, Rick told Johnny over the phone that he wasn't a great pitcher anymore. Johnny said he didn't need him to be a great pitcher. All he needed was a .500 pitcher who knew his craft and could bring with him a certain presence and be a stabilizing force for the mound staff. I think every manager and front office in the league had been impressed with the way Jack Morris had joined Minneapolis from Detroit in 1991 and led that young Twins staff to the World Series. I don't know whether Johnny felt we could go to the Series in '92, but he felt that Rick could help our young pitchers in a similar way. They needed someone to lead by example; if Rick could do that, we'd have a chance.

Johnny was persuasive, Rick signed with Baltimore, and he did lead by example. Dwight Evans was gone after just the one year—released in spring training, a move that surprised me—but Rick moved in as a veteran presence from the first day. There was no get-acquainted period with Rick. His boisterous personality couldn't wait around for that. He even tried to take charge of a lot of the dinner checks. We sparred over a few of those, because I also liked to pick up some checks for the younger guys. Maybe both of us liked to play the role of big shot.

Rick did instill a sense of unity among the pitchers. There's no question about that. They got so cocky they started calling themselves the posse. Don't mess with the posse—if you cross one of us, you cross all of us—if you weren't a pitcher, you were the enemy: that was their thing, but the rest of us weren't too concerned. In the event of open warfare, we had 'em outnumbered. One afternoon in spring training, Brady Anderson was lolling around sunbathing on the field on his day off while the pitchers were still at work. Johnny Oates liked to give his players a full day off, and Brady was rubbing this in, looking for trouble with the posse. He got it when they charged and "de-pantsed" him on the spot. Another time, after Joe Orsulak received rude treatment at the hands of the posse, he corraled Sutcliffe by the pitching screen and got a good headlock on him. Trying to get free, Rick twisted his neck and was out for a week, missing a start or two. The details probably didn't make the papers. During the season, the posse tied me to the training table. I submitted without much of an objection. Let them have their fun.

Rick's strong personality was the catalyst for all this. He's a take-charge guy, one reason Johnny Oates picked him to start on Opening Day—*Grand* Opening Day—in Camden Yards. I thought that was a really smart move. Of course, Rick had thrown a lot of openers in the past because he'd been his team's ace, but he wasn't the ace on this Orioles staff. That would have been either Mike Mussina or Ben McDonald, two really young guys. However, Rick had loads of experience. He was the one who wouldn't be upset if he pitched a great game but lost because the other team's ace had also pitched a great game. For the first couple of months, Johnny wanted his young starters to have a better chance against the other teams' third, fourth, and fifth starters. Rick, he felt, could handle the aces. And Rick did, especially on Opening Day, when he shut out Cleveland, my brother laid down a perfect suicide squeeze, and the Orioles won 2–0. We went on to win 10 of our first 11 in our new home, and the stage was set for an exciting season.

From the dugout, Rick called some pitches for the rest of the staff that year. I did, too, especially with Ben McDonald, and maybe now's the time to tell that story, which has been the subject of rumors in Baltimore ever since. To do so, I have to set the stage by flashing back to the mid-eighties, when Storm Davis was starting out as a power pitcher for the Orioles and having some trouble against the Red Sox and the Yankees, as I recall. Those two teams had Storm's number, for some reason, and he came to me and asked if I'd help with his pitch selection. Rick Dempsey was doing most of the catching in those years, and he called a perfectly good game, but Storm wanted to break out of his rut, so I sat down and wrote out how I thought he might pitch those lineups. For the Red Sox, I suggested starting off Wade Boggs in the first inning with a fastball down the middle, because Wade takes the first pitch ninety-five percent of the time. Then come in on the inner half of the plate with another fastball, which he's likely to fight off, then go for the strikeout on the inside edge. As luck would have it, Storm got Wade with these exact three pitches, and when the infield was tossing the ball around, Storm and I exchanged a glance. He went on to get a complete game victory in Fenway, and we came up with a simple set of signs I'd flash from my position when he was in a jam. He started having better luck with these teams, but this wasn't a matter of my pitch selection so much as the fact that Storm had broken a pattern and gained some confidence. Maybe if Boggs had doubled off one of those first pitches in Fenway Park, Storm would have considered my advice much differently! To my knowledge, no one else knew about our arrangement, and that's the way it should have been.

With Ben McDonald half a dozen years later, the problem was the one big inning which could determine the game. Ben was a young pitcher who was learning at the big league level after being the number one draft pick in the country. When he became a starter with the Orioles in 1990, we sat down with our catchers, Bob Melvin and Jamie Quirk, and the four of us went over the hitters. We did the same thing the following year with Chris Hoiles, our newest catcher. Two very young players feeling a lot of pressure, they were unsure what to call when things were critical. I started going to the mound to join their conferences, but after a while this arrangement became unwieldy, and one time it even caused a slight problem. We were playing Oakland, Brent Gates at the plate, runners second and third, and I went to the mound and told Ben, "Throw a curve. If it's a strike, throw another curve. If it's a strike, throw another curve." The first curve was a called strike, the second one was pulled foul, then the third one was pulled foul again, weakly. When Hoiles called for another curve, Ben shook him off, and Hoiles put down fastball away. I called time and returned to the mound. Ben said he didn't want to throw a fourth consecutive curve, so I gave him an option: either that fourth curve or go for a fastball *inside*, not outside, because Gates could slap that outside pitch to left field while protecting the plate. Ben selected the fastball inside, but it sailed too far in and hit Gates on the wrist. The next day Tony LaRussa tracked me down and wanted to know what was going on out there. He said it didn't look too good when I went to the mound and then his man got hit by the next pitch. Tony had a point—I hadn't thought about how these mound trips must have looked—and I told him the whole story. Then Chris, Ben, and I came up with a better system. If they wanted my suggestion, they flashed a sign to me, and I flashed one in return to Chris, who relayed it to Ben. When Jeff Tackett joined the Orioles in '91, Ben wanted to make sure I had my signs down with Jeff, too, so I went to him and said, "Jeff, I've been helping Ben out with pitch selection. It gives him confidence, and that's what counts, as you know." So I worked with Tackett, too.

Then, when Rick Sutcliffe joined the Orioles in '92, he *also* called some pitches for Ben and some of the other pitchers on the staff. We had signs all over the place, which sounds ridiculous, but it worked fine. Rick and I had a lot of experience—about twenty-five years between us—and our pitchers and catchers had almost none, for the most part. This was our way to help out.

One year after a career season, I was ready to go again in 1992. Then something happened that surprised me as much as anybody watching: with the Orioles playing solid baseball, I struggled for much of the year, and at times things seemed to spin almost out of control. At some point, my supply of confidence—built up in '91 and continued with a really good spring training—just ran out. I know at least one major reason why I struggled: I made the terrible mistake of letting the business side of the game clash with the baseball side.

My four-year deal was due to expire at the end of the season, and the Orioles' president Larry Lucchino, my agent Ron Shapiro, and I all wanted to hammer out a new agreement before the season started. Ron had some good negotiating points: my '91 season, the explosion in free-agent salaries the previous winter, the union's victory in the collusion case against the owners, and the boom in attendance at Camden Yards. But the Orioles had a great bargaining point as well: they knew I didn't want to leave Baltimore. The best way for a player to maximize his leverage is to go into the free agency period, but as I've said, I don't believe in filing for free agency as a negotiating ploy. If you do that you have to be willing to leave, and I wasn't. I'd always been able to live where I wanted to live and play where I wanted to play—*Baltimore*—but now if this contract didn't go through, I was going to have to pull up stakes. I would've been able to deal with the change—you deal with what you have to in this life—but I didn't *want* the change. I'm a Maryland man.

The Orioles understood this. On the other hand, the players' association wants the biggest possible contracts. They want Ryne Sandberg to crack the $7 million barrier, Ken Griffey, Jr., the $8 million barrier, Albert Belle the $10 million barrier. I felt in something of a quandary: I wanted to consider what I believed was best for me and my family, and I also felt a responsibility to the association and my fellow players to negotiate the best possible contract I could. Over the winter and into spring training, maybe Ron and I did hold a bit of a hard line, or maybe I didn't convey a strong enough impression to Ron that we were almost "there" in March, or maybe the Orioles played a little hardball themselves, knowing I wanted to stay home. The bottom line was that there was no bottom line and the deal didn't get done before the season started. In the past, I'd always wanted negotiations concluded in the off-season, keeping the business and the playing separate, but Eli Jacobs, the New York financier whose group of investors had bought the club from Edward Bennett Williams's wife, was supposed to be having cash flow problems and was already talking about selling the franchise. If he did, perhaps I wouldn't fit into the new owners' plans. It was possible. Since I knew that Jacobs wanted me, it made sense to keep negotiating after Opening Day and make a deal with *this* owner.

That decision to proceed—Ron wanted to wait until the season was over—was one of the biggest mistakes I've ever made. Everything was up in the air and profoundly unsettling for me while I was trying to play baseball. Some guys can use this kind of limbo situation as incentive and motivation. I can't. I like to know where I stand. I get too upright otherwise. Looking back, I would have handled everything differently. There aren't too many times in my life about which I'd say that, but 1992 was one of them.

I tried to keep an even keel, but it seemed like there was a correlation between negotiations and performance: I'd hit well for a few games, negotiations would heat up, then Ron would call and say bluntly, "The talks broke down." And I'd go hitless for a few games. This was probably fantasy on my part, but that's how my mind was working. This up-and-down scenario played out four or five times the first half of the season.

The newspapers were full of speculation, and there were leaks, which weren't fantasy on my part, and they bothered me. I don't like negotiating during the season, and I don't like to negotiate through the media. I've always been careful about that. *I* didn't say anything to the media about the negotiations. *Ron* didn't say anything. Who leaked? John Feinstein wrote about these negotiations in *Play Ball*, his book about the 1992 baseball season, and Larry Lucchino complained after the book came out that Ron had given Feinstein his notes to use. Ron did give Feinstein some access after the negotiations were over with, but John got information from elsewhere, too. He wrote in the book that the Orioles were leaking details on the negotiations to *The Washington Post* in order to get back at *The Baltimore Sun*, which had blasted the team for not signing me earlier. Interesting. A year later I heard another explanation for the leaks: the Orioles' front office wanted to deflate the notion that they weren't seriously negotiating.

After the first six weeks or so of the season, there was a long layoff. The sense Ron and I got from the Orioles was, We'll see you at the end of the year. That was helpful for me, actually. They said it, I didn't, and I started to get some control before I dug myself too deep a hole. Thanks to a 16-game tear, I got my average up to about .290, got some home runs and RBIs, helped win some games. Then there was a little lull before the All-Star break, but my numbers at the break were pretty good. After all that had gone on, I was still in position for a really good season if I got hot. More than that, the Orioles had a shot at a title this year. We were in first place in June. At the break we were four games back of Toronto. Getting ready to leave Baltimore for the game in San Diego, I was in a good frame of mind. All quiet on the negotiating front, and just as well.

That's when club president Larry Lucchino dropped his bombshell, a letter hand-delivered to me in the clubhouse in Baltimore by traveling secretary Phil Itzoe. In the letter Larry told me that now was the time, the Orioles really wanted to get this done *now*, during the break from the championship season. Ron learned of this letter at the last moment. If he'd found out earlier, he would have tried to stop it. "Ron," I said from an airport lounge in Dallas en route to San Diego, "I don't know if it's been our fault or their fault or nobody's fault, but let's make a deal right now. I want a deal."

"Fine," he replied, "let's go to work." Over that All-Star break we spent hours on the phone putting together a complete deal. We made some concessions, but I didn't want to promise a personal services contract after I quit playing, which they wanted, and there were a few other issues. To me, all of these questions could be ironed out easily enough. I thought that these professional negotiators should be able to solve things so that everyone left the table feeling good, not feeling that they'd been "taken deep"—ripped off. Tactics and strategy could be called "playing games," I realize, but I don't think playing games has a place in negotiation, especially one like this that should be a win-win situation, as Ron would say. He's writing a book on the subject. (You might want to check it out.)

The team opened the second half on the road in Texas. Ron and I took about a week to dot the *i*'s and cross the *t*'s on our proposal. We genuinely believed this was the deal and the Orioles would sign off on it. We had to give them a week to ten days to respond, but I naively thought they'd call almost immediately and say okay. I was tremendously relieved in one way, but I also found myself standing out there between innings *wondering*. We're waiting for the reply and I was trying to play baseball. I try to learn from my mistakes on the field, and I've learned my lesson from this situation, too. I'd never allow it to develop again. It doesn't work for me.

After ten days of high anticipation, we heard nothing, so Ron had to call Larry Lucchino, who acted like our new proposal had been the same old story. The negotiations were dead again. I was dumbfounded. Before that letter arrived out of the blue before the All-Star break, I'd been reasonably content to put the whole issue on the back burner. Then the negotiations had become a priority again, Ron and I had worked hard, then waited, then—*nothing*. Now my frustration turned to anger. Sheer anger. I get angry all over again thinking about it. Why send that letter? What had changed between then and two weeks later? I threw up my hands—to put it mildly—and said, "That's it. It's over." I decided I no longer wanted to negotiate or to know about any negotiations. If Larry and Ron felt like talking, fine, but don't even tell me. Nothing until the season's over.

Right in that period I went out to lunch in Seattle with Storm Davis, who was back with us for just that one year after having been with San Diego, Oakland, and Kansas City since 1987. He and his family still lived in the Baltimore area, so Storm still played in our off-season basketball games, but it was great to have him back on *both* teams, and he pitched well for the Orioles when he was healthy. During a rain delay earlier in the season I'd quizzed Storm about free agency, because he'd been through it twice, and now we sat in the restaurant in Seattle for hours, and I let everything spill out. Storm probably didn't get in ten words edgewise. He did say it wouldn't seem right if I wasn't playing for the Orioles.

I agreed—but.

I couldn't tell you what the Orioles' logic was right then. I just don't know or understand, and it was especially frustrating because here we were a contending team again, Mike Devereaux and Brady Anderson were going like wildfire, the new ballpark was a tremendous success. You couldn't find tickets anywhere. It would have been great to contribute and concentrate on *just* baseball. I totally blame myself for getting into that position in the first place. I should have known better.

Over the years I'd been a steady performer for the Orioles. My batting average had fluctuated, that's for sure, but I could be counted on to be productive, whether it was home runs, extra-base hits, or RBIs. Now, however, it was early August in 1992 and my average had dropped into the .240s, with well over 400 at-bats. You need a long hot streak to come back from that, and I hadn't hit a home run in a while, either—a long while. July had been entirely without homers, my first such month since my rookie year. It was alarming. People tweaked both my brother and me about his having more homers over the stretch than I did. I was tinkering with my stance, but not much, but it must have *looked* a lot different because people commented. Basically, I was hitting from the same stance as '91, but without consistency, sometimes lunging at the ball like I'd done with the *old* stance in 1990. I couldn't get my head together. Hitting is not an exact science, and it requires all your concentration, not just at the plate, but in preparation. When you step to the plate, of course you're thinking about hitting, but where was your mind beforehand, when you could have picked up key information? If your head's not totally into it, you haven't seen what the pitcher's "out pitch" is tonight, you don't know whether he's getting his breaking ball over with consistency, you don't know if he's changing speeds well, and you don't remember what he got you out on three weeks ago. This is information you need! You have to be focused. I wasn't, my average proved it, and I was hearing about it from all sides.

"Longest stint of Cal's career he hasn't hit a home run."

"Hasn't done this."

"Hasn't done that."

"Last year must have been a fluke." (I usually keep my ego in perspective, but this particular remark rankled with me. Sure, 1991 had been a great year, but what about my overall numbers for the past ten years?)

"He's already gone from Baltimore. He's trying to sell his dream house." (Kelly and I had been looking for property for a new house for several years. Our first one had been my house, basically, and designed for a single guy. Now we had Rachel and hoped for more children, and Kelly had her own ideas about a house. Finally we gave up the search and decided to remodel. Our looking had nothing to do with the contract situation.)

"You're tired, Cal, take a day off."

Everybody was talking. About the only thing I didn't hear was trade talk; I don't think the Orioles were trying to trade me that year. Of course, thanks to my contract, they would have needed my permission. It was a tough period, but at least I was able to play sound defense. I ended up getting my second Gold Glove that year.

Then all of a sudden Ron called and said, "We have a deal." He gave me the specifics and I said, "Fine." I would have agreed to anything (though Ron wouldn't have). As it turned out, and after a couple of dozen meetings altogether over almost a full year, he and Larry Lucchino had finally closed the negotiation beside the pond at Ron's farm north of Baltimore. I was still bothered, I couldn't help that, and I was disappointed with myself, too, for the season I was having.

Then, when Larry and Roland Hemond, the general manager, paraded me out before the full house, showed a videotape of the official signing in the offices before the game, and announced the terms over the PA system—"Cal signed a five-year deal worth thirty-plus million"—I was plain embarrassed. I hated it. What was management trying to accomplish? I wasn't sure. It was almost like they were declaring a victory, even though it hadn't been a war in the first place. To me, standing out there in a sensitive mood, the crowd reaction at the announcement was mixed at best. It wasn't "Yeaaaa!" It wasn't

"Booooo!" It was just . . . okay. Ever the optimist, Ron tried to tell me later how positive it was, but I didn't buy it. Maybe I was just exhausted by the process. In the game, I went hitless and made an error.

At the time, we were still in the pennant chase. More than that. Returning home from California in late August, we were only half a game behind Toronto. I slowly started to get the feeling with the bat and finally homered again on September 14, to end the string of 73 homerless games, but now it was time for the whole team to slump offensively. Incredibly, we went three weeks in September without scoring more than four runs. We lost 15 of our last 27 games, fell out of the race, and at season's end trailed Toronto by 7 games. The Blue Jays were just dominant, pouring it on in September when they had to. But we still ended up eight games over .500. It had been a great season for the Orioles, 22 games better than '91. There's no question that Rick Sutcliffe, who won 16 games himself, was a factor in the rapid development that year of Mike Mussina (18-5) and Ben McDonald (13-13). The staff ERA dropped eight-tenths of a point, a huge achievement. With my new contract in hand, I looked on the bright side: in Baltimore, the Birds were back.

Chapter Fifteen

No sugarcoating these facts: while my team had been going strong in 1992, I finished with 14 home runs, the first time in my career I'd had fewer than 20; I had 72 RBIs, my lowest total by far; I hit .251. This was my worst season. And after being the MVP in '91, it was really disappointing. Then, to top off everything, my father was fired by the Orioles in the post-season, for the second and last time.

I knew it was likely. During the last series of the season, Johnny Oates had asked me out to lunch in Cleveland and warned me that some people in the front office didn't want my father back. "I'm fighting for him," Johnny said, but he also warned me that he couldn't put his own job on the line by saying, "Rip comes back or you lose me." I understood that. If push came to shove, Johnny said, if the organization refused to have Senior back as third base coach, he hoped he could retain him as his bench coach.

Much later, Johnny told me that in the big organizational meeting after the season, the executives said they'd think about the bench coach possibility in the time it would take Johnny to drive to his home in Virginia. When he got there he called the office and got his answer: "No." When Johnny called my father after the news had been officially delivered, Johnny told him pretty much what he'd told me, that this job offered him a chance to send his kids to college, and he couldn't afford to quit, or even threaten to quit. Knowing Dad, I'm sure he threatened Johnny with his life if he *did*.

Johnny has always given my father the credit for making him into a big leaguer in the first place. He had come to the Orioles as a catcher out of Virginia Tech, but he didn't know much about the position. Dad put him behind the plate in Florida and hit hard fungoes from the mound and said, "If you can block these, you can block any pitch." Then Dad took his bat to the infield and hit hard fungoes and said, "If you can handle these, you can handle any throw from the outfield." They worked hard and talked baseball for hours, and soon enough Johnny was a student of the game. I met my future manager when I was a kid hanging out with Dad at the Instructional League fields at Jack Russell Stadium in Clearwater. I'd kicked a soccer ball against the outfield wall waiting for Johnny, who was usually the first player to arrive. Then I'd approach timidly and ask, "Mr. Oates, wanna have a catch?" Johnny has probably told that story dozens times.

In 1988, he managed the Triple-A franchise in Rochester the year Senior managed the big club for the infamous six games. For the four prior years Johnny had been a coach with the Chicago Cubs, so that spring he worked especially closely with Senior. He didn't want to send anyone up to Baltimore who didn't know the Orioles' plays. When the two were both coaches on the Orioles, Johnny, who has a passion for tomato and mayonnaise sandwiches, lived for the day in July when Dad would bring the first box of his Better Boys into the clubhouse. Johnny and his wife, Gloria, and their two kids spent some of the off days in the summer in my parents' backyard in Aberdeen, barbecuing and swimming and throwing horseshoes.

The two men were good friends, and to this day Johnny will tell you that he doesn't talk to my father as much as he'd like to because he's embarrassed about what happened in 1992.

The club told Dad he could have some kind of consolation prize, probably a job in the minor leagues. My father, who's not a diplomat, said he'd think about it, but he didn't think about it very long. He said no thanks.

What happened between Dad and the Baltimore Orioles organization? Well, there was tons of speculation, of course. It was said that the organization didn't like his old-school approach, the way he rode the umpires, for example, although he rode the umpires less than Earl Weaver had. Or that the club wanted Johnny Oates to establish himself as an independent force with the team, without Senior at his side. Or that my father had never released his bitterness over the firing after six games in 1988, and had withdrawn from the players.

Lots of explanations, but I didn't buy any of them. I still don't. I think the firing was wrong, but I'll never know the complete story. I hate to believe the decision had anything to do with the one play in late September that got so much press at the time, and then came up again later in the postmortems. That was when Senior held up Tim Hulett at third base in the ninth inning of a game against Toronto, with us on the short end of a 4–3 score. It was a big series: we were five and a half behind the Blue Jays and couldn't afford many losses. With one out, Tim represented the tying run when Mark McLemore lifted a fly ball to short center field. On any kind of decent throw, sending Tim was suicidal; a bad throw and he *might* have been safe. With a good arm in center fielder Devon White, with Brady Anderson coming up next, Senior elected not to take the big chance. He held Tim, and when the throw came in way up the third base line, some of the crowd groaned. Brady then walked and Mike Devereaux popped out. John Feinstein wrote in *Play Ball* that Larry Lucchino watching from the press box screamed about "coaching malpractice." I don't know about that, but even if the club president or someone else in the front office thought that Senior had made a mistake on the play, you don't get fired for one "error." So I don't believe that can be the explanation, either.

Looking at the big picture, maybe the situation boiled down to this: a lot of changes had taken place in the Baltimore organization and across professional baseball, and my old-school father no longer fit in with the *business* of baseball. Maybe it's as simple—and as complicated—as that.

A couple of years after Dad was relieved of his duties, Bob Costas was on *Nightline* discussing with Ted Koppel the problems with the national pastime post-'94 strike, and Bob said, more or less, that the main problem is that some of the people running baseball and baseball clubs today have either forgotten, or in some cases never even knew, what it is that makes this game special. I think Bob was drawing the same distinction I draw between the business of baseball and the game on the field. What's special is the game on the field. Everything else should serve the purpose of this game, but does it? Could Bob be correct? Let's consider the situation.

There's no doubt that the major league game has evolved into a major form of entertainment, and there's no doubt that the growth of the business has introduced millions more fans to the beauty of baseball, in person at the ballparks, over the airwaves, and in the newspapers. This is great, and I think this popularity can only increase. At the same time, we might as well acknowledge that this market growth has inevitably brought to the *forefront* the business side of the game. Ironically, some of these businesspeople may look at the game on the field as *only* a game, not as a demanding vocation that requires and rewards expertise from the scouts, coaches, and other people who have made it a career. Individuals who wouldn't dream of walking into a courtroom and telling their lawyers what to say may feel perfectly qualified to make major decisions about baseball talent after just a year on the job, thereby devaluing the decades of baseball experience and savvy of career baseball men. So who's making the baseball decisions, baseball people or businesspeople?

I wonder.

In any event, my father and his thirty-six years of experience and old-school craftsmanship were deemed expendable by the organization. I don't know any other way to look at it. What's more, the Orioles also let my brother Billy go after the '92 season. A lot of people around town, including myself, naturally wondered whether there might be more than coincidence here. Should I resort to the ballplayer's standard lament? Probably so: "I'm just a player, I don't know, I do what I'm told."

I was more puzzled than angry or resentful about my dad and my brother. I didn't understand, and still don't completely, although I do know that the business side *directly* affected Billy's career and the careers of many, many other players around the league. In the nineties, management has tried to defeat the arbitration process by releasing players when their contracts expire, thereby making them free agents almost automatically. The team could lose the player, but it could also "start over" in contract negotiations, in effect, and get him back at a much lower salary, especially in a flooded market. Back in the late eighties, the collusion cases had been clear-cut. What has been going on in the nineties could be collusion, but the owners could also claim it's just smarter business. One thing is clear: the trend was and is to devalue the importance of the middle-salary player and to eliminate his salary, strictly as a financial move. This is a fact.

On the Orioles, Mark McLemore, Sam Horn, Randy Milligan, Joe Orsulak, Bob Milacki, and my brother were all released in one way or another after 1992. (McLemore then re-signed with the team for '93.) Billy said they were trapped in baseball's twilight zone. Early in December, our friend Keith Mills, a television reporter in Baltimore, called Billy at 10:30 a.m. Keith calls Billy all the time, but usually not in the morning. He passed along the word that the Orioles were going to sign Harold Reynolds and release Billy. This was out of the blue. My brother had had no indication he wouldn't be tendered a contract. In fact, he thought he had *more* job security that year than he'd ever had, because he and Mark McLemore had been such a solid platoon at second base in '92. After the deed was done, Billy pointed out this irony (he's always pointing out ironies): every prior winter he *had* been rumored to be leaving the Orioles; this was the first time there hadn't been any rumors at all. After the warning call from Keith Mills, Billy drove over to my house for the regularly scheduled basketball game, but when Ron Shapiro called—Ron handles Billy, too—with the official news, he left after one game. The rest of us kept playing, but it wasn't a lot of fun.

That was a rough winter for my brother. At least Dad had some finality. He was no longer with the Orioles or with anyone else in baseball. He told me he'd take a year off to figure out what to do, but he was very possibly out of the game for good. At fifty-seven, he could retire. His youngest son was just twenty-eight. Billy received the pink slip on his birthday, in fact; he should have years and years of good major league baseball in front of him. At first he wasn't too worried that someone would want him, but as time went along and the holidays came and went and the phone at Ron's office was quiet, my brother began to worry. Finally, in January, two calls came in. Oakland first, then Texas. Oakland under Tony LaRussa? Billy was definitely excited. The two men talked on the phone. Billy wasn't promised a starting position, but he thought he could make the team and get playing time. Then Texas' Jeff Frye blew out his knee in January and the Rangers needed a *starting* second baseman. Billy went with Texas, of course, agreeing to terms on Super Bowl Sunday during the annual party he throws for that occasion.

As luck would have it, the Orioles hosted the Rangers on Opening Day 1993. There was my brother trotting out from the third base dugout for the introductions of the visiting team, and it was gratifying to hear the cheer he got from the Orioles' fans. They know Billy and what he brings to his team. Standing on our respective base lines during the ceremonies, I caught his eye. Strange feeling for both of us. We had grown up together, teased and tussled together, started side by side in 634 major league games.

But that's baseball.

Our parents stayed away from the game.

Has respect for the *craft* of baseball been compromised because of the growth of the business side? That's certainly one explanation for the fact that players with proven skills and experience have been devalued in the first place. It's also one explanation for the fact that the quality of instruction in the minor leagues has gone down in recent years. How do I, a major leaguer, know this for a fact? Because more teaching of fundamentals is now required in the *major* leagues. No one in the game disputes this observation; it's become a cliché. I see it every spring. In the minors, the guys aren't learning what they need to know. In addition, players are sometimes rushed to the majors before they're ready, another sign that the crucial role of the minors is devalued, or at least misunderstood. Is the minor league system seen as a nagging above-the-line expense rather than as the *heart* of the organization, and worth its weight in gold? In a lot of organizations, I suspect this is the case. It has to be one factor.

Regarding baseball, at least, I'm a conservative, a stickler, and there's no doubt I acquired this trait from my father. Maybe I've overstated my ideas here; I probably have, in order to make my point clearly. I don't want to sound like I know everything in this area, because I don't. I have more questions than answers, and I guess I'd have to spend a season roaming the minor leagues to get a complete picture of what's going on, and I can't do that. But there are also some telltale indications that really make you wonder about the craft of the game, fundamental failures like messed-up rundowns and outfielders missing the cutoff man (a *daily* occurrence). And think about the increasing number of successful trick plays in the major leagues. A good example is the double steal, runners first and third. This should be almost suicide at the big league level because it depends on a failure in execution by the defense, but it works with some regularity now. There are also more circus-type innings than there used to be, more "Little League home runs," you might say, with multiple mistakes, throws going every which way, bases left uncovered, and the guy just keeps running. All this is entertaining, but it isn't good baseball, and there's only one plausible explanation: minor league instruction hasn't covered all the bases.

There's no doubt that young players today are bigger, stronger, faster, and more talented in every respect than their elders, with remarkable combinations of speed and power. Sixty home runs seems almost inevitable sometime soon. Conditioning is vastly superior. All I'm saying here is that the *craft* of the game has slipped a little overall, and craft reflects instruction, pure and simple.

Another inkling of a basic problem is uncoachable players. I know my old roomie Floyd Rayford, now managing the Batavia Clippers in upstate New York, believes he sees more of these players—and Sugar Bear's not even an old-timer. He has a novel explanation: too much attention in the training room, which leads to too much babying overall. I don't know about that, but I've seen one or two uncoachable players as well, and there must be some truth to the theory that this is probably a young guy with dominant physical talent who has been catered to, maybe all the way back to Little League. I'm not a sociologist, this is not my area of expertise, but the situation must also reflect what's going on in society as a whole, with pressures exerted by everyone for kids to succeed at an early age. For the coach, this is the kid who can take him all the way, so rather than coach, he caters; rather than risk alienating, he indulges. If this goes on until the kid is no longer a kid, until he reaches the high minors or even the majors, he might not be coachable at all, and you can't blame the player entirely. If I'm the teacher and the student doesn't learn, I'd blame myself.

What about the highly touted prospect who seems to want it all and want it now, who thinks his signing bonus is a free pass to a long-term contract in the majors? Floyd Rayford believes he sees more of these players, too. I know I've seen guys in spring training play a night game followed by a day game who are then ready for a day off. Where's the mental toughness? But I also believe there are just as many or more guys who have been ill-served by their amateur and minor league experience.

They haven't been *taught* to care.

Okay. If the instruction and development and assessment of players in the minors is not up to par, it stands to reason that this deficiency would spill over into spring training. I think it has in some cases. More and more often, you read where someone says, "We're going to see who performs in camp. We'll see who makes the club." As far as I'm concerned, if you're really looking for your team in spring training, you're in trouble, because you can't bring lots of players to camp in the hopes of getting quality out of quantity. Furthermore, it's dangerous to use a player's performance in a single spring training as an accurate measurement of anything. You should use spring training as part of an ongoing evaluation. An organization should already have the book on the prospects *before* bringing them to camp. The evaluation should be well in hand, based on a player's long progress through three or four years in the minors. The last Triple-A season is more important than one major league spring training performance, when, for starters, the pitchers aren't really pitching to the hitters. They're working on getting into shape, working on their pitches, and aren't necessarily trying to exploit the hitter's weaknesses. Some players have come from winter ball and are ready to go from the first day, some have come from warm-weather climates, some have been shoveling snow. This last group may be behind the others in their training. I've seen zillions of players who are world-beaters in spring training, but only spring training; start the season and it's a different story. And I've seen the opposite. Shouldn't every organization understand this?

One final point: as minor league franchises have become more successful and valuable, with many of them building new stadiums, pressure is put on everyone involved to produce winning seasons. This is a fact of life now in baseball, but, ideally, the emphasis for the big league organization should be on developing talent to win at the *major* league level. Winning seasons in the minors don't prove a thing in this regard. They definitely don't prove that good things are going on, development-wise. In fact, a winning record might be *totally* the opposite of the truth. The Orioles did have winning teams in the minors, for the most part, during their heyday (my dad had 11 winning seasons out of 14), but this was a result of good scouting for talent, and then good coaching. You want a winning environment for the minor leaguers to grow up in, but making every last move in order to win every game is not the point.

What's more, it could be that some minor league managers are now managing for themselves and their résumés, and not to develop their players. They're managing to win. They pinch-hit, platoon, send pitchers out on three days' rest—anything to win. How do you even begin to find out if a guy is a good clutch hitter if you immediately pinch-hit for him in A-ball because you're trying to win that game? How does this guy *learn* to control his emotions and hit in the clutch? Or maybe a manager chooses to keep a slightly better player coming out of college over a more talented but necessarily less developed eighteen-year-old coming out of high school.

Sorry if I sound negative here. I don't intend to. I'm just concerned, because baseball has been my whole life. If you want, blame my parents for getting me into this. I do sit around and worry about botched rundown plays; I don't like to see them even from the other team. I've had the opportunity to learn the game in many different ways, from many different perspectives. I think of myself as having carefully observed four generations in the minor leagues: while I was growing up all over the country, while I played in the minors, while my brother came up through the ranks and I got his reports, and now as I see the latest crop of graduates. I've been able to translate instruction into actual experience, so I have a lot of firsthand as well as secondhand knowledge, and next—in the fifth generation, so to speak—I'd like to see some changes.

Throughout baseball today, front office people are always proclaiming that they're going to build their major league team through the system and rely less on free agency. For one thing, building from within gives the front office better fundamental options. "Payroll containment" was the buzzword in the labor-management disputes, but there's a legitimate way to utilize payroll containment. Now I guess I sound like management, but I don't see any contradiction between turning a profit and maintaining a quality system and a quality product. There's no inherent contradiction between the business side and the baseball side of the game. The Orioles were known for years as a club with a low payroll. But, you counter, that was before free agency. True, but it's a fallacy to believe that a small-market team can't compete in this era. A small-market team with a sound minor league system could compete. The Orioles competed in the early years of free agency.

How do you build "through the system"? You have to have knowledge and commitment. The phrase "Dodger Blue" wasn't a slogan dreamed up by some marketing whiz. It was created through hard work; the same holds for the Oriole Way. So how many people can still do this work? I think there are plenty. You also have to have *stability*. There was a time in the Oriole organization when the same men were in just about the same positions throughout the system for six or seven years, and I'm betting the same was true with the Dodgers. This is the way you get your teaching system down. But is that kind of stability even possible today? According to everyone I've discussed the subject with—players, coaches, trainers, anyone who'll listen—it would be tough. Tough, I agree, but doable. For starters, you commit real money to upgrade salaries for the minor league staff—instructors and managers. You deem the rookie ball manager just as valuable as the Triple-A manager, because he is. You do a million things that don't cost a lot of money but that instill pride and purpose. You hire men who want to teach, and know how to.

In a very small nutshell, those are a few of my thoughts on the state of the game. The future of professional baseball is unlimited, I'm convinced, and all I want is for the game on the field to match in all respects the better-than-ever talent of the players. I think it's possible with the right direction, focus, and hard work. Someday, maybe sooner than I think, I'd like to test my knowledge and ideas. But would it be a real test without ownership? Now, there's a lofty goal. I like the idea of putting together an organization, or getting a good organization back to the way it was—just the baseball side. I'd love the opportunity to test my ideas with the Orioles, obviously, but anywhere, if necessary. Starting from scratch with an expansion franchise? *That* would be interesting.

While we're on the subject of change: in 1993, I started staying in a different hotel than the team in some cities, at my own expense, of course. In the contract negotiations the previous year, I more or less reserved this right if I felt it was necessary, mainly when my wife joined me on the road, but at other times as well. Kelly and I had already been doing that occasionally, and she suggested it as an option for me at other times. After thinking about it for a while, I agreed, because with or without her, I needed peace. Call it a weakness if you will—I do—but staying elsewhere was much more peaceful than staying at the team hotel. For the ten or more hours I'm at the ballpark, I give everything I've got to baseball. So do the other guys. Beforehand and afterward, I need my time to regroup. I'm that kind of person. In the minors and in my early years in the majors, I'd been a fanatical card player, but when life became more complicated, I cut way back. I no longer wanted to "kill" time; I wanted to *maximize* it. Some things that shouldn't have bothered me did bother me. Some people can shrug off stuff a lot easier than I can; stuff bugs me. I guess that's clear by now.

It all happened by accident. Toward the end of '93 the team was staying at the Grand Hyatt in New York (that's no secret; the list of the Orioles' hotels is printed in the media guide), and I was elsewhere on the East Side. (I've been tracked to the new place, but I really like the hotel and the situation isn't out of control.) At the last minute my wife had to cancel her planned visit, so I was all alone for that series with the Yankees. I have the clearest memory of coming downstairs in the morning, buying a newspaper, sitting in the restaurant catching up on the scores and the news, looking around in total anonymity and privacy—or, if not anonymity, at least privacy—and then walking out the front door for a tour of the neighborhood streets. I'd forgotten what this could be like, and I thought, This is nice. This is *really* nice. Even in the middle of Manhattan, the feeling that I could pick and choose what to do was so peaceful. For my frame of mind—for my *peace* of mind—it has made all the difference.

Of course, now I look back at some of the crazy and funny things that happen in hotels and laugh about them. Example: at 2 a.m., there's a knock on the door. Get up, look out, nobody there, go back to bed. Then there's another knock on the door. Ignore this one but call security. Then *security* bangs on your door. Example: several times around the country, people convinced the staff at the registration desk that they were relatives of mine and that I must have forgotten to make the hotel arrangements. Not only did they manage to talk themselves into the adjoining room on each side of my own room, but then they left the door open to each of those adjoining rooms and kept a lookout, so they'd know when I left or returned.

A lot of players have to use an alias when they register, to cut down on the unwanted phone calls, but even if you use an alias, the moment a room service person or bell captain comes up, you're busted. The list of room assignments for the players was readily circulated, and sometimes this list had the name *and the alias*. Or if twenty-one players have actual names and four have aliases, the aliases and their room numbers are easy to pick out. The keys to the rooms are put on a table in the lobby when we troop in from the airport, and people watch as you pick up your key.

If you don't want phone calls, even with the alias, turn the phone off, but then your real family can't get through. Ask the operator to hold all calls except for your wife, but that doesn't always work; I'm not sure why, but it often doesn't. And then there are the radio stations. Calls from them at 7 in the morning, maybe even earlier, became really fashionable at some point. On the Orioles, my brother Billy became a favorite target.

"This is your wake-up call."

"I didn't order a wake-up call," Billy would say, according to his favorite rendition of this story. "I don't *want* a wake-up call."

"Well, this is WUFO, and *you're on the air!*"

"Oh, yeah, well @#*# you!"

Of course, the station got exactly what it wanted, a crude response they could *bleep* and have some fun with. I swear someone was being paid by the stations to provide the room numbers. Then there was the time in Texas when the guy hid behind the ice machine on my floor—the episode I mentioned in the first chapter. I think Texas was a hot spot because of Nolan Ryan mania. The memorabilia and collectible business is much bigger in the Arlington area than in most others. Anyway, your guard is down, all you want is some ice, then all of a sudden you see blurred movement and a guy steps out wielding a baseball bat at 1 a.m.! Maybe he was about to knock on my door when I surprised him by coming out, so he ducked into this little room off the hallway where the ice machine was. But there was nowhere to hide except behind the machine. When he knew he'd been discovered, he came out.

One year in Seattle I stayed in a hotel right around the corner from the team hotel and got cornered even though I'd been extra careful. I offered a trade with these guys: "My autographs for learning how you found me." Turns out they had divided into teams of two, equipped with cellular phones, and staked out every plausible choice (in Seattle, there aren't that many).

I knew my teammates didn't care where I stayed—nothing happens at the hotel anyway, no one has a roommate, guys scatter—but I polled them anyway, just to make sure. What I thought was unfair, what hurt me, was when a few people (no teammates, incidentally) said that my staying at a different hotel in some cities affected team chemistry. This boiled down to an attack on me as a teammate—as a team player. How does sleeping in a different hotel affect team chemistry? When the team is playing at home—half the season—we all sleep in different homes. Does this affect team chemistry, or is there chemistry only on the road?

What is team chemistry, anyway? Is it rah-rah, American Legion–style camaraderie with everybody sleeping in bedrolls on the floor while sharing the same hotel room during the big tournament? Is it being a group of twenty-five good people? Is it getting along with and liking your teammates as friends? Is it eating in restaurants and going out to movies with them? I don't think so. I believe chemistry is formed mainly at the ballpark: on the field through the experience of success and failure, then in the clubhouse by talking about and analyzing these successes and failures. Winning instills confidence and provides a blueprint for the future; losing teaches you how to cope and regroup. To me, chemistry is a blending of individual responsibilities into a team focused solely on winning. Everything is directed at winning. Stability within an organization and team helps build chemistry. You know the guys, they know you, you know how to deal with them, they know how to deal with you. You focus on good communication. Misunderstandings are cut to a minimum. Without a doubt, constant turnover does impede chemistry.

Chemistry is a necessary part of winning, but not the largest part. Talent is. Talent rules in big league baseball. Without it, you can't compete over the 162-game season. As an exercise before every season, my father and Jimmy Williams used to match up for each team in the league the eight starting position players, the designated hitter, role players, five starting pitchers, middle relievers, and the closer. I've also done these match-ups. If you like the Orioles' guys in eighteen of the twenty-five positions, you have to like the Orioles to beat that team in the standings. I'm not saying that the final standings will reflect the match-ups in every instance, because a lot of match-ups will be close, some guys will have unexpected career years and others will have off-seasons, but talent does come first. All the intangibles and team chemistry and managerial magic in the world can accomplish only so much. A team can overachieve only up to a point.

When Senior took over as manager of the Orioles in 1987, he was adamant about preparation and the execution of fundamentals, but when he was asked if he was the kind of manager his players would run through walls for, he quipped, "Rather than have twenty-four men run through walls, I'd rather have fifteen who hit it over the wall."

Given the talent, you need experience, individually and collectively. To win championships you have to win one-run games, and talent and experience allow you to execute at a high level. In a bunting situation in the eighth inning, runners on first and second, the winning team has the ability in August or September to pounce on anything but a perfect bunt and turn it into a force at third, and maybe a double play; it has the talent, experience, and guts to make that play. I think immediately of the great play the Yankees' Andy Pettitte made against the Atlanta Braves in the fifth game of the 1996 World Series, throwing out John Smoltz at third on the attempted sacrifice in the sixth inning. Pettitte is a young guy, but he had the poise to make that play anyway, one of the big turning points in that Series. On a championship team, poise is contagious.

I choose a defensive play as the example because in professional baseball pitching and defense win games. Especially pitching, because pitching *is* defense. The pitcher makes the rest of the defense good. The Dodgers won for years with that formula, but name the team that has won with *offense* alone. I don't think you can. The Yankees and the Red Sox have been known for offensive teams, especially the Yankees, who scored 800-plus runs almost every year in the Mickey Mantle era. But look at the pitching on those teams: in 1956, Yankee pitching was second in the league in ERA. Over the following eight years of that dynasty their pitching was first, first, third, first, second, second, second, and third in the league. When Boston finally had a chance to win it all, in 1986, they had pitchers who kept them in the game and gave them a chance to win on a daily basis, led by Roger Clemens. Their team ERA? Lowest in the division. A decade later, in 1995 and '96, Cleveland's offense got most of the credit for that team's success, which they deserved, but their starting pitcher was good and their closer, former Oriole Jose Mesa, was untouchable. In 1996, the world champion Yankees won with pitching above everything else, including their untouchable bullpen. Mariano Rivera was awesome—the most dominant performance by a middle reliever I can recall.

One reason some people might not see that talent seasoned with experience rules is that they focus on short periods of time: a red-hot April or May, or a ten-game winning streak in June or July. I don't play a lot of golf, but apparently golfers make the same mistake, remembering their two or three best shots in a round and thinking that these indicate their true talent level. They don't. The true talent level is the final score over a period of time. The handicap takes into account the bad shots as well as the good shots, the ability to handle a long iron out of the rough, the mental lapses, the ability to make the shot under pressure. In baseball, fans and sometimes management, too, see the team leading the league on June 15, only to fall back and end the season eight games out, and they conclude that the talent had been there but that something else went wrong. They'd do better to take a closer look at the actual talent level, especially in the pitching and defense departments, which always comes to the forefront later in the season.

Now, it's true that there are teams with lots of talent that don't win. The talent does have to blend together to form a team—that's how I define chemistry. Many baseball people believe they can build team chemistry just by carefully selecting the players, but I don't believe anyone is smart enough to know ahead of time who will mix and match and blend. It's almost impossible. On the other hand, you *can* know who has a specific talent and how this fits on your twenty-five-man roster. So when I think about the makeup of a ball club, the Orioles or any other, I don't get carried away looking at personalities and off-the-field habits. I imagine there *are* a few players around the league I just wouldn't want on my team, if I had my choice, but I also know that one or two of them have a World Series ring and played a big role in their team's winning it.

Peaceful teams have won the Series and teams that seemed to be coming apart at the seams have won the Series. In 1996, the Orioles made it to the American League championships after a year with quite a bit of controversy. In short, all kinds of teams have been successful—all of them talented, but with very different chemistries. I sometimes wonder: is chemistry only truly defined by *winning*? good question by JR.

Recall the hotel situation? There's a sidebar to that one: transportation. At some point early in 1993, somebody observed that I didn't leave the airport on the team bus, but stayed behind and then drove away in a town car. The rumors started immediately. "Cal has changed," they said. "He's taking limos everywhere. His big contract has gone to his head."

But the issue was simple: I had to get to my hotel somehow, and I was told the airports wouldn't allow regular cabs on the tarmac. It has to be a specially licensed car. I eventually wound up with just a licensed van with writing on the side, because there was no way it could be confused with a limo. And in New York, for the sheer fun of it, I went one step further. I called the car company and asked if they had a paneled station wagon, preferably one with some rust on the side and with the driver in a fishing outfit, maybe, with flies and lures stuck all over his hat and vest, the whole bit. They fixed me up, and when this model pulled up beside the plane, the players started laughing. I said to myself, "Perfect." For the next three days that's what I drove to the ballpark in.

I think Brady Anderson was the only player who knew I did this to make a point. Speaking of Brady, his family was in town for the games that weekend at Yankee Stadium, and on Saturday they were going out to eat after the game. Brady splurged and asked the clubbie to call him a limo—a real limo. I was taking a while to come out of the locker room after the game, as I always do, sitting around talking about the plays, so Brady walked outside before I did to meet his family. The driver of my ride—a new guy—mistook Brady for me (lots of people say we look similar—except for his sideburns, I guess) and walked up to him to direct him to the Ripken vehicle. What was Brady thinking? He had ordered a limo but he and his family stepped inside this ratty-looking station wagon instead and rode off. When he presented the driver with his credit card, the guy said the car was paid for, but he called his dispatcher on the radio to make sure. When Brady heard the name "Ripken" during this conversation, it dawned on him.

When I heard about this snafu, I said to Brady, "Wait a minute, you'd seen the car at the airport, you laughed along with everyone else, didn't it bang you in the head that this was *my* car?" He swears his explanation about all the confusion outside the dressing room is plausible, but I don't buy it. I haven't let him forget this screwup. Meanwhile, I was now stranded back at the stadium because Brady had my station wagon, and I was going out to eat with ballplayers Rick Sutcliffe and Mark Parent, a New York friend, Bobby Zarem, and a friend of Zarem's. Five altogether, maybe a sixth, and at least three of us were big guys. We wound up in Zarem's friend's hatchback, really smashed in. And what happened to the limo Brady had ordered? That's a mystery to this day.

Did I say I hit rock bottom as a hitter back in the 1990 slump, or maybe in the '92 slump? Well, I *really* hit rock bottom in May '93 when my average sank below .200. That's riding the interstate, as in I-99, and I had over 150 at-bats. A serious hole. I'd worked hard in the batting cage over the winter to keep the better feeling I'd had at the end of '92. I'd had a strong spring training, I felt great, I was excited about the season and about Kelly's and my second child, due in the summer. I had a strong first week or so—and then, nothing. All of a sudden I couldn't hit, and I was very stubborn about my squat stance. As I've explained, when I get excited at the plate I don't relax, I go after the ball too soon, my body gets out front, and I can't buggywhip from that position. One way I had learned to control that tendency was to spread my stance and squat a little. That's what I had worked on with Frank Robinson that second half of 1990 and then carried over into '91, when I hit everything hard.

In '92, the squat worked off and on. Now in '93, I just couldn't find the feeling at all with that stance. But so what? It's not how you start the swing, it's how you hit the ball, and if you compared videotapes of the different swings of any particular hitter, these swings would look remarkably the same when the bat hits the ball. So if one trigger's not working, why not try another trigger? But I stayed with the old one, maybe exaggerating the squat even more. It took me a long time to admit that I couldn't bring back the MVP numbers with the MVP stance.

And so much for the theory I read somewhere that the dimensions at Camden Yards had been tailored after those at one of my favorite hitting parks—the Metrodome in Minneapolis—in order to assure good times for me on my new home field. According to this theory, the short foul lines in old Memorial Stadium had supposedly enabled the left and right fielders to shade a step toward the gaps, hurting line-drive gap hitters such as myself. Well, it's true that Earl Weaver, taking into account our good pitching staff, liked to play his outfield deep to cut down on extra-base hits. Playing deep at Memorial Stadium, they therefore also played over in the gaps a little. Mainly, though, they were playing deep. On the other hand, Jesse Barfield with the Toronto Blue Jays played almost on the right field line because he had Devon White in center field, who caught everything between left-center and right-center. There wasn't just one way to position the outfield at Memorial Stadium.

As I see it, I hit well at the Metrodome mainly because of the artificial turf. I don't think my success has much to do with the dimensions. A field designed for me and all the other ground ball and line-drive hitters would have, first of all, a fast infield and outfield—artificial turf, ideally. You hear that Camden Yards is a great hitter's park, and for home run hitters you could make the case, but for the rest of us, this isn't particularly true. It's a slow infield. But this wasn't my problem in either '92 or '93.

If you have major league talent, hitting is mostly mental. The confidence factor can't be overestimated. I'm so analytical and such a worrier sometimes that I can get caught up in the finest points of technique and forget to let my natural talent flow. It's frustrating, but it's the way I am sometimes. My manager Johnny Oates said at some point in '93 that maybe I just wasn't going to hit home runs anymore. So I was washed up as a pretty good power hitter at the age of 32?

Reporters and fans suggested that I was putting too much pressure on myself to justify the new contract. Yes, I felt some pressure to have a good season, and maybe I did feel a little extra pressure, but I can't swear to that. Any extra pressure in 1993 was more likely because I wanted to be sure to make the All-Star team, since the game was being played that year in Baltimore, *my* city. I'd thoroughly enjoyed every All-Star appearance, but I really wanted to be in this one.

Frank Robinson was still with the organization as assistant to the general manager, and I worked with him on my hitting. I worked with Greg Biagini, our hitting instructor that year. I talked with my father on the phone. I hit a lot of balls off the "T," which I've always thought helps me.

Last, but definitely not least, I wondered—like everyone else—whether the streak of consecutive games was the source of most of my problems. In my mind, this became the focus. I had read or heard about Billy Williams and his streak, which he voluntarily ended at 1,117 games in 1970 because the pressure got so great. Billy found himself saving a little energy from *this* game in order to have some left over for the *next* game. One afternoon at Wrigley Field he settled for a double on a drive that might have yielded a triple, and that's when he realized he had had enough and said so to Leo Durocher, his manager. As Steve Garvey's streak of games kept growing, he started having dreams about bizarre things that ended it, like the one in which he was driving on the L.A. freeway at 3 p.m. on his way to Chavez Ravine for the night game and hearing that the *afternoon* game was already in the bottom of the ninth. I didn't dream about the streak I had going, not that I remembered, but I did get paranoid about the starting times. I was extra careful about twilight games and Wednesday afternoon day games.

At the All-Star game in 1986, I asked Dale Murphy about the streak of 740 games he had recently voluntarily terminated. Dale said he'd just gotten tired of dealing with it, but he urged me not to sit down for the same reason.

By June '93, I was thinking about doing just that. My spirit was zapped a little. In times past, I'd always laughed when Kirby Puckett pulled up at second base after yet another double and called over to me, "Cheer up, Cal, just four more years and you can have a rest!" In '93, maybe I didn't laugh very hard.

Those first months of the season were the only time in my career I ever got so discouraged that I asked myself, Am I *still* doing the right thing by doing the right thing—playing every day? The only comparable time was during the bad patch in 1990. At Memorial Stadium, I used to walk out to the center field fence for some quiet time. That spot was pretty isolated, and I'd lean against the wall and think about things and try to straighten them out in my mind. One afternoon I spotted Brady Anderson walking in my direction, and he kept coming even after I tried to signal that I needed to be by myself. Brady can be a forward kind of guy, and he didn't retreat, and just as well, maybe. For quite a while we talked about the situation and I asked him what the streak meant to him. Did it mean anything at all in a *baseball* sense? Was it even meaningful that I played every day? Brady said, "It's one of the great- est records in baseball history. You'll be considered one of the greatest players ever to play." Brady says I shook my head negatively. I'm sure I did, because his answer made no sense to me. I was supposed to be one of the greatest players just because I'd played all these games? No way. I'd always thought my approach made perfect baseball sense. But did it really? My doubts remained.

Three years later, I was even more doubtful. In Oakland, I believe, I got word that Barry Bonds had taken a day off for the Giants and his father Bobby had criticized me for never doing the same. "If I were his manager," Bobby said, "he'd be out of there. He's hurting the team and showing that personal goals are more important. He wants to break Lou Gehrig's record even if it costs Baltimore the pennant." Bobby soon sent word that he'd been misquoted, and there was some irony here, too, because Barry began his own streak of consecutive games later that season that stretched to 357 before a pulled muscle stopped it in August 1996.

During this period, *Sports Illustrated* ran a piece titled "Solitary Man." All in all, it painted a pretty sorry picture of me and my "somber solitude." But I didn't live in somber solitude. The fact that the consecutive games streak was beginning to define me about that time, as I stated in the story, didn't mean that I was retreating from the world. Nevertheless, an *SI* piece gets your attention, and the timing of this one contributed to my concerns about my hitting. I was getting seriously worn down, and one afternoon I said to Rick Sutcliffe during batting practice in Cleveland, "Sut, let me talk to you a minute." Sure, Rick said, and we stepped to the side, and I said, in so many words, "All this stuff is really bugging me. I don't know what to do. Am I doing the right thing? Maybe I should take a day. I'm thinking I should get this over with. Just one game and all this stuff will be gone. If I *knew* that sitting down would break this slump and end all the constant talk, I'd do it in a second. I hate to capitulate. I'm paid to play, but maybe I should sit down. Maybe it's the only thing left to try."

Rick looked at me like he'd heard dumb statements before, but nothing quite this dumb. Then he said, "We need you in the middle of the lineup, in the middle of the field every day. The only problem you're having is your hitting. Fix your hitting and all the other stuff will go away. Just fix your hitting. The answer has nothing to do with taking a day off." Then he added, "Or do it when I'm not pitching." He wasn't smiling, either. "I'm pitching tomorrow night, and your name's going to be in the paper one way or another. You're either going to be in the lineup or in the obituaries."

As you can see, Rick is a plainspoken guy and he'd gotten himself worked up. For myself I was thinking, Fix my hitting? I wish it were that simple.

Rick turned more lighthearted and said, "Look, can you get *one* base hit tonight? If we're down nine to one in the eighth inning, can you get a bunt single?"

"What do you mean?"

"Cal, if you go just one-for-four, nobody's going to mess with you after the game. Nobody will say you're tired. Look, you've spent your whole life worrying about the Orioles. Why don't you take the next two weeks and just be selfish, get one hit a night no matter what it takes."

Of course, it's not selfish to get a hit. Rick was just trying to channel my focus, sort of like I'd been able to channel Mike Boddicker's focus years earlier by telling him to forget about winning, forget the final score, and just concentrate on limiting the other team to three lousy runs.

What Rick said was just what I needed to hear at that time. I would have had no problem if the streak were broken because I pulled a hamstring or caught the chicken pox from Brady Anderson (actually, my mother reassured me that I'd had it already), but in my heart I knew that sitting down for a game as a way to break a slump would be so foreign to what I believe that it might put me in a worse slump. To me, this is running away from the problem instead of facing it.

I didn't sit down. Instead, I won a round with my stubbornness and altered my stance a little, stood more upright, and almost immediately began to relax at the plate. I hit .280 the rest of the '93 season, and with good power, and ended up with 24 homers and 90 RBIs. Before that, at midseason, I was voted onto the starting All-Star squad as well, although I got such a late start averagewise that I thought about declining. I was hitting about .215 when the teams were announced, Travis Fryman had the numbers that year, and one part of me thought the thing to do was somehow to let him have the honor of starting the game. But I couldn't really do that. The voting can be controversial, but I think it's great that the fans make the decision, and two million of them had taken the trouble to vote for me. And I've admitted it already—I did want to be on that team. Everybody does, despite what guys occasionally say about not caring, about being just as happy to spend three days at home.

By the time of the game, I had gotten hot and collected my 2,000th hit, off Wilson Alvarez, and my doubts about starting the game eased. As part of the pre-game festivities, Michael Jordan participated in the celebrity home run hitting contest (in which Tom Selleck was the only participant who actually cleared the fence), and Michael collected auto-graphed bats. I was honored to give him one of mine, because I've always admired him. But the greatest honor I received that day was the standing ovation during the introductions. This was overwhelming. Along with September 5 and September 6, 1995, that evening was the most thrilling, gratifying experience I've had in baseball. After all that had gone on in my career for the past bunch of years, after the terrible start I'd had in '93, to have the fans give me an overwhelming vote of confidence was just unbelievable. I felt that the ovation wasn't for that year, but for my whole career.

My emotions almost got the better of me. They *did* get the better of me at the plate, where, naturally, I wanted to do something great as a way to show my appreciation. But I couldn't control my excitement. Jumpiness doesn't translate into good hitting or good fielding, and I struck out once and grounded out twice, while my friend Kirby Puckett picked up the slack for the good guys with a homer and a double.

Around Baltimore, by the way, that's the famous All-Star game in which American League manager Cito Gaston didn't pitch our Mike Mussina. After Cito put his own pitcher, Duane Ward, in the game in the ninth inning of a 9–3 American League blowout, Mike got up in the bullpen and started throwing, getting in the work he needed. I never understood the brouhaha that followed. Cito hadn't been snubbing Mike, and Mike hadn't been trying to incite the fans against Cito, but for some reason that's the way Cito took it, and Mike did nothing to correct this impression. This controversy really sparked our fans, and when we got as close as a half game behind Toronto in August, Baltimore fans had visions of a beautiful revenge series at Camden Yards to close out the season. But the Blue Jays again poured it on, just like they had the previous two seasons, while we dropped 14 of 22 and slipped a full 10 games back.

My wife entertained forty people at that All-Star game in a skybox at the stadium. A couple of weeks later, on July 26, she delivered our second child, Ryan. People said how fortunate that it was an off day. More than fortunate, it was *planned*, and it happened to be during one of my road trips. I hoped I could sneak in, sneak out, and nobody would be the wiser, but it didn't work out that way: after the delivery in the morning, Kelly saw the report on the noon news. As always, the stats were instantly available, this time about our big baby boy. As with Rachel, we hadn't known whether we had a boy or a girl, and didn't want to know, although I have to admit that when I sat in on a couple of the sonogram sessions I couldn't help studying the screen looking for some little indication, one way or the other. But, again, what did it matter when the first cry rang out in the delivery room?

And then I was gone. I'd flown in from Minneapolis early in the morning and had to leave again late that evening for Toronto. I did *not* want to leave. Make no mistake, the separations throughout the season from Kelly, Rachel, and Ryan are the toughest thing about this game. I love baseball, it has provided a wonderful life for my family, but as I'd found out from my father, the scheduling is tough. This particular departure and separation was the toughest of all for me. I was a little rueful while passing out chocolate cigars in the visiting clubhouse at the Skydome the following afternoon.

Chapter Sixteen

June 6, 1993. Camden Yards. Although Seattle's Chris Bosio had thrown behind a couple of our batters, it hadn't occurred to me that retaliation might be in order. But with two outs, our Mike Mussina plunked Bill Haselman with a fastball on the shoulder in the seventh inning. Haselman charged the mound. I was running toward the mound from shortstop to help protect our pitcher when my foot slipped as I turned to face the wave of Mariners arriving at the scene from their dugout. I heard the pop in the right knee, then I ended up on the bottom of the pile with a couple thousand pounds of players on top of me. The knee wasn't particularly painful; it was just strange, more than anything, because most of my previous injuries had been my ankles. This was the first time anything at all had happened to a knee. It felt okay after the two teams were finally separated, and I stayed in the game, which we won. In the training room afterward, I guess I down-played the situation. Dr. Charles Silberstein, the Orioles' orthopedic surgeon at the time, poked and prodded, nodded his head, and I iced the knee.

I drove home with no particular concerns. When I woke up the next morning and put my right foot on the floor, I winced. I couldn't put any weight on it. Almost none at all. Like all players, I'd played through a bunch of little stuff, but my first reaction that morning was, There's no way I can play tonight. That's what I told Kelly, and what happened next has been written about a hundred times. She got a really sad expression on her face and said, "Couldn't you just play one inning?"

I thought, You too? If I can't play nine innings, I'm not playing at all.

I was bewildered by Kelly's reaction, especially since this was the first time the subject of the streak had ever come up in a conversation between us. The first time. No wonder some people in baseball had doubts about the streak if my own wife thought I'd play one inning just to keep it going. No way, even if Lou Gehrig had. I knew that Gehrig had taken innings off here and there because Johnny Oates, as a way to induce me to sit out more innings, had researched Gehrig's streak. He probably got hold of Bob Davids's data. Davids is the founder of SABR, the baseball research organization, and one of the leading authorities on Gehrig's streak. According to him, Lou made one strictly cameo appearance, in consecutive game number 1,427. Down with a bad back, Gehrig was put in the lineup by Joe McCarthy, his manager, as the leadoff batter, then lifted for a pinch runner after he'd singled. In three other games Gehrig played one inning; in two games, two innings; sixty-eight incomplete games total, along with a host of minor injuries, including multiple broken fingers.

But so what? I wasn't competing with Gehrig. Sure, I wanted to play that night, but not just one inning. Nor would I have DH'd if this was just a manager's way to keep the streak rolling. I was exasperated by Kelly's question, she dropped the subject, and I limped to the telephone to call Richie Bancells, a guy I'd grown up with in the Baltimore organization. My first day in rookie ball in Bluefield, West Virginia, in 1978 had also been his first day with that ball club, after being the assistant in Miami the year before. After Bluefield our career paths split off before coming back together in Baltimore in 1983, when Richie came up from the minors as Ralph Salvon's assistant. He took over as head trainer in 1987. For years he and his wife and their three kids have come over to our place once or twice every summer—maybe more than that—for a crab feast and swimming party, and he used to play in some of the basketball games in the gym, too. Very fundamental, nothing fancy: that's how I'd describe Richie on the court and in his training room, too.

I call him all the time, but not usually at nine o'clock in the morning. When he answered the phone and heard my voice, he probably knew something was up with the knee. The first words out of my mouth were, "I think I have a problem." No need for greetings.

Richie told me to get off the leg, ice down the knee, and meet him at the park early, 2:30, I think it was. I called my parents and told them I was hurting. I didn't know what the future held, I just knew this seemed like the worst injury I'd ever had, and I thought they'd want to know about it. An hour later, they pulled up in the driveway. I was surprised, but now that I think about it, I shouldn't have been. It was totally in character. We may not be the most expressive family—we're not the most expressive, I'm pretty sure—but family is *family*. I was very touched they came over to lend support, and we sat on the front porch and talked about anything and everything while I iced the knee for twenty minutes. Then the three of us would take a short walk down the driveway. These little walks were my idea, not Richie's; I was already thinking about whether I could play. The combination of ice and walking seemed to free up the knee.

Richie alerted Dr. Silberstein, of course, and when I arrived at the park at the appointed hour, everyone gathered around for a look. The diagnosis was simple enough—sprained medial collateral ligament—and the prognosis not all that good. That ligament is a major stabilizer for the knee. I knew that much without asking, and I knew that as a big guy playing a position that requires a lot of lateral movement, I needed my knees. Richie and Dr. Silberstein didn't say a lot, but I could tell from their behavior that this was going to be tricky. If the training room had been a hospital, my condition in terms of playing baseball five hours later would have been listed as "Guarded."

My attitude was, Let's do everything we can for the next three or four hours, then I'll test it out. Richie used every "modality" in his books: cold whirlpools, muscle stimulation, ultrasound. I hogged his attention that afternoon, no doubt about it, and word spread. The other guys couldn't resist peeking through the doorway. There wasn't a lot of conversation. There was a mood of concern, I guess you'd say.

After all the treatment, I suited up and walked out to the tunnel to make some moves by myself and see how the knee felt. When I passed that test, I went out to take some BP and infield. The knee was not wrapped, and it didn't feel bad at all. I was even a little surprised. I jogged a little, took a couple of sprints, tried some quick starts and stops; I took some swings in the cage and fielded some ground balls in the field. When Richie asked me what I thought as I walked off the field, I said I thought it was going to be okay. Roland Hemond told me later that he'd been watching from his office in the old warehouse beyond right field. He'd been notified about the problem. Other front office people were probably watching as well.

Richie was in a dicey situation. The trainers around the league feel that the decision to play is the player's, because we're the ones making the living. The trainer gives us the risk factors and helps us make the decision. But if the trainer feels a player wants to play ill-advisedly, he'll tell the manager. When I asked Richie about the downside with my right knee, he told me I could get caught in a bad position and tear the ligament. A mild injury could become a lot worse, and that would mean the loss of a lot of days. I understood that, but I also felt that if I absolutely should not be out there, Richie would tell me.

Johnny Oates also watched me take infield, seemed satisfied with the result, and told me to let him know the score before he walked out to home plate with the lineups. It wasn't until I was working on this book that I learned that both Johnny and Richie felt under pressure that afternoon, and were happy enough to leave the decision to me. I didn't feel any pressure at all. Both of them trusted that I wouldn't do something completely stupid, and I trusted myself not to do something completely stupid. If I could play, I would. If I couldn't, it wouldn't be the end of the world. I'd get back to work the next day, or as soon as possible. I was all right with the situation. I was almost tranquil. I don't know why, but this must have had something to do with the fact that I really didn't consider myself a prisoner of the streak. Other people said I was, but I never felt that way.

Ten minutes before game time I stuck my head in Johnny's office and said, "It's a go." He nodded. The knee felt pretty good, and when Lance Blankenship hit a hopper with topspin in the hole in the first inning, I knew I'd made the right decision because I planted my right leg without a problem. I was thankful for the test *early* in the game; my concern lifted, because now I knew I could make the play in the ninth inning of a close game. I ended up running the bases three times and made a final throw off my right leg in the ninth inning of the one-run game. (A footnote to my story, but much more than that for the Orioles' story in 1993, is that Mike Mussina hurt his throwing shoulder when he landed on it during the same brawl and a couple of weeks later went on the disabled list and stayed there six weeks.)

Contrary to what some have suggested, I don't have a bionic body. That twisted right knee was not my first injury, by a long shot. I've had lots of twists and bruises and sprains and foul balls off the ankles that I thought might have broken a bone. In 1985, I twisted my ankle on a pickoff play against Texas in April. The next day was an exhibition game against the Naval Academy, and Ralph Salvon told me to take the day off. In fact, I spent the day in the hospital wearing an inflatable cast and getting X rays and treatment. Would Ralph have told me to take the day off against league competition? Sure, he wouldn't have had a choice, and it wouldn't have been any big deal for him or anyone because nobody was thinking about a consecutive games streak in 1985, although it stood at 444 at the time. Streakwise, that was a lucky break with scheduling.

It's probably true that there have been a bunch of other times when certain other players might have taken the day off with some problem I had. Everybody has a different threshold. That's what Richie Bancells says. Based on his experience in the training room and, I suppose, conversations with other trainers, Richie also believes a few major league baseball players don't really enjoy their work. They play because the pay's good and they don't know how to do anything else. But if they don't feel just right physically, they might opt out of a game. Other players *want* to play, but their mental makeup is such that they need to feel almost one hundred percent before they can. And, Richie says, some guys don't care how they feel; they just want to play. I'm somewhere in between. I do care how I feel, and if I think some little ache has gone on longer than it should, I get treatment. Almost every season Richie has to manipulate my lower back, sometimes three or four times in a season. I have a slight curvature of the spine, and if it gets out of alignment too much and the muscles spasm, Richie knows what to do. If he gives me a treatment program for anything at all, I follow it to the letter. Why wouldn't I? He's the pro. But some players don't follow their programs.

There's no question that some guys are more susceptible to injuries than others. They have muscular imbalances, skeletal imbalances—and bad luck. Paul Molitor has been on the DL for the equivalent of way more than two years' worth of games over his nineteen-year career. In the eighties, he missed about twenty-five percent of all the Brewers games; at the end of one season, he had surgery on three different body parts at the same time. Most guys have pulls and sprains, but Paul has breaks and tears. In Kansas City, George Brett missed almost twenty percent of the games altogether. Mark McGwire, who has the second-best career ratio of at-bats to home runs (12.7; Babe Ruth is first at 11.8), has been hurt dozens of times, DL'd eight times. Texas Rangers slugger Juan Gonzalez, who won the MVP Award in 1996, has had more than his share of problems.

Richie does acknowledge that I might be a "quick healer," whatever that means, but I'm not a freak of nature. In 1995, reporters were always asking Richie whether I had some secret workout. No, Richie said, just basic baseball fitness. Actually, he feels that more amazing than my lack of serious injury for fifteen years has been my good fortune regarding illness. Well, he's right in that I haven't had anything drastic—I've never had to play with a 104-degree temperature—but I've had all the regular stuff that anyone gets while traveling around the country all the time. I have been lucky regarding food poisoning, which I've never had during the season, to my knowledge. The year before the knee injury, in fact, a bunch of players picked up food poisoning from the sandwiches served at RFK Stadium after the exhibition game against Boston, two days before our Grand Opener at Camden Yards. Rick Sutcliffe was able to start that game, and win it, but some other players were really sick. I ate the same food and felt fine. The one part of me that may actually be made of iron is my stomach.

My good health is good fortune on my part, but my former manager Joe Altobelli makes a related point: how many managers get sick during the season? Hardly any. Of course they only have to sit in the dugout, but still, they don't get sick, and Joe's theory is that they don't *let* themselves get sick. They're so focused on the job they build the fortitude to keep going, *then* they catch a cold a week after the season's over. I hadn't thought about this, but how many games do managers miss? I can't remember any manager of mine losing one day for a regular illness.

Richie also agrees with me that injuries are less likely to happen when the game is played correctly, with intensity and focus. Molitor and Brett are definite exceptions—along with many others, these two guys do play the game right in every respect but still get injured—but, generally speaking, the quickest way to get injured is to go through the motions, and I know exactly when I learned this lesson. I was eighteen years old and waiting for my own full-court basketball game when a half-court game needed one more guy, and the players looked at me. I said okay, and played at half-speed. On rebounds, I thought I'd just go up easy and come down easy. In fact, I came down on another guy's leg and my left ankle twisted badly. This was ten days before my first minor league spring training camp in Florida in 1979, but I wanted to play in the full-court game so badly I tied the shoelaces tighter on my hightops and kept going. When I finally took the shoe off, the ankle blew up—one of many sprains that have weakened both ankles permanently; they click as I walk. If I'd played my normal game that afternoon, I would've put a hip on my man, boxed him out, cleared more space, been more aware in general, and therefore more likely to come down on the floor, not on the other player. In our off-season basketball games now, I play hard not only because I'm competitive, but also because I feel this insulates me from injury.

Three days after the brawl in Camden Yards, the Orioles got into a mini-knockdown contest in Oakland—one incident on each side. After Rick Sutcliffe had located a fastball up and in against A's catcher Terry Steinbach, and then struck him out, Bob Welch hit me on an 0-2 pitch with an inside fastball coming right at my coconut. I instinctively got my hand up to protect my face, and the ball caromed off my left wrist into my jaw. The jaw was fine but the wrist did hurt. Intentional? Seemed like it to me. Later in the inning, I came around third on a hit by Mike Devereaux and found Steinbach blocking the plate with the ball, and I was perfectly willing to run over him.

I made a clean play, but afterward I wondered whether it was *completely* clean. I hadn't done anything wrong, but was my anger misplaced on that play? Probably. At the All-Star game the next month at Camden Yards, I tried to explain to Terry, but he said, "Hey, that's the game. Don't worry about it."

As it turned out, those two episodes marked the beginning of the end of the doubts and negative sentiments about the consecutive games streak. In Baltimore, commentators put that Steinbach collision together with my participation in the brawl at the pitcher's mound and said that Ripken must mean what he says: he plays every day because he *can* play every day. He's not trying to protect himself from injury, is he? Then came the tremendous reception a month later at Camden Yards at the All-Star game, which I've described. After that night, no one in Baltimore complained about my playing every day. Then again, they didn't have a batting slump to trigger the discussion. The second half of '93 was solid.

So Johnny Oates had done his research on Lou Gehrig, and he wanted me to take more late innings off when we were in blowouts. Johnny's theory was that if it was good enough for Lou, it was good enough for me. I didn't argue with him; in the mid-nineties, I probably did sit down for a few more late innings than I had missed in the eighties. Johnny asked what I thought about playing just the first inning of a Wednesday game that was followed by an off day Thursday. That would, in effect, give me both Wednesday and Thursday off. I appreciated his concern, but it wasn't necessary. On the other hand, one night we had a 10-run lead against Oakland in the eighth inning, I believe, and I went to Johnny and asked, "You want these last two innings, Johnny?" What a surprise when he said, "No, I'm not comfortable." After I hit a three-run homer, he came up and said, "Now I'm comfortable."

Johnny and I had a bunch of conversations about the streak in general. The subject was on his mind. I told him that as far as I was concerned, he was the manager, I was the player, and if he ever felt he was hurting the club by playing me, I wouldn't be in the lineup. But let's face it, practically speaking Johnny would have had a very tough time sitting me down, barring injury. He even made a statement to the effect that "Cal's streak is bigger than baseball." That was in Detroit, and he took some heat from a local writer who argued that no one player is bigger than baseball. But Johnny hadn't said that *I* was bigger than baseball. He said that my *streak* was bigger than baseball, and that he didn't feel baseball—the tradition, the fans, the media—gave him the freedom to sit me down. Richie Bancells was operating under the same constraints. He admitted after the brawl episode that it was unlikely anyone else in the major leagues would have played the following night. He said it was unlikely he would have *let* anyone else on the Orioles play. I had no idea at the time.

I played my 2,000th consecutive game on August 1, 1994, in Minnesota. The day before, the Orioles celebrated the 1,999th game with a fifth-inning video salute at home at Camden Yards, and the crowd really got into it. When I got the same kind of reception the next day in Minneapolis, I was pleasantly surprised. Other than the record-breaking week in Baltimore the next year, that's about the only streak milestone I remember; some of the others I've tried to forget. I never wanted whatever hoopla there was, that's for sure, but it was gratifying that everyone seemed to be behind me now. It's true that I was hitting .315 and driving in runs in 1994, but I also like to think that people finally understood what the streak was all about. For quite a few years I'd been thinking of it as a negative, mainly; I'd had to defend playing every day. Now it seemed like the streak had turned into a positive thing for me and for baseball.

The two "2,000" celebrations gave me a hint of things to come. For thirteen years, I'd just ducked my head and met the challenges of each day. I hadn't thought about the future or about actually breaking the record. Before, Gehrig's number had seemed hypothetical, even inconceivable, but now the number 2,000 made the number 2,131 seem much closer. For the first time, I had a clear realization that it *was* possible, and I also now understood that fans *wanted* me to do it. Kelly had surprised me by flying in to Minneapolis for the game, and we had a quiet dinner for two afterward at one of Kirby Puckett's favorite local restaurants. We talked about how things were shaping up, and I said I wasn't going to do anything different. I wasn't going to play it "safe" for the sake of the record. If at all possible, I wasn't going to think about the record at all. Let the chips fall. However, now I did feel some pressure, and this was a little scary.

Who would have guessed that consecutive game number 1,999 would be the last game in Baltimore in 1994? Not me. I was driving back home after shooting a commercial at Adventure World when I heard that Bud

Selig had announced at a press conference that the rest of the regular season as well as the post-season had been canceled. Like everyone else, I was stunned and angry and sad. How did the labor situation in baseball ever come to this? Collective bargaining is a necessary part of the business side of the game, but I looked at these negotiations the same way I looked at my own negotiations, as win-win situations. I felt that we—the players—had established reasonable starting positions and then bargained in good faith, but one theory held that a group of owners was determined to break our association and start all over.

Both sides were trying to use public relations to gain leverage across the table. I don't believe in that, but nobody was asking me. If the owners really weren't interested in negotiating, if they wanted to break us, it made sense to go public, and I have to admit they did a good job. The way to break the union was to break the leadership, and players read so much in the papers about everything being Don Fehr's fault, a few began wondering, *Is* it Don Fehr's fault? I'm as frustrated as the fans. Maybe the owners are right.

The owners were able to define the terms of the debate, and by focusing on the question "How much is enough?" instead of "What's a fair share?," by hiding the whole history of baseball salaries (Lou Gehrig's *highest* salary was $37,000 while playing for the wealthiest organization in professional sports), and by alienating the fans from the players for the sake of the negotiations, they did gain a short-term advantage that fall. But if they were trying to break the union for the sake of business, what about the long-term damage done to the game *and the business* in the process? Was this ever taken into account?

You never know where you're going to get into a debate about athletes' salaries. My biggest surprise in this area came quite a few years before the '94 meltdown, at a dinner party at George Will's house in Georgetown. One of George's other guests that night was Jack Kemp, former congressman, former quarterback for the Buffalo Bills, future Republican vice presidential candidate. At some point, Jack tried to involve me in a discussion of federal housing policy. As the Secretary of the Department of Housing and Urban Development, he knew this area; as a baseball player and also as a citizen who admittedly doesn't follow politics closely, I didn't. So I didn't have a lot to contribute to that discussion. But eventually the conversation turned to baseball—or salaries, at least—and it turned out that Jack didn't understand the salary his son, Jeff, was drawing as the backup quarterback sitting on the bench for the Seattle Seahawks. I replied to Jack, more or less, "He's not 'sitting on the bench.' He's playing a role on the team—a very important role. And how did he arrive at this position? By earning it, by being one of the top football players in the country." Finally Jack just threw his arms in the air and said, "Well, say what you want, but how can they pay four hundred thousand dollars to someone who hasn't taken a snap?"

I was really confused. This was his son we were talking about. George joked, "You have to excuse Jack. He just discovered economics two years ago." Of course, George was one of the most prominent supporters of the players during the strike four or five years later.

I never believed we'd lose the season in 1994, and then once it happened I didn't realize that my streak would briefly become a focus of the media. However, when the owners threatened to start the '95 season with replacement players, the question came up immediately: would I be given special permission by the association to join the replacement players for the sake of my streak, which stood at 2,009 games, two-thirds of a season short of Gehrig's mark? Various players were quoted saying they'd understand if I chose to play in replacement games. At a meeting of the players in September in New York, Mark Belanger, by now working as a special assistant to Donald Fehr, and a couple of other union people asked me what my feelings were. Well, fourteen years earlier I'd told Mark I wouldn't be a replacement player in that earlier dispute, and nothing had changed my mind, but I hadn't intended to say *anything* publicly. I'd sneaked into the meeting through a back door after taking the train to New York and then going to the midtown hotel in a nondescript van (I was still sensitive on the "transportation" question), and I wanted to leave town the same way. I had even discussed with the association how I could pull this off, because I had come to be informed, not to inform.

It didn't work out that way. First, a group of photographers was ushered into the meeting room, which surprised me. Then, after the meeting, the path to my van via the back door was blocked by a group of reporters. What could I do? I stopped on the sidewalk and said, "If it's replacement players, it's not major league baseball, and I won't be playing."

If they played and I didn't, would the streak be over? I didn't really care. Let the baseball historians argue over how those games with replacement players would have affected my streak. Matters became even more complicated when the Orioles' owner Peter Angelos announced that he wouldn't even field a replacement team, and he cited my situation. He said he'd forfeit all the games if he had to—a *strong* show of support. I appreciated this.

Looking back, I'd say that maybe the players should have finished the '94 season. Looking back, practically everyone would have to admit that, I guess. But I don't fault the decision to strike in August, because striking was our last resort to force the owners to negotiate, because real negotiations weren't taking place. Once the '94 season was history, I just wanted to get the issues resolved and get back to work. As the time for spring training approached, I was driving Kelly crazy, working out for six hours a day, taking phone calls on the progress of the negotiations, gearing up for—what? I didn't know. It was rough. The whole thing was just a terrible mess. Just two years after the long strike in 1981, the Orioles had drawn two million fans for the first time, but in 1994, Tony Gwynn lost his chance at hitting .400 for a season; Ken Griffey, Jr., Matt Williams, and Frank Thomas lost their chances to challenge Roger Maris's record for home runs in a season; Frank Thomas lost his chance for the Triple Crown in hitting; with 16 wins and an ERA of 1.56, Greg Maddux was having the best season on the mound since Bob Gibson in 1968. A great season had been ruined, and we couldn't take for granted that all the fans would return immediately. I don't know whether everyone in the game understood this, but most of us did. The game was going to have to do some serious rebuilding to earn back the faith of the fans.

Nobody understood that climate better than Jim Traber, my former teammate and basketball and hockey competitor whom we've already met in these pages. By this time, Jim was a radio personality in Oklahoma City after finishing a baseball career that, like so many others, didn't work out quite like he would have wanted. In 1988, he was sent down to Rochester the same day Senior was fired, then called back a couple of days later, then sent down again after a few more games. Back and forth the whole season, and that's how things were going for him with the Orioles. Of course, a major part of his problem was being a first baseman in the same organization as Eddie Murray. Many times he asked to be traded, but it never happened. If he had come up through another organization, who knows, Jim might have had a long career as a first baseman, because he had good numbers when he got sustained playing time. He wishes he'd gotten a better chance, but at the same time he doesn't have patience with players who whine about how things turned out. That's the nature of the professional game, Jim says. Some guys—I'm a good example—are in the right place at the right time, and some aren't.

Finally, though, Jim finally found what might be his natural home, on the radio. "I was a pretty good ballplayer," Jim likes to quip, "but I'm *terrific* on the radio." During the strike he got an earful on his talk show at KXXY in Oklahoma City, and he still gets it almost every time the subject of baseball comes up. Why does there seem to be so much more anger at baseball than at the other sports, all of which have also had their labor problems? One obvious answer Jim hears is that the other labor hassles have done a better job of staying behind the scenes; crucially, those sports never lost their equivalent of the World Series. Beyond this, Jim has figured out that people feel baseball is *easier* to play than the other games, and they don't think ballplayers should complain or negotiate for still more money while already making a lot to play a game that doesn't look all that difficult. Jim runs into this attitude all the time, and his listeners aren't impressed when he tells them that he played basketball at an All-State level in high school, that he was the starting quarterback at Oklahoma State University, and that neither job or sport is nearly as difficult as being a consistent hitter in professional baseball.

By the time we finally did get back to work in 1995—no actual contract, of course, just a favorable court ruling for the players—the Orioles had a new manager. Johnny Oates was out, Phil Regan was in. Johnny had done a good job with us, but the front office people don't consult players before they fire managers, nor should they. When I heard the news in September, I called my former boss to tell him good-bye. I told him it wasn't his managing that kept us from winning a title from 1991, when he took over from Frank Robinson, through 1994. Maybe we would have won in '94. When the strike began we were in second place in the AL East, only six and a half games behind the Yankees. We had a good record, 63-49. We had had winning records in '92 and '93 as well. But for whatever reason, it didn't work out for Johnny. Managers *are* hired to be fired—and it seems as if this is even more likely these days.

Phil Regan had been the pitching coach for Cleveland, where he was responsible for shifting Jose Mesa from the starter's role he had struggled to fill in Baltimore to the closer's role he excelled at with the Indians. Jose had always had a great fastball, but as a starter, he'd had trouble getting his curve over. As a closer, forget the curve and gas 'em for one inning. That was a great move for Phil, Jose, and that ball club. In Baltimore, when spring training got under way three weeks late in 1995, Phil and I sat down to discuss the team and the streak. I was scheduled to pass Gehrig's mark in September. Phil said he'd probably sit me down in the late innings of blowouts. I said fine, and that was probably the last conversation we had on that subject until the week of the celebration, although there was one little blowup when Phil told some writers one afternoon that someday, after the streak was over with, I'd have to take a day off. The story came out, "Regan says Cal needs a day off."

Until the big numbers went up on the warehouse beyond the right field wall at Camden Yards, ten games before the big night, a visitor to the Orioles clubhouse wouldn't have known any kind of record was in the works for one of us on the team. Hank Aaron had feared that his quest to break Babe Ruth's home run record had been distracting for the Braves. I didn't want that to happen with the Orioles in 1995. My situation was a nonsubject on the team. I'd realized the year before, when I reached the 2,000 games mark, that this all might build up into a pretty big deal, but I hoped the Orioles would be playing well enough so that all the focus come September would be on the pennant race. It didn't turn out that way. We struggled until the last month or so, when it was too late.

Things would be normal for the team, but I realized from the first day in Florida that they weren't going to be normal for me. I walked onto the field in Sarasota for the first time and photographers were everywhere. Chaos. Bedlam. I gave the eye to John Maroon, our new director of public relations, and said, "John, I thought you'd be more prepared." I was joking, but I guess we didn't know each other well enough yet, and he took me seriously. He'd been hired less than a week earlier; when the strike was called off—not settled, called off—all of us were on our way to Florida on a few days' notice. John and I had talked for a grand total of about ten minutes on the flight down. By the end of the whole thing, we knew each other very well.

But how could John have been prepared? No one knew what to expect. On the field that first day, John got things organized quickly, and then we had the first official press conference—fifty reporters and twenty cameramen, all jammed into a little room. I announced that I was going to retire in order to play professional basketball, everyone laughed, and I understood right then that the coverage was probably going to be supportive. In fact, that support even increased as the year progressed, and as everything built into a huge deal, I came to a deeper understanding of the power of the media. It would be easy to think of it as a little scary.

By comparison, *The New York Times* featured this headline on the front page of the sports section on May 3, 1939: "Gehrig Voluntarily Ends Streak at 2,130 Straight Games." The following day there was a small follow-up piece. That was it for the moment. The big headlines came weeks later when the diagnosis was announced.

Once the season started, John Maroon approached me with the idea of meeting with the local media on the first afternoon in every city we visited. He got that idea from the PR guy with the Texas Rangers, who had dreamed up the format for Nolan Ryan on his farewell tour of the league. The press conference would be the perfect way for me to get all the streak questions out of the way on the first day, so I could then have the next two days "off." The PR guy for the home club would make an announcement about the press conference to all the media. The local radio and TV women and men would get a quick pre-game interview; other than that, no one-on-ones. All other questions during that series would be about the ball games, assuming I didn't fall and break a leg.

It seemed presumptuous to me. Who said the local media in every city would be interested? John pointed to the scene in Florida and suggested that I'd be naive to think they wouldn't be. He was persuasive, but I stalled until Minneapolis, where there was a lot of interest on our first road trip.

After that scene, John asked me quietly, "Can we just try the press conference idea for one trip?"

"Yes."

The plan worked great. If the team bus was scheduled to arrive at 4:30, we set the conference for an hour earlier in the dugout, where I thought I'd be most comfortable. We'd also be in and out of the dugout before any of the other players came onto the field, so there would be no disruption to them. John used a device called a multibox, into which every reporter plugged his or her microphone, and I wore a single clip-on mike. That was great, especially considering the alternative: a dozen mikes in my face. The average turnout around the league for this local press conference was fifteen people, and the format worked out perfectly. The reporters got what they wanted and needed, and I was still allowed to play baseball.

The questions were pretty much the same in every city:

"Do you know much about Lou Gehrig?"

"Are you going to end the streak when you've broken the record?"

"What about the suggestion that you take a seat after you've *tied* the record, as a way to honor Lou Gehrig and the other old-time players?"

"What was your closest call with an injury?"

I tried to think about each question in a new way every time, so I could answer it as if I'd just heard it for the first time. I believe I succeeded, for the most part. My inherently analytical makeup served me well. Every time, I explained that I had intentionally avoided learning a great deal about Gehrig because I wasn't playing in these games to break his record. I really wasn't. At the time, I only knew the rough outline of his story. I mainly knew that he was one of the greatest players ever, and that it was strange to be compared to him in that regard when the only comparison I could see was our love of playing the game.

Now I know a lot more about the Iron Horse. His disease, unidentified at the time, struck quietly in 1938, when he was only thirty-five years old—my age in 1995. His numbers were good that year, but Gehrig wasn't good, he was great. A hitter with a lifetime average of .340 hit .295 in '38. His power was down. Something was wrong, and by the following spring, he could no longer play the game at all. On April 30, he told Joe McCarthy he couldn't continue. The following day was an off day, so May 2, 1939, in Detroit was the official end of the streak, the first game since May 31, 1925, in which Gehrig hadn't played for the New York Yankees. The answer to the trivia question about the man who replaced him in the lineup that day is Ellsworth "Babe" Dahlgren, who in 1995 lived in California, where the press found him. He died in 1996.

At some point in the hotel in Detroit, Gehrig began an unfinished letter to his wife. It's now in the library at the Baseball Hall of Fame in Cooperstown. It reads in part:

> My sweetheart—and please God grant that we may ever be such—for what the hell else matters—That thing yesterday I believe and hope was the turning point in my life for the future as far as taking life too seriously is concerned—It was inevitable, although I dreaded the day, and my thoughts were with you constantly—How would this affect you and I—that was the big question and the most important thought underlying everything. I broke just before the game because of thoughts of you—not because I didn't know you are the bravest kind of partner, but because my inferiority grabbed me and made me wonder and ponder if I could possibly prove myself worthy of you—As for me, the road may come to a dead end here, but why should it?—Seems like our backs are to the wall now, but there usually comes a way out—where, and what, I know not, but who can tell that it might not lead right out to greater things?—Time will tell. . . .

The Iron Horse had character. I was interested to learn that many doctors and nurses who treat Lou Gehrig's disease today say the same thing about the great majority of their patients. These men and women always seem to confront their situation with grace and dignity.

A lot of people may not realize that the end of Gehrig's streak of 2,130 consecutive games was also the end of his career. He played three more innings in an exhibition game in Kansas City, and that was it. Within a few weeks he was diagnosed at the Mayo Clinic in Minneapolis with amyotrophic lateral sclerosis, an incurable paralysis that soon became known as Lou Gehrig's disease. There was and is no cure, and the former first baseman knew this. He spent the rest of that year sitting on the Yankees bench in his uniform. July 4 was Lou Gehrig Appreciation Day at Yankee Stadium, and the honoree, normally a man of few words, responded with a thank-you speech that no one who heard it or has seen Gary Cooper deliver his slightly modified version in *The*

Pride of the Yankees would ever forget. Gehrig said, "Fans, for the past two weeks you have been reading about a bad break I got. Yet today, I consider myself the luckiest man on the face of the earth. I have been in ballparks sixteen years, and have never received anything but kindness and encouragement from you fans." Then he gestured toward his current and former teammates on the Yankees and said, "Wouldn't you consider it an honor just to be with such great men for even one day? Sure I'm lucky! . . . When you have a father and mother who work all their lives so that you can have an education and build your body—it's a blessing. When you have a wife who has been a tower of strength and shown more courage than you dreamed existed—that's the finest I know. So I close by saying that I might have had a tough break, but I have an awful lot to live for."

Babe Ruth, four years into his own retirement, was present that afternoon in the house that he built. The two men were not close friends, but Ruth hugged Gehrig and cried. Three months later, behind Joe DiMaggio, the Yankees won their fourth consecutive World Series, with Gehrig watching from the bench. Two years later, when they won their next title, Lou Gehrig had already died.

I told the reporters that I believed sitting down after I had *tied* Lou Gehrig's mark—one "respectful" suggestion—would *dishonor* both of us by implying that the record was a purpose and not a by-product of my simple desire to go out and play every day, which had been Gehrig's desire, too. Lou Gehrig would *not* have wanted me to sit out a game as a show of honor. No athlete would. Take that to the bank.

Someone will break my record one day. Nobody believes me when I say that, but I do believe it, and I want this guy to *break* the record. I don't want him to *tie* it.

The moment the strike was lifted in 1995 and the quick calculation revealed that I'd break the record in September of that year, if all went well, the phones started ringing in the office I'd set up a couple of years earlier as the streak publicity began to build. I do enjoy certain elements of business, and I guess I'm technically a businessman, although I'm one hundred percent baseball player during the season. Baseball I understood and knew how to handle—most of the time—but what about all this other stuff? I hired Ira Rainess, a lawyer out of my agent Ron Shapiro's office, to help me exercise some control over my business affairs and requests for my time. Early in '95, our small staff answered phones all day long and still found it literally impossible to handle the rising tide of incoming calls. So we began putting together a bigger staff to get to work. Now I don't know how I'd get along without this special crew; they do a great job and often carry the ball for me for quite some distance. During streak summer, working in partnership with the Orioles' PR staff, they made everything go unbelievably smoothly. They worked sixteen-hour days, seven days a week.

I also saw some of these business opportunities outside baseball as opportunities to set up life *after* baseball. I don't know what that life will be, but I won't sit around the house all day, that's for sure. I've been fortunate, and financially I'll be comfortable and secure, but my makeup is to do things. I've focused all my energy and dedication for my whole adult life on baseball, and I'll have to refocus in some other area at some point. I like the idea of developing relationships with a variety of people in a variety of fields in order to create a variety of options for my second career. This is typical of me: plan, sort through, know my options. I've got a lot of resources, and it makes sense to explore.

Kelly and I had also set up a foundation, and business deals would help to fund our projects. We had established the Ripken Learning Center, an adult literacy project that was doing great work. In 1989, Mayor Kurt Schmoke announced a war on illiteracy, declaring that Baltimore would become The City That Reads, and Kelly and I came up with another program to tie in with this initiative: the "Reading, Runs and Ripken" program that cashed in with contributions for every homer (now RBI) I hit. I hosted a Winterfest for Literacy that raised $225,000 for the learning center.

In my elementary school "autobiography" I wrote, "Reading is essential to become a baseball player. You have to be able to read a contract and other important papers." True enough, but you have to be able to read proficiently, period, and I was surprised to learn from touring a couple of reading centers in Baltimore that a lot of adults cannot read. And they want to. They understand how important it is. Kelly and I wanted to get involved in the mayor's initiative.

I didn't really enjoy reading in school, mainly because I had so many other things to do. It was in the minor leagues that I learned to love to read. I specialized in thrillers. Now I read better books. I may tackle a novel like *Atlas Shrugged*, recommended by center fielder Brady Anderson, who's read that huge novel at least twice. When Rachel started reading, I shopped in bookstores around the country to buy books for her and got into the habit of buying books on tape for myself. With these, I'm eclectic. I'll take on anything from Tom Clancy to Ross Perot. One advantage of these recorded books is that I don't have as much time to read now as I did in the minors, or as much as I'd like. Part of my problem timewise is that I have this weird theory about *focus*. Simply put, I think we humans have only so much focus available to us in a twenty-four-hour period. If I need mine at night for playing baseball, I don't want to squander it during the day. Reading requires focus, so I don't read much before ball games. (Of course, family matters always take top priority, no matter what's happening on the baseball end of things, and they also require focus; if we can, Kelly and I try to make the more minor decisions about house matters, etc., on the off days, when I can apply myself to smaller matters more easily.) In fact, I don't do much of anything before games, and this is true of a lot of players. I can read on the airplane *after* the game. I think this issue of focus also explains why so many ballplayers are into movies and, formerly, the soaps. On the road, I'm likely to watch two movies straight from 10 a.m. to 4 p.m., with a break for room service. When I was in the minors, motels didn't have movies on demand via cable, and television had only the three major networks. So we watched the soap operas.

Now, thanks to my kids, I know more about the Cartoon Network than about the soaps.

As the season rolled along in 1995, the phone was ringing off the hook in the office, "good luck" mail was pouring in, mostly c/o the Orioles, and everyone in my family was busy with interviews. Kelly had dozens. Mom and Dad did five television shows in one day, dozens of interviews altogether in July and August. Elly and Fred did somewhat fewer, but plenty. Somehow the family stories didn't come out quite the same every time—they never do, in any family. Someone must have done a little embellishing now and then. People were always driving slowly past Mom and Dad's house in Aberdeen, and a few got up the nerve to go to the front door asking for autographs. Playing for the Buffalo Bisons, Billy did forty-seven radio interviews. He kept count. Five in one day in August.

Wait a minute. The Buffalo Bisons? How had Billy ended up in the minors in '95? Well, he'd been hurt for a good portion of the '93 season in Texas and for most of the following year, too. He played well when he could, hitting .309 in 32 games in 1994, and figured Texas would want him back for 1995 after the strike. But they didn't. Now his options were to sign a Triple-A contract with Buffalo in the Cleveland organization or go to the camp in Homestead, Florida, for all the players who didn't have contracts, and work out and see if anyone wanted him. Neither option was all that great. Billy wanted to play in the big leagues, of course, but if that wasn't possible in the short run, he'd have to play somewhere else. He had to prove himself, and Buffalo would be good for that purpose because they needed a shortstop. Credentials at that position as well as at second base might come in handy someday. So Billy signed with Buffalo.

After seven and a half years in the majors, the most important thing then was his attitude. This is what slows down some major leaguers when they go to Japan, usually at the end of their careers: attitude. Same thing with winter ball. But Billy kept his good frame of mind and proved all over again that he's a good ballplayer. Written into his contract was a window of opportunity for July 1–10: if a major league team wanted him, he could leave the Bisons, no strings attached. As July 1 approached, he talked with every opposing manager and third base coach he could, asking if their organizations needed help in the big leagues. Ron Shapiro handled a few calls of tentative interest before July 1, then the phone went dead, and this silence really took the wind out of Billy's sails. He admitted it. He was surprised and upset. As well as he'd been playing—he wound up hitting .292 in 130 games—he thought someone would need him. But apparently they didn't. During the run-up to September 6, Billy was joking that he was getting more air time and print in one season in Triple-A while talking about me than he had in seven seasons in the majors. Toward the end, he complained about the well being dry and threatened to type up a response sheet and just fax it out to one and all.

Floyd Rayford, former roomie and the last man to replace me in the Orioles lineup, said he gave seventy-five interviews about me and the streak over the summer. Seventy-five? Sugar Bear . . .

As for myself, I didn't mind all the press conferences and interviews for the national magazines. In fact, I enjoyed them. For years I'd resisted almost every reference to the streak, because it either treated the streak as a goal, not a result, or it turned out to be negative. What's more, I'd always been very "territorial," not just about my position but about my baseball responsibilities in general. I wouldn't compromise my baseball work, and at first I was fearful about having to make those compromises in 1995. Then I accepted the situation. I got less rigid about my schedule. I realized I'd use more energy trying to overcontrol things than I would by going with the flow. I wasn't going to fight the coverage this year. I wasn't going to analyze every question to death. Usually, Kelly and I had long discussions on whether I or we should do this or that magazine piece, but this year we agreed to do almost all of them.

In fact, it was Kelly who set the tone for my new attitude. When she came down to the abbreviated spring training for a weekend, she had given me a note that read: "For once in your life, enjoy it. Let them tell you how great you are. Go with the flow." I thought she was a little hard on me with the "for once in your life" needle, but I got her general point, although I don't think people actually wanted to tell me how great *I* was. They wanted to celebrate baseball. A few writers said that just like Babe Ruth had saved baseball after the Black Sox Scandal in 1919, Cal Ripken, Jr., would have to save it this time around after the 1994 strike. That idea was silly, I thought—my mother had even stronger words—but I do think my situation became something of a focus for fans' *positive* feelings about the national pastime. They— you—were angry at all of us, but they—you—still loved baseball, and here was this streak of games that in a very tangible way tied modern baseball to old-time baseball. And the streak also tied baseball to other jobs and careers. Newspapers and magazines were full of stories about people who hadn't missed a day of work in three, four, five decades. A contest in *USA Today* declared the winner to be Herbert Christiansen, who hadn't missed a scheduled day at the hardware store in Chicago since he started the job on April 1, 1936. Unbelievable.

Ernie Tyler of the Orioles was another one of these people. Ernie is the umpires' attendant at Camden Yards, and, before that, at Memorial Stadium on 33rd Street. (He's also the father of Jimmy Tyler, our club-houseman, and Fred Tyler, who runs the visitors' clubhouse at Camden Yards.) My 2,131st consecutive game in an Orioles uniform was Ernie's 2,810th consecutive game seated behind the backstop.

I had never considered myself a prisoner of the streak, but now I did surrender to the celebration.

Chapter Seventeen

In the beginning of my career, the modest fame—a word I'm not comfortable with, but I don't know what else to call it—that came my way as a major league ballplayer in Baltimore verified that I was doing well in my chosen career. At least that was my perception, and I soaked up the attention. I really did. The appearances in shopping centers and lumberyards and the publicity caravans for the Orioles and all the TV and radio interviews were new, and I was saying yes to everything. Everything. I thought this work was part of the responsibility of being a major leaguer; I wanted to do it. But after the '83 season, when we won the World Series and I won the Most Valuable Player award, I was saturated and a little overwhelmed and really glad to get to spring training the following year. I was forced to learn how to say "No, thank you," and I said that a lot for a year or two. After regrouping, I then reemerged with a better understanding; a lot of it was just age and maturity.

In 1991, with the All-Star game and the MVP award, attention moved up to another level, and in 1993, as I've explained, it moved up to yet another level still as the consecutive games streak became a focus. By 1995, I'd gone from regular baseball fame to being more of a national figure, and this afforded me two opportunities: I rediscovered the relationship between the players and the fans, and I had a terrific opportunity to promote the game.

At the same time, I had to accept the fact that the streak had become (and still is) who I am in the public eye.

I overheard people whispering, "That's Cal Ripken. You know, the baseball player who's going to break that famous record."

"Oh, yeah. Him."

Some people would label me a "celebrity," but that's a description I'd never be comfortable with. I'm well-known in some circles, but I'm still a regular guy—a profoundly regular guy. However, I realize that sometimes people don't see me that way. They see me differently. All in all, over the past fifteen years I've seen a steady progression of changed expectations on the part of some people I meet and, sometimes, on the part of people I've known for years. It seems to me that people stereotype "fame."

In a restaurant one morning during spring training in Florida the waitress approached halfway through the meal and asked, "Are you a very famous person?"

I suppose the fact that she asked the question proved that I'm not, but I answered, "Depends on what you mean."

"Is your name Carl?"

"Cal."

"Oh, right . . . but you're such a nice person!"

You see, there's an assumption that if you're "famous," you're egotistical and not polite, maybe even arrogant. There's that stereotype, and I suppose some people who become well-known do act more important than they had before, but I hope my actions and words demonstrate that I don't believe I'm different from everyone else. Some of the things that have happened to me are unique, but, basically, they haven't changed me. And now, post-streak, it might be even harder for people to think of me as ordinary folks, the old Cal, whereas that's exactly how I think of myself. This is why it's always a pleasure to hear someone call me Calvin: they knew me, or knew of me, before I became a professional ballplayer.

One time in spring training a guy had five pictures to be signed. I asked, "Why five?" Well, he said, one was for a paraplegic, one was for someone who was getting a kidney transplant, one for this, one for that, and this guy himself had just found out he had MS. He said I was a motivation for all these people, and I believed him, but he was so anxious making his points that I might have wondered. Often I think to myself, Calm down, please, what's the big deal? Sometimes I'll say, "Believe me, I'm not worth getting excited over." By mentioning something that also relates to them, I try to get them to understand I'm no different than they are. If they have along a toddler at the potty training age, I might mention these hassles, and then I can see this woman or guy thinking to herself or himself, *You* change diapers? Yes, I do, and boys are harder to potty train than girls, in my limited experience.

On the other hand, I think I have a sense of what's happening in people's perception, because I'm the same way with professional basketball players. It's hero worship on my part, in a way. I elevate these guys to another level, and I don't really have any idea what they're like as people. I know Michael Jordan is a regular guy, but I just can't see him that way.

Maybe there's more to the idea of people "changing" than meets the eye. For one thing, all people change anyway as they grow older. You become the person you are as a result of the path you walk, your opportunities and experiences, the people you meet and come to know. It all shapes you and changes you. Certainly the money that has come with my own situation has afforded me certain opportunities and experiences I otherwise wouldn't have had. Travel is a good example, and my wife, Kelly, and I really enjoy our opportunities to see the rest of the world. We've been to London, Paris, Italy, Japan twice on baseball tours (and myself a third time), the Caribbean a number of times, Hawaii, a few other places.

However, people think the life of the "celebrity" is more exciting than their own. That's the impression I get. But in the end, it's not true. In fact, I'm pretty sure that my life right now isn't more exciting than most lives. It's probably more *complicated*, certainly more complicated than it used to be, and more complicated than I'd like it to be. My life growing up on the road as a kid was complicated logistically, but otherwise it was simple. Everyone in the Ripken family relied on each other. Life is a little more complex now, and for someone who prefers order, this can be uncomfortable. I've decided that the pluses that go along with fame far, far outweigh the minuses, without question, but mainly I've decided it's not nearly as great or as big a deal as a lot of people apparently believe. I wouldn't have any problem returning to anonymity.

Who I am as a person deep inside? Income and fame don't change this. They don't change basic attitudes. And they definitely don't make you or me "happier." People dream that they'd stop working if they hit the lottery. But would they really? It's a nice lump sum to put away. Most people aren't going to quit and lie back on the sofa for the rest of their lives, but they believe they would. You don't just work for a wage. You work for yourself—if you enjoy your job. As I've said, that was always a big issue with my parents. They tried to provide a stable path, but when the time came for Elly, Fred, Billy, and myself to map out our interests and figure out what we were going to do, they were going to be supportive of our choices. Dad said, "It's better to make less money and do something you really want to do."

But people apparently do believe that money will make them happier. They believe that money will solve their problems, and there's no doubt that money does solve some of them. However, there are a lot it doesn't solve, *cannot* solve, and there may be some it causes. The issues that face someone in my position may be different than those my mother and father faced while they were raising their four kids out on the road, but they're issues nevertheless. Money does not change the fact that life can be difficult. Maybe life *is* difficult, basically.

During the run-up to the streak and even afterward, my brother Fred was profiled several times as the one man in the Ripken family who wasn't into baseball. In one of these stories Fred remembered saying to me years before that he wasn't interested in getting rich, and that I'd replied that everybody wants to be rich. I don't remember saying anything like that, but when I was young and didn't understand much, I might have said something he could have interpreted that way. Fred's a motorcycle mechanic, and we've talked about finances, and in stories about the family he's talked about the lean times over the winter, waiting for the bikers who gear up in the spring and bring business to the shop he works at in Delaware, across the state line from where he and his wife and their two kids live in Havre de Grace, which is right up the road from Aberdeen. I know making a lot of money isn't important to Fred, but I've also said to him that I don't understand why he doesn't take his wonderful talent and bend it a little somehow and figure out a way to make a little more money. There's a big difference between wanting enough money to have a nice life and wanting to be rich.

A reporter asked Fred if he's envious of me. That made me smile, because at times I've been a little jealous and envious of him, especially in the mid-eighties. Fred was already married and had a child, and I felt that he had happiness and peace. Everyone wanted a piece of me then, this was a new experience, and his life looked simpler than mine. I wondered whether he understood more about the secrets of happiness.

I wasn't surprised that his long answer to that question about envy came down to one word: No. Why would my brother be envious? He sees my new situation, and he sees what goes along with it, too. I make more money than he does, but he doesn't care. Fred was ribbing me about my salary long before I was making much of a salary. My brother is a neat guy, a really neat guy, and he has very high moral convictions (after all, he punched a fan who was riding me hard in the early days at Memorial Stadium!) and high standards for everything he does. He loves his work and his family. He's a Ripken, no doubt about that, a younger version of our dad.

• • •

For the first two or three years I was in the majors, until I started dating Kelly seriously, I spent a lot of time in Aberdeen hanging out with old buddies Tony Canami and Donald Paunil. They didn't care whether I was now a baseball player. After I started dating Kelly, I got up there less often. I never returned to a high school reunion. Usually I was playing a game, of course, but the fifteenth reunion, in 1993, was in the fall. I wanted to go, but I hesitated because I wanted to go just as myself—as *Calvin*—but was afraid I couldn't. That's exactly the kind of social situation I hold back from. I wonder whether I stayed away to preserve the old memories, so that I wouldn't be confronted by different treatment. The last thing I wanted was to "make an appearance." In the end, I chickened out. I decided not to go. One old pal, Mike Thomas, flew in from the West Coast, and the afternoon of the reunion he joined our basketball game. That night he called from the party to reassure me that everything would be great if I dropped by. By then it was too late—I had baby-sitting responsibilities—although I did talk to a couple of the guys on the phone.

As it turned out, I did have a reunion of sorts two years later, in the off-season after I broke the record. I hadn't planned to, but on short notice I attended a fund-raising banquet for the Cal Ripken Museum in Aberdeen. A bunch of my high school friends had made a surprise videotape about the old days—something of a roast. Afterward, we sat around and talked privately. We had a great time. Nothing had changed. And yet it had, of course, for all of us, with jobs and families.

Maybe this sounds like a contradiction coming from a reserved person, but one of the social situations in which I'm most comfortable is signing autographs. Somehow it's easier when people come to me. My dad always told me that when I meet a baseball guy, don't hassle him, just try to learn from him. So I didn't collect many autographs, and I don't really understand why it means so much to people to have a name signed on a piece of paper, but autographing is part of baseball, and there's a flavor to it and it belongs in the game. I don't fight it at all. I accept it, and I really enjoy it. I love the banter, and when a kid's face lights up with joy, this makes the whole thing go. It's a selfish pleasure on my part, I admit, but how many opportunities do most people have to make someone so happy for even a brief moment? I see the look in the eyes. I also see the look in the eyes of the Make-A-Wish kids and their families when I meet them before ball games. The big picture with these kids is heartbreaking, of course, but I try to focus on the here-and-now, just like they're trying to do. It's all they have, really, and if I can help make it better, I will.

Before I got married, I sat in my car in the parking lot and signed after games, sometimes for an hour or more. After the wedding, this became more difficult, obviously, but I did what I could. On most nights, I got home way after midnight regardless. The situation was manageable. But starting in 1991 it became less so, and I shifted my signing inside the stadium so I could incorporate it into my pre- and post-game routine. In 1995, I signed for an hour after some games; sometimes two hours. I signed before games if I had the chance. I was treated all around the country as if I were a hometown player, and I rediscovered the beauty of the relationship between fans and players.

I sign balls, bats, baseball cards, scorecards, snapshots and big glossy pictures, homemade and commercial posters, magazines, *Time* Man of the Year mock-ups, books (except unauthorized biographies), ticket stubs, jerseys, sweaters, caps, gloves, helmets, pennants, Wheaties boxes, a million other items, and—my favorites—little scraps of paper and smashed popcorn boxes with sneaker prints that can have only one purpose: holding a real memory for someone, maybe for a lifetime.

If I'm signing in blue ink, someone will want black. If I'm signing in black ink, someone will want blue, emphatically: "No! Blue ink!" Occasionally someone calls me "Mr. Ripken." More often it's, "Nice and big, please, Cal."

"Please! Please!" I can hear the anxiety behind the voice. This person has been waiting two hours before the game, and he's being crushed by the hundreds of other autograph-seekers who got there later and are trying to make up for lost time.

"I've been here two hours!"

"I've been here three hours!"

"I've been here *four* hours!"

"Cal, I can't reach!"

"I love you, Cal!"

"Quit pushing me!"

"I was here first!"

"No, I was!"

"For my sister's best friend's brother, Cal!"

"Don't yell! He's right here!"

"Have a good season!"

"Gonna make the squad this year, Cal?"

A wiseguy.

"Marty Kaminsky, Cal. Remember me? I interviewed you two months ago on the telephone."

"I'm stretching my memory." (Without success.)

Sometimes fans ask me to sign money, and I will sign a dollar bill. I won't sign a $100 bill. I have a problem with that—too much money—and sometimes people don't understand.

"Please reconsider," they urge.

"I'm sorry you don't understand, but please consider my feelings. Don't you have anything else at all? I'll sign that. Maybe your business card."

It's always something while autographing. Some people will say anything to get the autograph, I know that. But I usually sign anyway. It's a game, and I think everyone has fun. I know I do.

"Can I have this for my brother? He's sick."

"Yeah, what's he sick of?"

"Oh, he's got a fever."

"Well, what is it?"

"Whadya mean?"

"Is it ninety-nine degrees? A hundred and one? Hundred and three?"

Now all the other people are laughing, and he says, "No, really," and I say, "I believe you." Maybe I do, maybe I don't.

Or, "This is for my friend in Edgetown, Maryland."

"You mean Edgewood? Or maybe Edgewater? Or Edgemere? I've never heard of Edge*town*."

I do have to leave, eventually—maybe my Grand Slam breakfast has worn off, and I might have gone from early morning until late afternoon without a meal—and when I start thinking about this, people will sense it, and things can get hectic. Inevitably, someone has an objection. I say, "Ma'am, I'd like to please everyone, but I don't know how to do it. Do you have any suggestions? How can I make everybody happy?"

That's another one of those questions without an answer. I'm happy and willing to give people as much time as possible, but I do have to leave eventually. I do have to eat! I take the time to explain the situation. I don't think I've ever gotten angry even if I thought someone was hassling me unfairly. I hope I haven't. I've developed patience. I think I'm a good person—I think most people are—and I try to do what I believe is right, because I am sensitive to what people think of me. I know that a thousand hours of politeness can be wiped out by two seconds of doing bad. I watch what I do.

Today my own experience autographing and bantering with the fans is almost always great, but back when either the team or I or both were struggling, there was a good chance I'd hear about it, something like, "You know, Cal, you need to take a day off. You're really hurting the team."

I wish I could have said what Dad said—"That's your opinion, which doesn't make it a fact"—but I was more polite.

Or the guy might have said, "You know, Cal, you haven't hit a homer in twenty-six games."

To that I might have answered with Larry Sheets's favorite line: "Thanks for reminding me." I might have been aware of the slump, but maybe not the exact number of homerless games. I might also have said, "Sir, I guarantee you I'm trying and working hard to correct my problem. Can you guarantee me that if I take a day off the next day will be any better than today was? I don't believe that. I work extra hard. I don't want to run away and hide from either you or the pitcher."

But who wants to put himself in that position? There are times when it's tempting for a player to hide from the fans, even though this takes him away from the people—kids—who want the autograph for all the right reasons. Besides, the windows of opportunity for signing before games is very small, and I don't think fans understand this. They see guys run into the dugout an hour before the game and automatically figure they're ducking the autographs. Maybe they are, but maybe they aren't. Maybe they have to get treatment or attend a meeting. After the game may be the time for more treatment or an exercise regimen. I've always been pretty accessible, but I'm also serious that my baseball work isn't compromised. All the guys are.

I know some people in baseball have talked about establishing a built-in time for autographing for all players. As a post-strike policy, a few organizations send out a small, rotating group of players before every game. This is okay, but if a guy doesn't believe in autographs, for whatever reason, I'm not challenging that. For one thing, if the player doesn't want to be out there, is it going to be fun for the fans? And a lot of guys are turned off by the memorabilia market—the fact that they're asked for an autograph not because they're appreciated but in order to create value for a product. I say the autograph has been part of the game forever; its *meaning* may be different for some people. And I don't want to develop a prejudice against collectibles because fans' interest in collectibles is genuine, too. I don't claim to understand passionate collecting, but I respect it and I appreciate it.

On the other hand, I don't like to be *overly* targeted by the dealers, and a beneficial by-product of signing in the stadium is that collectors have a tougher time. But it happens. I've watched kids come up, I sign for them, they go back behind the crowd, and soon here comes another kid from the same spot behind all the other people. The guy wants to be out of the way, but close enough to keep an eye on his courier. This doesn't have to happen very often before I know that a dealer is back there paying a little kid one or two bucks, sometimes five, I've been told. Sometimes I'll see the exchange. Usually someone with the Orioles or a security guy tries to monitor this, and they'll let me know. I try to recognize the collectors and get a feel for their items, and I try not to let them hit me too hard. But I'm not going to get paranoid about collectors.

Wayne Radi, a fan in Thurmont, Maryland, west of Aberdeen, opened a Cal Ripken Museum above his Signature Shoppe. In Pennsylvania, Bill Haelig, a commercial insurance underwriter, has what's supposed to be the world's largest collection of Cal Ripken stuff—over five thousand items. That makes him the king of the Cal-ectors, to use the term favored by Cal-ectors. I've met Bill briefly a couple of times here and there—a nice guy. Other collectors all over the country are supposed to be close behind him in number of items owned, some of them spending thousands of dollars for various items. Carolyn and Don Harrison in Hampton, Virginia, publish an illustrated index of Ripken memorabilia. It's eighty-four pages long. A couple of the rarer items are the 1988 "Ripkin" typo card printed by Classic but never sold, and the Ajax dog food card, an unlicensed item from 1983.

Why should I penalize someone who really wants an autograph enough to pay for it? I shouldn't, but it's hard to differentiate the good from the bad in the market. There's forgery and money changing hands all the time in various cons. I don't like to be in that market, and that's why I have a contract with a company that sells *authorized* autographed baseballs commemorating the streak. It's easier and up-front. The signature is guaranteed to be real.

One place I'm a hard case is in a restaurant with my wife and/or kids. If I'm alone or with another player, I'm fair game, but I try to maintain some normalcy as husband and father, and signing autographs is not normal. I could pass along a lot of restaurant stories, but I'll restrict myself to one of my favorites, because it has such a strange kicker. One night in New York, right when things were really taking off in 1995, Kelly and I, Brady Anderson, his girlfriend, and a couple of other friends were at a restaurant on the Upper East Side in New York, after a game at Yankee Stadium. The minute we sat down the requests started coming in. People outside the restaurant were telling sad stories to people coming in, trying to get these other diners to ask me for an autograph. And these people in the restaurant were doing it!

"There's the cutest little kid outside. His parents asked me to do this for him."

I had to explain that this group outside was a remnant of the same crowd for whom I'd just signed at the stadium. I didn't want to bring attention to myself and involve the entire restaurant in my situation. That would have been pretty rude. In the end, though, the entire restaurant *was* involved, and I thought people were wondering why I wasn't signing autographs. When our party left, everyone inside was looking out the window to see what was going to happen next. There was a big crowd out on the sidewalk. A real New York street scene, and by this time, of course, I felt some pressure to sign because everyone both outside and inside wanted me to. I told everyone on the sidewalk that if they allowed me to do this calmly and stay under control, fine, I'd sign. And I did.

Now here's the weird kicker. In the men's room, Brady ran into a guy claiming that all the people outside the restaurant were waiting for *him*. He was bragging, "How did they know I was here? Gee, I can't go *anywhere*."

Chapter Eighteen

Despite the ceremonies for the 2,000th game the year before, despite the steady buildup during the summer in 1995, breaking the Gehrig record remained somehow *hypothetical* in my mind until the huge banners with the number 2123 dropped onto the brick wall of the old warehouse just beyond the right field fence at Camden Yards on August 29. Only eight games to go? Breaking Lou Gehrig's record was no longer hypothetical. This number on the wall made everything very real, and now I did feel real pressure to go ahead and finish this business off. What if something happened this last week? It would be ridiculous. John Maroon, the team's PR guy who had been at my side for the whole summer, more or less, said he could tell that the dropping of the new number every night of the homestand "hit me hard," and he was right. That was a powerful emotion.

The banner numbers were a great idea, a takeoff on what the Indians did in Cleveland as Eddie Murray approached his 3,000th hit, but I was skeptical about the idea at first. As with the press conference in every city around the league, it seemed a little presumptuous, but everyone assured me otherwise, and I guess they were right. These last games of the streak, concluding with 2,131, the record-breaking game, were a homestand for the Orioles against the West Coast teams, and this scheduling wasn't completely an accident, as I understand it. The Orioles wanted the two big nights to be at home, and of course I wanted to break the record at home, if at all possible. This was a consideration, and I'm pretty sure the timing of 2,131 as the last game of a homestand was also intended. But the danger with this schedule was that any rainout earlier in the season would push the record-breaking game into our next road trip. There was a lot of concern about this a few times. We probably played a couple of games that would've been postponed by rain if it hadn't been for this consideration.

For the first night or two of the homestand at Camden Yards, the fans didn't know what to expect with the numbers, but after the pattern had been set—first the John Tesh music when the game became official, then the explanation on the scoreboard of what constitutes an official game (four and a half innings if the home team is winning, five if the visitors are ahead, and even I got confused once or twice when a particular game was official)—the fans were primed for the unfurling of the new number. I was usually in the field, embarrassed, of course, not really knowing what to do other than doff my cap. Different moments from my career flashed through my mind every night. I remembered stuff I hadn't thought about for years, some of which I've now written about in this book. It became a time of reflection, mainly, but when the more emotional memories came up, I tried to fight those back. I was still on the field, active in a game, and I didn't want to get emotional in the middle of some crucial play. In that sense, the countdown was usually counterproductive for me.

For weeks prior to the final nights, I'd been doing five or six interviews or *something* before each home game, starting in early to midafternoon, with almost everything done at the ballpark. Only a few interviews or photo shoots were at my house. At the ballpark, the locker used for most of these shoots was actually a prop installed in the auxiliary locker room down the hallway from the Orioles clubhouse. This locker looked perfectly authentic, complete with uniforms, gloves, shoes, boxes of supplies, a change of clothes, unidentifiable odds and ends. A couple of times in August there were two setups at the same time: one photographer or TV guy working at my "locker," another one set up across the room with a different prop, waiting.

Just like with the press conferences, I put a new twist on every answer to the same question by thinking about it differently every time. Or at least I tried to, because it didn't seem fair to shortchange the fourth or fifth interview of the day simply because it *was* the fourth or fifth interview. That summer happened to produce a bumper crop of fruits and vegetables in the Aberdeen area, so the lucky reporters left Camden Yards with a box of Senior's delicious Better Boy tomatoes.

As you'd imagine, there was press everywhere as we approached the final games. John Maroon had anticipated issuing 350, maybe 400 media credentials for those games. He handed out 750. Right in the thick of the buildup, John surprised me by saying one afternoon as we trooped around, "Don't take this the wrong way, Cal, but I'm not sure I'd want to be you." I answered, "Well, it's a trade-off. Some things I can't do now, but people treat me very well." I *was* treated wonderfully everywhere I went in 1995, and one way I thought I could reciprocate was to sign as many autographs as possible. Earlier in the summer I had started signing for an hour, occasionally as long as two hours, after the games. I decided to do this on my own; I didn't consult anyone, but just started telling the security guards before the game that I'd be signing after the game. But in early August, the club asked me to stop doing it because the security people couldn't control the crowd, which started lining up in the third inning above our dugout on the first base line. By the late innings the line went all the way up through the box seats and then out through the concession arcade. Nice and orderly, but when the game ended, fans who had been sitting in those first base box seats rushed forward for the best position at the rail, and the fans who'd been in line for five or six innings got angry. Two women duked it out, I was told, so I understood the decision to call off the post-game signing sessions, but the announcement over the PA system didn't provide any explanation and left the impression, to my mind, that this had been an arbitrary decision on my part, an untrue impression that I regretted.

Maybe a week before the end, I stopped doing the pre-game interviews, substituting one big post-game interview. And one camera followed me everywhere. Otherwise, I held to a pretty routine schedule, trying to focus on baseball but also flashing back every night when the number dropped.

However, I did have to write the thank-you speech I would give after I broke Gehrig's record. I try to be disciplined about my obligations, but for some reason I had put this off until almost the last minute. After our game with Seattle on Sunday, three days before 2,131, Ira Rainess sat on the stool by my locker and took notes as I outlined what I wanted to say. The following afternoon—Labor Day—I met with Ira, Ron Shapiro, and the folks who work in my office to hammer out a real draft. It was a miserably hot day, and, because of the long holiday weekend, the air-conditioning in the building had been shut off since Friday. It may even have been hotter inside the building than outside, and don't ask me why we didn't do the smart thing and adjourn to a cool restaurant or somebody's house, because I don't know.

The group wrote three or four drafts altogether, with me practicing my delivery aloud, tailoring the words as we went. I'd given a lot of speeches over the years, but never before an audience this size—a full house at Camden Yards and a national television audience. Even without the sweltering conditions in the unair-conditioned office, I was already sweating bullets, worrying about whether I'd be thrown off by the public address system, which causes a brief delay between spoken word and broadcast, worrying whether I'd be able to talk about my parents and my family without my emotions getting the better of me. I did not want to break down on the big night.

So whom to thank? I thought about this question two ways, in terms of who I am as a person *and* as a player. The answers were pretty clear to me. As a person, I'm totally indebted to my parents, my wife, and my children. Obviously, I would try to convey my debt and appreciation and love to them. As a player, well, from Senior I'd learned how to play the game, and from Eddie Murray I learned how to be a major leaguer. Eddie was the man. Eddie was the reason I played all these games, because he played all the games when he wasn't hurt! Here was a guy who epitomized playing and winning at the major league level. As the great clutch hitter, he was expected to be on the field on a daily basis, and he impressed on me the same responsibility as a shortstop hitting in the middle of the lineup. If the manager wants you to play, you have to play if at all possible. As I've said many times, the streak was an *approach* to the game, which was much more important than the fact that I was lucky enough to play all these games in a row. Eddie taught me this approach. Thanking Eddie Murray was a privilege.

Acknowledging the great fans of the Orioles was another easy call. And finally, of course, Lou Gehrig, who was called on to be courageous in a way that most of us can only hope we'd measure up to.

I had wanted the Orioles to be in the pennant race on the nights of September 5 and 6. For one thing, it would have been the best possible way to keep the focus where it belonged, on the ball games. Unfortunately, we were more or less out of the race by mid-August, if not mathematically eliminated, although in late July we'd been in the hunt, four or five games behind Boston, playing .500 ball. Then there was a steady slippage. By the time of the record-breaking homestand the first week in September, we were sixteen games behind the Red Sox. Honestly, I would have traded all the hoopla for an exciting pennant drive, but that wasn't to be. That's the reason the streak week games had an atmosphere something like Opening Day and the All-Star game—celebrations of baseball—as opposed to the atmosphere at the playoffs and the World Series, where there's also a real seriousness and something truly at stake. I'll always wonder how that week in September would have played out if the Orioles had been playing for the pennant.

If we couldn't be in contention, second best would be for the Orioles to play well those two nights, at least, and for me to play well, too, and this scenario played out perfectly. It couldn't have played out any better, in fact, beginning in the second inning on September 5 against California, when Chris Hoiles, Jeff Manto, Mark Smith, and Brady Anderson hit solo shots, and the crowd went wild. The streak celebration would have been fun regardless, but I think it helped that the fans had some good baseball on the field to celebrate as well. The players were pumped up, too, by now, and they wanted to perform well before the full houses. And they did. Those four homers set the tone. Then Brady Anderson caught the fly ball that ended the top of the fifth inning—Brady still has that ball—making the game official since we were ahead. I had tied the record. I was back in the dugout for our half of the inning when they cued the John Tesh music and the number 2,130 dropped into place and Camden Yards just exploded. Exploded! In the dugout, there were handshakes and hugs all around and I came out for the first of I don't know how many waves to the crowd. I waved to my parents and Elly and Fred and Billy, and I caught Kelly's eyes, sitting in the box to the left of the dugout.

All of the emotion of the year was wrapped up in these two or three seconds between my wife and me. As I've said, during the baseball season it can be hard for a player's family to get in sync, especially with kids. The guy's playing all over the country and they're at home doing their own thing. But, ironically, maybe, all the streak business and preparations and interviews that summer made that part of my job a lot easier. In 1995, baseball brought Kelly and me together, and somehow those few seconds of eye contact summed up a season for us. It was a surprisingly private moment in a very public place. For Kelly, that night was bigger than the next one when I broke the record, which she described as getting married for a second day in a row. I noticed her tears.

The next inning I was fortunate to put the icing on the 2,130 cake. Mark Holzemer hung a slider to me and I got just enough of the pitch to lift it over the left field wall. When I hit the ball, I didn't think it was

going out. When it did drop two rows beyond the 364 sign, that was gratifying, because I did want to play well in these games. In the first place,
I've never been a great spotlight performer. I've talked about how I generally struggle when I'm really trying to do well, especially in All-Star
games, and this was probably a bigger spotlight than I'd ever had. And I
was thinking about the remark I've mentioned to the effect that the
streak was a matter of will, not talent. The streak had become who I was
as a baseball player. Performing well in these games wasn't a *necessity*—
I thought my overall record as a shortstop and a hitter should speak for
itself—but my performance had been overshadowed in recent years. To
be able to hit a homer on September 5, after hitting one the night
before as well, and for us to win this game 8–0 behind Scott Erickson—
great, really great. I probably can't over-emphasize how important that
was to me going into this series with the Angels. It would have been a
lot different—for me, definitely, and I think for the fans as well—if I
couldn't get the ball out of the infield and the games were miserable for
the Orioles.

I knew that an assortment of gifts were going to be presented after
the record-tying game, but I didn't know what. Usually, I would have
insisted on knowing, but as with everything else that year, I decided to
set aside my penchant for analysis and control. Kelly had been involved
in this part of the week's activities, and everyone promised I wouldn't be
embarrassed, so I was ready for anything, even the PG-13 spoof by two
of the actors on *The Young and the Restless*, one of Mom's favorite
soaps—and mine, too, in the minors—in which Melody Scott Thomas
is impressed by Brad Carlton's description of my Iron Man's endurance
and stamina. Don Diamont, the actor who plays the hunk role of Brad
Carlton, is a good friend who's played some basketball with us at the
gym. When he showed up one year at brother Billy's Super Bowl party,
Mom whispered to me, "Is that who I think it is?" I said, "I think it is."

I got a lot of cool gifts that night, including, compliments of Dave
Letterman, direct from the home office in Grand Rapids, Michigan, my
very own Top Ten list of reasons I needed a day off (number one: my

jock was full of stadium mustard); one of Joan Jett's gold records; jerseys from Hammerin' Hank Aaron, Ernie Banks, Baltimore Colts' immortal quarterback Johnny U. (Unitas, of course), University of Maryland coach Gary Williams, and number one NBA draft choice Joe Smith; a speedskating uniform from Bonnie Blair and a jacket from *Grease*, one of my favorite Broadway shows; a bat from Tom Selleck; a bag of team balls from every NBA squad, delivered by the Admiral himself, David Robinson; a HERE flag from Frank Robinson (a replica of the original banner that marked where Frank's drive cleared not just the fence but everything at Memorial Stadium); a Brooklyn Dodgers cap from Rex "THANK Yoooooou" Barney at the microphone in the press box; from Pam Shriver, a part-owner of the Orioles, a signed poster from all the tennis players competing at the U.S. Open that week in New York; and from the visiting Angels, delivered by former teammate Rene "Gonzo" Gonzales (the guy who tied my unofficial record for leaping the steps at the Metrodome in the fewest strides), a Walt Disney animation cell of Pluto standing on top of a pile of trophies.

And one more gift, which really touched me. Jim Gott's first victory in the major leagues with the Toronto Blue Jays was also the first game of my streak, on May 30, 1982, and Jim walked onto the field at Camden Yards to present me with that game ball. I couldn't believe this, because I know what these "firsts" mean to a baseball player. I whispered to Jim that he shouldn't do this, but he told the crowd that it was an honor to be part of what I'd accomplished. It was pretty incredible to me that he wanted to do this.

When did I finally get home that night? Late, and I collapsed, and somehow the alarm clock either didn't get set or malfunctioned, and it was a scramble to get Rachel ready for her first day of school. All of us were excited about that, and as I told one of the press conferences, Kelly had made the connection for Rachel that she and I were each having a special day on September 6. Driving her to school, we chatted about how much fun this was going to be for her. We'd already talked about some of the concerns I'd had at school, although I did withhold the information that I'd tried to run away from first grade several times. I didn't want to plant that idea in her mind.

With the rarest of exceptions when I'm in town during the season, I wake up to take Rachel to school, because this is really the only chance I get to be with her during the week. Then I go back to sleep—or try to, which was the case on September 6. On the other hand, after I gave up trying to sleep, I was pretty relaxed around the house that day. Only twelve hours and one speech to go. It was almost over.

At the park—well, I don't remember much at the park before the game. I guess I was relaxed but keyed up at the same time. Or maybe I was relaxed before I arrived, then got keyed up wondering what this night was going to be like. And I wasn't feeling great. I was hot and sweating, and our trainer Richie Bancells gave me an aspirin for the fever and a gallon of Power Ade. When President Clinton and Vice President Gore came through the clubhouse to greet everyone and congratulate me, I was embarrassed to be sweating so much. I recalled the scene from *Broadcast News* in which the character who has worked his whole life to get in front of the camera as a newscaster finally achieves this goal, but then he's sweating so much the debut performance is a humiliating disaster. Strange thought. My mind can come up with a ton of them at the oddest times.

For this night, Rachel and Ryan were down by the field with Kelly, and they threw out the first balls. Nice pitches, too, especially considering that the southpaw, Ryan, was just two years old. I was still sweating; after I kissed Rachel, she wiped off her mouth. And I was still sweating in the bottom of the fourth, with a 3–0 count against Shawn Boskie. Rafael Palmeiro had homered in the first inning to tie the game 1–1, then Bobby Bonilla in front of me in the fourth to put us ahead. I've never been much of a 3-0 hitter, and normally I would have taken that pitch, but this time I stepped out and said to myself, Keep your concentration, act like it's 2-0 if you have to, calm down, see the ball, put a good swing on it. I thought I might even be able to pull this off, because it was weird how well I was hitting the ball, starting two days before, with good focus and concentration, a state of relaxation at the plate. I'd been seeing the ball great the whole series, and I saw this one great as well, a fastball right down the middle.

On September 5, I hadn't been sure the ball was going to leave the playing field. On September 6, I was sure, because I nailed that pitch, and what a thrill that was. Going out in style, so to speak. This was extra sweet, no doubt about it. Fred told me later that he'd called both that homer and the one the previous night. Had that feeling, he said, calling each of the homers *on the pitch*. My brother the psychic.

Then Manny Alexander, playing second base, caught the third out in the top of the fifth inning, and it was official: I was the new Iron Man of baseball—or the Iron Bird, as at least one sign said. What was I expecting next? I didn't know, of course, but something like the previous night, I guess, a lot of cheering and curtain calls and an all-around great time. Our starting pitcher, Mike Mussina (Moose had calculated in July that he should have this start), had joked earlier that there'd be an hour delay. That possibility shocked me. I had tried to end the previous night's fanfare quickly, because these games were huge for the Angels. They were leading their division by five and a half games, down from eleven a month earlier. We couldn't ask Shawn Boskie to wait around for an hour for this Ripken business to conclude before pitching the bottom half of the inning.

I waved to my parents. I caught their eyes. I walked over to the box and took off my jersey to reveal the special T-shirt I'd been wearing, made by Kelly—"2130+ Hugs and Kisses for Dad." I hadn't planned this, but it seemed like a good idea at the time. I gave the jersey to my daughter, the first-grader. In the dugout, Butch Burnett, one of our clubhouse guys, was just bawling. We hugged, and now I was trying to hang on myself. I emerged from the dugout and tapped my heart with my right hand. What more could I say than that? What more could I *do*?

Rafael Palmeiro knew the answer. "You're going to have to take a lap," he said. "That's the only way they'll quit." This was one streak-related suggestion I *did* resist. Like extended antics after a home run, a "victory lap" is not exactly old-school. It was something I would never be comfortable with. And yet, maybe Rafy was right. Ten minutes after the number dropped, the fans were still going crazy. Finally, he and Bobby Bo pushed me to the top of the dugout steps and sent me on my way around the park.

On the videotape, my body language is pretty obvious. I didn't know about this at all, and at first I just wanted to get it over with. The game was waiting. But then something remarkable happened, at least it seemed that way to me. As I got close to the fans and recognized some of them and looked in their eyes and saw how happy they were and how much this moment seemed to mean to them, I was overwhelmed. By the time I had looped around the outfield and started coming back down the third base line, I slowed down. Another point of surrender to the celebration. I forgot we had four more innings to play. Let this go on forever. And right about then, the "backstage" crew played the Whitney Houston ballad, "One Moment in Time," over the PA system. I wasn't even aware of this at the time—I wasn't hearing anything—but did the music and the lyrics soak into my subconscious somehow? Were they one reason I settled down and slowed down?

Then again, I was also tired, running on empty. As I came along the third base line, I shook hands with Ron Shapiro and his associate Michael Maas and with my brother Billy and with the umpires. By that time I wanted to shake hands with each one of the forty-six thousand people in the stands, but I couldn't reach that far. I didn't have time. The Angels lined up in front of their dugout and congratulated me. This was really special, because these were my peers in the game; these were the guys who were in a pennant race and trying to beat the Orioles that night.

I had been in something of a dreamlike state when I got married, when Rachel was born, and then again when Ryan was born. This night at Camden Yards made the fourth time in my life for that strange sensation. I was *there*, and I knew it, but I was also somewhere off in the distance, surveying the scene. Not an out-of-body experience, exactly, as I understand that phenomenon, but maybe something close.

•   •   •

The Orioles went on to win the game, 4–2, with Mike Mussina getting the victory. Afterward, waiting for the on-field ceremony to begin, my parents and I visited in the tunnel behind the dugout, just the three of us. Sharing the moment, pure and simple. We didn't get into the big questions, like "What did you feel out there?" Small talk about the hot weather is more the Ripken style. To me, actions and presence speak louder than words. However, I also knew it was almost time for words from me. Mom and Dad assured me I'd be fine.

I appreciated the remarks of Mike Mussina and Brady Anderson on behalf of the Orioles—most of the other great gifts I got are in the trophy case on one wall of the dressing room in the gym, but the big rock with the number 2131 chiseled on it, a gift from my teammates, is going by the pond in our front yard—and the congratulations of all the other speakers as well. Then it was my turn, hoping I could keep my emotions under control. I had a lot of surprises that week, and one of the most pleasant was how relaxed I felt as I began by saying that the fans in Baltimore are the greatest, and this *is* the greatest place to play. For me, that's totally true. I was able to thank Mom and Dad, and Kelly, Rachel, and Ryan without choking up. I was home free! After that, thanking Eddie Murray was easy. And after acknowledging my debt to the great Lou Gehrig, I concluded, "Some may think our greatest connection is that we both played many consecutive games. Yet I believe in my heart that the true link is the common motivation of a love of the game of baseball, a passion for your team, and a desire to compete at the very highest level. I know that if Lou Gehrig is looking down on tonight's activities, he isn't concerned with someone's playing more games than he did. Instead, he's viewing tonight as just another example of what's good and right about the great American game. Whether you're name is Gehrig or Ripken, DiMaggio or Robinson, or that of some youngster who picks up his bat or puts on his glove, you are challenged by the game of baseball to do your very best, day in and day out, and that's all I've ever tried to do."

Then I felt mostly relief. Pure, blissful relief. A really sweet feeling.

Then I screwed up, unknowingly. We'd already decided that I wouldn't do any of the morning talk shows the next day—I was really, truly exhausted, and thought, Why not let the celebration and the event stand alone, on their own? Plus, it wouldn't have been fair to pick one over the other and I couldn't do them all, so we decided to do none. But at 2 a.m., who shows up outside the clubhouse door but Bob Costas, one of the best broadcasters in the business, along with a camera crew. Bob asked John Maroon if he could have an interview, and John asked me, and I said, sure, why not, one last time. The hoopla had died down by then, and I was feeling fine. I just thought of Bob as representing sports and baseball in general. Maybe he wasn't even there for the *Today* show, I don't know, but the interview ended up on that program, touted as an exclusive interview with the new Iron Man. I guess the other networks felt they got the shaft from me. It never ends.

After *this* game, Kelly did wait around for me. Not much said on the drive home. Both of us too tired, trying to put everything in perspective. In fact, we're still trying to do that, and, for my part, at least, I haven't gotten much beyond the few words Kelly and I did exchange in the car.

"Big night at the ballpark, huh?"

"Sure was."

Chapter Nineteen

The following spring, it was business as usual on the baseball field—except that it was never business as usual in 1996. There were a whole string of mini-controversies with the Orioles, and I was involved in a few of them. So much for my wish for a nice, calm season in which winning was the only exciting thing going on. Of course, the Orioles had a new manager in Davey Johnson, who'd played second base for Baltimore in the late sixties and early seventies and had won the World Series while managing the Mets. Our fans had high expectations, especially given the addition of free agent Roberto Alomar at second base, without a doubt one of best all-around players in the league.

Fast forward to May 19, when Davey Johnson mentioned to me after a victory over Seattle at Camden Yards that he was considering shifting me to third base, with B. J. Surhoff, a free agent from Milwaukee, on the disabled list with a sprained ankle and Bobby Bonilla also nursing a bad ankle. Nothing definite, Davey said, just an idea, and we left it at that on Sunday night. The discussion was purely hypothetical—and, I thought, just between Davey and me. On Monday, I came to the park early and Davey and I had a much longer conversation in the batting cage beneath the stands, in which all the angles were discussed and analyzed. Again, I thought this conversation was just between us, although Davey warned me that the story could leak.

Well, that's exactly what happened. In fact, Davey was the one who gave the story to the media, and, right on cue, the reporters descended on my locker that very afternoon. I refused comment, because I didn't know the full story. I didn't know what Davey had said. Davey acknowledged that he understood I was "perturbed" by the leak. I was—not about the move to third base, but about what I considered a violation of trust. But what could I do? On Tuesday I said to the press, "Whatever the manager asks me to do, I will do. A player is a player and a manager is a manager." I'd moved to shortstop for Earl Weaver, I'd played a few games at third for Frank Robinson in 1989 spring training, and I would move back there for Davey Johnson, if that's what he asked me to do.

Davey and I then had another conversation on Tuesday, and left the situation open. He might move me on Friday for the first game of the series against Oakland, or maybe wait until the West Coast road trip the following week, or maybe not move me at all. My brother was playing a lot of third base, and playing well. (Billy was back with the O's on a one-year contract.)

All of this was grist for the mill, naturally. Scouts said on cue to reporters what they'd been saying on cue for a decade, that I'd "lost a step" in the field. Readers were reminded that on May 14 Davey had me batting seventh in the lineup, the first time I'd been that low since my rookie year, and that a couple of weeks before that Davey had used Manny Alexander to pinch-run for me in the eighth inning of a close game against the Yankees. In that game, I'd just dumped a single into right field when Manny trotted out of the dugout. Yes, I was surprised. I'm not the fastest guy in the league, but I'm a good baserunner, and for the first time since 1981, I was not in a game that was still in doubt. Weird, weird feeling. Not a great one, either. Anyway, with Bobby Bonilla on third, Manny, who was going to try to steal, got picked off instead. Back in the dugout, he sat down next to me and I didn't say a thing. What was there to say at that moment? Tino Martinez finally won the game for the Yankees with a grand slam homer in the fifteenth inning.

I knew that Manny, our backup shortstop who occasionally played elsewhere, was unhappy with his role, and that Davey had been saying since spring training that he felt sympathy for Manny's situation, stuck as he was behind me, and that maybe this was the year he should get his opportunity to show what he could do. All these issues were hashed out in detail in every paper and on every talk show in town. Everyone seemed to agree that eventually I'd end up my career at third base. (I felt the same way, if only because I'd been reminded about the subject every year.)

And what was the big deal anyway about changing positions? people asked. Veteran players change position all the time; Robin Yount had moved from shortstop to the outfield, where he won his second MVP award; every player should be willing to move for the good of the team.

In Baltimore in 1996, comments like that were a reference not only to me but also to Bobby Bonilla, who had come over in a trade with the Mets halfway through 1995 and whom Davey Johnson wanted to make the full-time DH in '96. Let me explain this situation. In spring training, Bobby worked overtime preparing himself at two positions, right field and shortstop. He played in "B" games, he played two games a day, maybe more than once. Then, just a couple of days before we broke camp and headed north, Davey told Bobby he wanted to try him at designated hitter. In that role, Bobby slumped. When his unhappiness came out in public, people said he wasn't a team player. When he'd come over from the Mets the previous year he'd been hailed as a great team leader, but now he wasn't any kind of team player at all. I couldn't disagree more. I think Bobby Bo's a *great* team player; he wants to be in the lineup every single day. He'd never been a DH and had never pictured himself as one, nor is he the first guy to have trouble with this adjustment. Mainly, though, he was upset that he hadn't known this move was coming and hadn't had a chance to prepare.

Some people also said if Cal Ripken doesn't agree to move to third, he's not a team player. But the issue was never whether I'd agree to move to third base. In the first place, I don't have to "agree." If Davey or any other manager says jump, I jump; if he tells me put on the catcher's gear, I look for a spare mask. The question I'd discussed at length with Davey, because he'd asked my thoughts, was whether my moving would actually be good for the club. My main point was that if I had to relearn a position after fourteen years elsewhere, I'd like for this change to be for a good reason, not just as a temporary fill-in until B. J. Surhoff could return to the lineup. And things weren't desperate as they were. We were a couple of games behind the Yankees.

As it turned out, Davey didn't make the move with me and I went on a tear on the West Coast, homering three times in Seattle, tying Eddie Murray's record for career homers by an Orioles player (333), driving in eight runs. People said this was a sign of relief about staying at shortstop, but in fact it was purely coincidental. The bat came around. On June 14 in Kansas City, I broke Sachio Kinugasa's world record of 2,215 consecutive games, set in Japan.

Advance the tape two weeks and shift the scene to New York City, when our owner Peter Angelos challenged my leadership in the press, after he saw comments attributed to me prior to this four-game series against the Yankees. I was quoted as saying that the team had a lot of new parts—front office, manager, coaches, players—and needed time to gel. Angelos immediately called up a reporter and said for the record, "To suggest the lack of familiarity with two of the most respected men in baseball, [Davey] Johnson and [Pat] Gillick, and the coaching staff, is a problem is simply off the mark. It's off the mark, but more importantly, it precludes one from capturing the underlying truth. . . . The truth is, this team is in desperate need of leadership on the field and in the clubhouse, and no one is more qualified to provide it than Cal Ripken. If Cal accepted that challenge with as much zeal as he plays, there is no question that the Orioles would reach their potential."

He noted accurately that the Yankees had a new general manager, new field manager, and new personnel as well, but they weren't asking for more time to gel, because they were leading the Eastern Division. I found out about this statement from the reporters after the game Friday night, and the first thing I said was that I wanted to see the story that Angelos was reacting to. Somebody produced it, and I saw that the reporter had taken my answers to four or five different questions and reshaped them into one nice story—inaccurately, to my mind. My main point in that interview had been that the Orioles would get better as the season rolled along, that we were getting better at the time, in fact. I wasn't making excuses for our *previous* performance as much as making a prediction about our *future* performance. I was making very positive, optimistic statements—and I was correct, as things turned out. I also downplayed the do-or-die significance of this series against the Yankees in late June.

When the controversy about my leadership made the headlines, some players said, Wait a minute, Cal is who Cal is, he leads the way he leads, it's silly to expect him to become a cheerleader-type all of a sudden. Others said that something was "missing" from this Oriole team. To me, these latter statements are just another example of what I feel is going on throughout society: deflection of responsibility. To me, statements about something being "missing" are an excuse rather than a solution. In my opinion, the solution probably lies in making the pitches and the plays at the plate and in the field. Be responsible for your play on the field.

After I tried unsuccessfully to reach Peter Angelos, Ron Shapiro arranged a conference call with me and Peter, and we thrashed everything out. Then we had another round of interviews with all the reporters, where I explained that I took Peter's comments as a compliment, referring to my stature and the positive influence I could have on the team.

A columnist wrote in *The Baltimore Sun*, "Ripken should realize that he's the emotional center of this team, and that if he doesn't confront an out-of-line teammate, he's ultimately condoning him." I disagree. I feel it's the manager's job to set the tone on what he expects out of his players. He has to know each player, motivate each player. That was Earl Weaver's specialty, knowing which buttons to push with which players. If things happen that the manager isn't aware of, then I agree, it is *someone's* responsibility to go to that guy and identify the problem, and on the Orioles, I'm likely to be the one. I've done that plenty, but not publicly, and not for credit. I'm never going to confront a guy on the dugout steps. I don't embarrass anyone in front of the team. A manager might do that with benefit, but not a player, at least not *this* player. The goal is to solve a problem, not create a new one. I'm not all that comfortable talking about the subject now, but I guess I have to, to some extent.

Society caters to the modern ballplayer. All this attention could work for the better, but I guess it's unlikely. The humbling process of baseball usually takes care of that problem, but there have been a lot of times when I've advised players for their own benefit and for the team's benefit that they might try looking at things in a different way. I don't approach them in a "Hey, you'd better shape up!" kind of way. I'm more likely to try to get the guy to think about the bigger picture, plus the fact that everyone—*everyone*—is replaceable. "If you don't do your job, you can be out of a job. Do you really want to be here? Do you care?" I make them think about how they might selfishly focus on their individual talents if they want, but what's really needed is to mold those individual skills into one team.

If my first approach fails, then I have to devise another strategy. Above all, leadership is having the trust and respect of your teammates in handling all situations. The leader doesn't need credit in the paper. That's a violation of trust. This is very important to me. If some episode with a player does make the papers, the player wonders whether the "leader" helped for the player's and the team's benefit, or for his own.

All in all, leadership, like chemistry, can be blown way out of proportion, in my opinion. Like chemistry, it's a lot easier to talk about than it is to understand. Generally, I think bad apples are more detrimental to a team than team leaders are *positive*, though there definitely are some leaders I'd want on my team. Rick Sutcliffe is an example. In 1992 and '93, he brought leadership and experience to our young pitching staff. But I also think about Mo Vaughn in Boston. Mo's leadership was given a lot of the credit for the Red Sox's great season and division title in 1995. The next year, Mo was the same guy, hit just as well, maybe better, but the team slipped back. Did Mo somehow lose his leadership qualities? There are better explanations.

When Eddie Murray came back to the Orioles in time to add the 500 home run milestone to his 3,000 hit milestone on September 6, he was given a lot of credit for being a stabilizing presence on the team. It's true, Eddie was great to have around. For his teammates, he's always great to have around, and as the DH for us he was there on the bench to add a voice of seniority. But the main contribution he made to stability on the Orioles was that his acquisition put the DH question to rest. Bobby Bo could rest easy. Eddie was our main man for that role.

One of the more interesting angles I saw on this leadership question as it pertained to me in 1996 was Tom Boswell's analysis in *The Washington Post*. Tom theorized that I'd learned to "disengage" myself from the won-lost record of my team back in the eighties, when the Orioles were pretty bad and I was eating myself up worrying about it. Boswell wrote, "Coaches and friends counseled [Ripken] to bleed orange-and-black a bit less so that he wouldn't end up an anxious, depressed .250 hitter." Well, Boswell is correct that I did eventually come up with a different strategy for hitting in those years—I've talked about it earlier—but that's very different from a strategy for coping with the inherent ups and downs of the long season. If anything, I learned these coping strategies in the early eighties when I was on *winning* teams, not when we were losing later in the decade. In 1983, when the Orioles won the World Series, we had two seven-game losing streaks, and I saw our veterans—Murray, Singleton, Dauer, Bumbry, Lowenstein, all of them—go about their business in the same way they always had.

I agree with the statement that on a confident team like those '83 Orioles, you couldn't tell in the clubhouse after the game whether we'd won or lost. I don't think any purpose is served if you panic after a loss or after a bad series; this only reveals a lack of confidence. Be consistent, approach the game on an even keel, do your best each and every game, and in the end the superior team will likely win. You can't get too high or too low during the season. In baseball, there are no special prizes for a wire-to-wire championship.

In my remarks that so upset Peter Angelos, I played down the significance of that series in New York in late June. If we didn't win, there was plenty of time, and if we *did* win, there was plenty of time to *lose* later. As it turned out, we split that series, but two weeks later, right after the All-Star break, the Yankees took four games from us in Camden Yards, a sweep that dropped us ten games behind them. We had played pretty well against the best pitching staff in the league, but the Yankees played a little better. When Dwight Gooden struck me out in the third game, he yelled something I didn't hear, but which I heard about in the dugout. Fine, Dwight was pumped, he blew me away; good for him. My next at-bat I had a little better luck and hit a home run; I was pumped; good for me. Sure it was a big series, and the clubhouse was pretty quiet after the last loss, but it was only July. Ten games out in July is not the end of the world. However, everybody wanted to see blood on the floor in the Orioles clubhouse. To me, that reaction just betrays a misunderstanding of the big picture. We had 75 games still to play. Who was to say we couldn't have a run in those last 75 games to match the run the Yankees had had in their first 75?

Why did some people seem so anxious to write off the Orioles midway through the '96 season? That's another question I wish I had the answer to.

Meanwhile, back at third base . . . After the last game of that sweep by the Yankees on our field, I was waiting around for an appointment for the final work on my nose, which had been broken during the pre–All-Star game photo session in Philadelphia. One of my less heroic moments. White Sox reliever Roberto Hernandez slipped while stepping off the risers, threw up his left arm in reaction, and caught me flush with an accidental forearm shiver. That made the news, you bet, but the nose was okay; one last adjustment was now all it needed. While I waited, Davey called me in and reopened the third base case. It had been decided—by whom? I don't know—to start the Manny Alexander experiment immediately, tomorrow night, against Toronto. I'd play third base.

Here it was. The next game. Now. After 2,216 games at shortstop, I have to say it felt strange. A horde of photographers followed me out to the new position for infield practice. Davey said I was an All-Star short-stop and I'd be an All-Star third baseman, if it came to that. In the first inning, Otis Nixon struck out trying to bunt against me. Batting second, Tomas Perez tried to bunt on the first pitch, too. That's when I looked into the Blue Jays dugout and wagged my head, laughed, and exchanged jibes with Cito Gaston, their manager. But in his position I'd have done the same thing. When a new cornerback steps into the breach, you work his area of the field. In the third inning, Charlie O'Brien cracked a shot down the line. I dove to my right, caught it, and threw Charlie out from one knee. A standing "O" from the fans, and I was happy, too. That's the kind of situation that kicks my always competitive juices to a higher level still. Move me to third and I'll try to be the best third baseman in the league.

In the end, Davey ended that experiment with Manny Alexander at shortstop after six games. Manny wasn't hitting, and Davey said later that the situation had probably been unfair to him.

We didn't catch the Yankees in the AL East, but we won the wild card race. We also set the major league record for home runs in a season, so I guess I should weigh in with my theory about the great power numbers throughout baseball in 1996, including the Orioles', led by Brady Anderson's 50. Among the theories was one about a tight, hopped-up ball. I don't buy that at all, because a tight ball would travel farther, wouldn't it? But I don't recall seeing *longer* home runs in 1996, just more of them. No, I think the homer derby was due to a combination of the strength of the hitters, some smaller parks around the league, and a decline in the *craft* of pitching. There's that word again. Pitchers are in better shape than ever, they have stronger arms and throw harder, but it seems like they're not throwing to the hitters' weaknesses but trying to trick us, beginning with the first pitch. Along with many other people in baseball, I think we're now seeing the end result of a couple of decades of aluminum bats in college, where pitchers are wary of coming inside on hitters because coming inside isn't effective against aluminum. These bats have such a large sweet spot they can produce a line drive on a pitch that would break wood. Since there's no reward for coming inside, the pitcher resorts to trickery. Therefore we have *lots* of deep counts in the major leagues today.

By the way, I think this is the main reason for slow ball games. There are many theories about this, but I think if you want to speed up the game, the answer is not to enlarge the strike zone but to *tighten* it. Calling a tight zone would keep the pitchers from trying to stretch, stretch, stretch an already pliable zone. Hitters would know they have to come to the plate ready to swing, and they'd know they're going to see legitimate strikes to swing at. Or, as Senior puts it, don't *let* the batter hit the ball. *Make* him hit it by throwing strikes in good locations. Outs—or hits—would be recorded earlier in the count, and the pace of the game would quicken.

The bottom line was bombs away for the Orioles in 1996 on our way to winning the wild card race. Some fans and reporters say that the wild card is a back door into the playoffs, but the players don't. You're in the playoffs, you're in the playoffs. No wild card team has yet to win the World Series, but it will happen, and when it does, will it be a tainted victory? Will there be an asterisk in the record book? No.

Of course, given the way things had gone for us that year, when we did make the playoffs the center of attention was not the good baseball we were playing on the field, but rather Roberto Alomar's spitting incident with the umpire John Hirschbeck in Toronto the last week of the season, September 27. What a terrible mistake, for which Robbie will be branded for the rest of his life, I'm afraid, because he really is a good, solid person as well as a great baseball player.

In the end, it was Robbie's flare to center field off Jose Mesa with two outs in the ninth inning that tied the fourth game of the Cleveland series, 3–3, and it was his homer off Mesa in the twelfth inning that won the game and sent us to Yankee Stadium to meet the Yankees for the AL championship. Not such a bad season for us after all. Some folks in Baltimore who had pronounced us dead and buried in July were now backing and filling three months later.

Yankee Stadium. Some people call it the Bronx zoo, but I don't. They just have great fans, that's all. I wouldn't say it is the most exciting place to play a big series, because every stadium is exciting when the games are big, but I can't imagine a *more* exciting one. It's intimidating, because the Yankee fan is loud and boisterous and into every pitch and every check swing. Every play is magnified. These fans react as a group like no others. They thoroughly enjoy getting into the game. They rag on you, scream and yell, and that's a sport in itself. "Hey, '95 is over, Ripken. Take a day! You're bushed!" Any bit of information or specula- tion in the papers will be picked up and thrown back at you: "You haven't lost *a* step, Ripken. You've lost *two!*" More of this in Yankee Stadium than anywhere, and I don't think of this as being treated badly. I think it's a neat part of the game, and if you can deal with it, it's great. No one can condone the batteries thrown from the stands, that's wrong and dangerous, but I love to go there. Nothing ruins the fun for me. Sometimes I'll even turn around and acknowledge a taunt. "Yeah, you're right. I'm tired. But would a day off really help me?" Many times I've stood out at shortstop or in the on-deck circle at Yankee Stadium and thought, This is a great atmosphere for baseball. I love this. These feelings are what you play for.

Not even to mention the sense of history. In Baltimore, we had that sense at Memorial Stadium, and a future generation of players will have it one day at Camden Yards. At Fenway Park, you have the Green

Monster and Ted Williams. Yankee Stadium would feel special if there wasn't a single fan in the stands. This is sacred ground, where Babe Ruth and, yes, Lou Gehrig played.

Those five games against the Yankees were full of what-if's and might-have-beens. Any series is, but this one was a *lot* closer than the 4–1 split might indicate. What if the famous kid hadn't leaned over the right field wall and caught the fly ball? If that had been an out instead of a tying home run, would we have won that game and then left Yankee Stadium up two games, because we won the next one anyway? In the third game, playing in Camden Yards, we were four outs from winning with Mike Mussina on the mound. They came back to win and go up 2–1 in the series. In the fourth game, when Darryl Strawberry hit two homers, we had the bases loaded, nobody out in the eighth inning, down 8–4 runs. What if . . . ?

In the end, it came down to the fact that the Yankees were a little bit better than the Orioles in 1996, just like I was a fraction late with my dive to the bag making the final out of the fifth game. Nobody wants to make the final out of the final game, but I wasn't worrying about this as I walked to the plate with the crowd screaming. Bobby Bo had just homered to left. If I could get on, Eddie Murray would come up as the tying run. How sweet that might be. But on the grounder in the hole I was two inches late diving for the bag at first. Or maybe one inch.

For the following year, 1997, Baltimore acquired Oakland free agent Mike Bordick to play shortstop. So ends my career at that position, and so begins, after fifteen-plus seasons, a second career at third base. The way I look at things, this isn't an end, but a beginning. Let's see what happens.

Afterword

When I woke up on Monday morning, July 14, 1997, I felt a dull ache in my left hip but dismissed it as a slight strain and then put it out of my mind for the game that night against Toronto—successfully, as it turned out, because I got three hits and we won 9–5. After the game, maybe the ache was a little worse; at home that night, worse still. Trying to sleep, I couldn't get comfortable in any position and finally got up at four in the morning and tried various positions and manipulations on the floor. Now I was concerned; Kelly, too. Next I tried the hot tub on the deck, where I was sitting when the sun rose. Kelly convinced me I had to call Richie Bancells, the Orioles trainer who'd been handling my aches and pains for a decade. Richie listened to my story, consulted Dr. Silberstein, the former team doctor who'd handled my knee episode four years earlier, and then called me back with instructions to meet the medical team at Johns Hopkins.

I went in the side door at the hospital, but people recognized me. The ones who thought I was there to visit a patient must not have noticed my limp. The doctors got their X rays and then an MRI, which didn't turn out perfectly because I couldn't lie completely still for forty-five minutes. But the diagnosis was clear anyway: herniated disc between the fourth and fifth lumbar vertebræ. The prescription was also clear: anti-inflammatories and four to six weeks of rest; within two months, with any luck, the problem would be completely resolved.

Of course, the doctors knew it wasn't quite that simple. At least one of them was thinking about the streak, which stood at 2,404 games, because he thought I might be able to DH. I wasn't thinking about the streak or the DH. I was thinking that the Orioles had a possible championship season in the works. We'd won on Opening Day and been in first place ever since. We were 56–33, five and a half games ahead of the Yankees. I was hitting pretty well—.286, with 58 RBIs—and had made the adjustment to third base. Earlier in the season, I'd had some unrelated back stiffness and soreness, which I think were caused by the deeper crouches and quicker reactions and lunges necessary at third. I'd misplayed some balls I was trying to block and made some throwing errors. Now I felt solid, and I'd just had a bunch of tough chances at the All-Star Game and made all of them, confirming, to me at least, that I belonged at this bag.

If I sat down now, it would be at least September before I was physically ready—no guarantees—and then I'd need a second, abbreviated "spring training." My season would be effectively over. That's the way I saw it. Plus, we'd already lost Eric Davis, who was undergoing chemotherapy for colon cancer, Roberto Alomar, who was missing a lot of time with a groin injury, and other guys off and on. From the Oriole's point of view, this was bad timing on the part of my back. Really bad.

All in all, I didn't think I had much of a choice. So I looked around at the team of doctors and asked, "What if I can endure the pain?"

Silence.

"Will playing make the injury worse? Will it heal anyway?"

They said it would probably heal anyway, whether I was playing ball, walking around, or lying flat on my back all day. I could tell they were also thinking: You mean you're thinking about *playing* in this condition?

I went to lunch with Ron Shapiro, my agent, talked with Kelly, talked with my parents over the phone, and finally I decided to do what I'd done in similar situations in the past: go to the park, get treatment, suit up, take some swings, field some balls, see how I felt. But this time I was much more pessimistic than I'd ever been. This was by far the worst injury I'd had—much worse than the knee, which had felt better as that day went along. This back was getting worse. The pain was bad.

Players peeked through the window while I was on Richie's training table. I told a few guys, "I don't know if I can go tonight." But after the treatment and after I worked out a little, I had a quick exchange with Davey. I was playing. The back hurt, but I could do the basic tasks. Between innings I either stood or kneeled down. I couldn't sit on the bench. I could swing the bat well enough, though I didn't get any hits. After the game I laid low but said to myself, "If it's worse tomorrow, I'm out."

It wasn't worse. It wasn't better. It was the same, so I played. No hits. I played for a week feeling about the same, explaining to reporters that I was missing BP because of back spasms, which, after all, I'd had off and on my whole career. In seven games, just two hits, but then the benefit of the anti-inflammatories kicked in and I felt some relief, and my hitting proved it: in the next seven games, six hits.

I needed that sign of light at the end of the tunnel. My left leg was aching, muscles were tightening up from lower back to shin. The big problems came when I had to put extra weight on the left leg. A couple of times I just flopped down while trying to make a play in the field. Overall, though, I was doing my job. Davey Johnson checked with me daily, and I got the impression that he wanted me to play if at all possible. And I wanted to, but I also knew I couldn't think about feeling like this for a month or two. I had to stick with the one-day-at-a-time philosophy that had served me well for two decades.

Two weeks after the first bad night we flew to the West Coast. On Saturday I had to come in hard to field a swinging bunt, and when I reached down to make the play, everything spasmed. *Everything*. My whole left side, from brain to big toe, or so it seemed. I couldn't make the throw, so I just tossed the ball back to Mike Mussina on the mound.

Right then I almost walked off the field, but I hesitated, looked around at the field, my teammates, the fans—the game I love so much—and reminded myself that if I left now, I wouldn't return for a while. There'd be no turning back. I reminded myself not to make rash decisions. That has never been my style, as you know by now. I had the presence of mind to realize that I was due up the next inning, and I convinced myself to see how that went.

It went well. Walking to the plate I thought about swinging within myself, and I did, lining a hard single to left. Standing on first base, I thought, Well, I guess I'm over this particular crisis. That hit was really big for my state of mind. The next day I hit a homer, which offset my frustration at flopping down on a fielding play. I hope that didn't look as bad as it felt.

In Oakland I had a long talk with Richie Bancells about "the big picture," as he put it, about not doing something dumb now that would have repercussions for the rest of my life. Didn't I want to play basketball in years to come with Ryan and Rachel? Didn't I want to dance with Rachel at her wedding? Richie wanted me to be careful, and these scenarios hit home hard. I sat down for a long talk with Kelly, who was on that trip with both the kids. At our next stop, Seattle, I was definitely feeling better, with more freedom of movement, fewer spasms, but I called the doctors in Baltimore anyway, wanting reassurance that I wasn't hurting myself long-term. They assured me.

In Anaheim, I had one bad moment in the field but three hits in the first game of the series and a home run to win the final one. We had a great road trip (6–3) and I was producing (twelve hits, with my average rising from .276 to .283). I wasn't going to give up now.

A couple of weeks later, right on schedule in late August, I was feeling pretty good, reflexes were better (although a second MRI showed no change). I had leftover secondary conditions—muscular tightness in my quads, left hip, left shin, and up the back, and weakness in the left leg overall—but treatment was keeping them under control. My average peaked at .294, which supports the theory that in baseball an injury can actually benefit the hitter by making him concentrate better at the plate. You want to put the ball in play with good swings early in the count, without dragging out the at-bat. You don't overswing. I buy this, mainly because of an episode early in my career, when I hyperextended an elbow sliding into second base. In the on-deck circle for my next at-bat, the pain was bad on practice swings. Whoa! I said to myself. What's this? But I learned quickly that if I hit the ball, the elbow didn't hurt; if I missed, it did. I immediately went on a tear. Coincidence? I don't think so. Good concentration.

The first weekend in September we took three out of four from the Yankees, who'd been applying serious pressure. Now we'd more or less clinched the wild card and had a big lead for the division championship: eight and a half games. The team was in good shape, I was feeling much better, I knew I'd make it through the season and into the playoffs—and then I slumped. Looking back, I think I'd worn myself out mentally fighting the injury. I needed a break mentally. The whole team took a break as well.

Because of earlier rainouts, we had to play five games in 50 hours, in which I had a total of one hit. My back was okay—the *best* game of the five was the last one—but a couple of reporters tried to link my recent slump to my bad back. They said it was time for me to take a seat. Suddenly, out of nowhere, there was an avalanche. The headline on the front page of *The New York Times*—the first section, not the sports section—read "Ripkin's Will Is Still Iron, but Not His Body." Columnist Dave Anderson came up with an extended analogy with Hamlet and me: "To be or not to be in the Orioles' lineup. That is the question."

Well, if I'd needed to sit down, six or seven weeks earlier would have been the time, not now. That's pretty much what I said. There was no need to sit now. And I reminded everyone that there had *never* been a time when just a day or two off would have been the answer. It had always been a *month* or two, according to the doctors. A day or two would have accomplished nothing. Ask them.

Davey Johnson was totally supportive during this firestorm. He said any decision to end the streak would be his and mine, not the reporters' or anyone else's. And he strongly implied that he wasn't going to do it. For one thing, he realized that if I sat out a game, *that* would become the story for the Orioles for the rest of the regular season. Not good.

Looking back, I have no regrets about hanging in. My batting average went *up* for the six weeks following the first symptom—the worst period by far—and we won the division going away. And on September 15, Eric Davis returned to the line-up—a truly emotional moment for everyone on the team and in the stands at Camden Yards. I don't think there were many dry eyes in the house when Eric walked to the plate the first time. This was a different kind of ovation from the fans, one of respect from him as a person. After all, he was *still* getting chemotherapy. During the summer he'd hung out with his teammates as much as possible. He went on a couple of road trips. He even taped his ankles before games, trying to keep in the spirit of things. And we knew he wasn't feeling great. We really admired and appreciated this kind of effort. Eric Davis was a big factor in our success in 1997.

In the playoffs I had the time of my life. For these games I felt fine, with good freedom of movement. There was only a dull ache in my left leg, which was still weak, though the only way the fan might have known this was to observe that I used my *right* foot and leg to touch bases. In normal times, I'd use either one. I had good range in the field, I was swinging the bat well, dove into second base a couple of times. No holding back, in short. I was letting it all hang out, and if I blew the back, I blew it.

We beat Seattle three out of four games—including Randy Johnson twice, with Mike Mussina pitching for us. Before that series, all the speculation was about our having to face The Big Unit twice, but we were thinking, wait a minute, *they* have a problem, too. They have to face Mike twice. Mike's not a huge, physically intimidating guy and he doesn't throw 100 miles an hour, but he throws hard—and soft, and in between, and on the corners. He's a complete pitcher. And in the regular season, he'd dominated the Mariners in an early-season matchup against Johnson, and then we beat Randy a second time. Overall, we knew we had the best staff in the league. As it turned out, we won three out of four against Seattle, beat Randy twice, with Mike winning both games in dominating fashion.

Then we played the six incredible games wth Cleveland. In a seesaw series, there's always the temptation to look for crucial turning points. In this case, I don't think there was one—or there were too many to count, whichever way you choose to look at it. Maybe the biggest of the big moments was Marquis Grissom's homer in the eighth inning to win the second game and take the series back to Cleveland tied 1–1. However, every game could have gone either way—all four Indian victories were by one run. Both teams pitched and played well. (Mussina pitched with really tough luck. Fifteen strikeouts in game three, eight shutout innings in game six, but two "no decisions" for Mike, and we lost both games.)

In that kind of series, every player can point to the one most exciting moment for him personally. In my case, that was in the eleventh inning of the third game, score tied 1–1, runners first and third, no one out. With the infield playing in because Omar Vizquel on third was the winning run, Randy Myers, relieved Arthur Rhodes in the middle of Kevin Seitzer's at-bat, with the count 2–2. On the mound Randy advised me, "First pitch slider." That's a useful tip. Batting righthanded, Seitzer would have a better chance of pulling Randy's slider than his fastball. And that's what he did, right down the line. I dove flat out, stopped the ball, then threw Seitzer out at first base. Lots of fun, and we got out of the inning but then lost in the twelfth on the missed squeeze bunt by Vizquel that bounced off Lenny Webster's glove.

By the way, I really believe that was a foul tip, not a passed ball. All in all, however, it's difficult to blame John Hirschbeck, the home plate umpire, because it was so loud you couldn't hear anything but the crowd. (The same thing had happened with me in Baltimore, tipping a slider off Paul Assenmacher that was ruled swing-and-a-miss, strike three. I squawked a bit to Jim Joyce, but if he didn't hear it, he didn't hear it. Before my next at-bat I mentioned to him that I should have asked him to check the ball. My black bat probably would have left a mark, but I didn't think about it at the time. Joyce said he hadn't thought about it, either. To me, these breaks are a small price to pay for being in those great situations in the first place.)

Losing that third game and, eventually, the series against the Tribe was disappointing, of course, but not crushing for the Orioles. We had had an extraordinary year, and we were proud of it. My attitude at the time: Let's keep this same group of guys and come back in 1998 and see what happens.

Well, Davey Johnson, for one, is gone—on the day he was voted AL Manager of the Year, in fact. That's baseball for you. Our pitching coach, Ray Miller, was promoted to the hot seat. My *new* attitude: I like our chances just as much with Ray. See you next spring.

Cal Ripken, Jr.
November 1997

Acknowledgments

No one is able to write a whole book by himself—least of all me—and the list of folks I'm indebted to is mighty long. Bear with me, because all these people played important roles in this fascinating process.

I begin with my family, all of whom worked with me on digging up, confirming, or refuting old stories and perspectives: my mother and father, sister Elly, and brothers Fred and Billy. My wife, Kelly, read drafts and offered a host of suggestions. My mother- and father-in-law, Joan and Bob Geer, are definitely part of this story.

I thank everyone who works professionally with me almost on a daily basis. They're all the best: Ron Shapiro and Michael Maas; Ira Rainess, Désirée Pilachowski, Blythe Hammett, Lanie Yerman, Susan Morris, and Gloria Dausch.

With the Baltimore Orioles, John Maroon, Bill Stetka, and Heather Tilles in the media relations office were indispensable. Tom Keenan in that office did a great job as the main fact-checker for this book.

For help with the text itself, I thank Patty Bryan. Jean and Nick Bryan, Nicole Bryan, Val and Steve Salinger, Joe Spieler, and Stephanie Vardavas contributed valuable support, as did my friends at John Brown's Store.

I have a pretty good memory, but it's not perfect, and I couldn't have written this book without the generous contributions of dozens of people who were there, too. I thank all of them for their time, and perspectives: Spiro Alafassos, Joe Altobelli, Brady Anderson, Richie Bancells, Rex Barney, Mark Belanger, Tim Bishop, Mike Boddicker, Bob Brown, Brooks Carey, Joe Castelano, Bob Davids, Storm Davis, Doug DeCinces, Rick Dempsey, Mike Flanagan, Scott Garceau, Will George (not George Will, who comes up later), Bill Haelig, Roland Hemond, Elrod Hendricks, Phil Itzoe, Reggie Jackson, Davey Johnson, Lenny Johnston, Tom Marr, Ben McDonald, Scott McGregor, Ray Miller, Keith Mills, Eddie Murray, Mike Mussina, Tim Norris, Johnny Oates, Buster Olney, Jim Palmer, Hank Peters, Kirby Puckett, Floyd "Sugar Bear" Rayford, Jamie Reed, Phil Regan, Brooks Robinson, Frank Robinson, Gerry Sandusky, Peter Schmuck, Larry Sheets, John "T-Bone" Shelby, Mrs. Short in Bluefield, Charles Steinberg, Vince Steier, Rick Sutcliffe, Jim Traber, Jimmy Tyler, Rick Vaughn, Julie Wagner, Earl Weaver, George Will (not Will George, who came up earlier), Jimmy Williams, and Gregg Zaun.

At Viking, I'd like to thank Assistant Editor Michael Hardart, and last, but by no means least, my editor, Wendy Wolf, who was great from beginning to end, in all respects, and amazingly tolerant as time was running out on her deadline ... then her next deadline ... then her *final* deadline.

FOR THE BEST IN PAPERBACKS, LOOK FOR THE

In every corner of the world, on every subject under the sun, Penguin represents quality and variety—the very best in publishing today.

For complete information about books available from Penguin—including Puffins, Penguin Classics, and Arkana—and how to order them, write to us at the appropriate address below. Please note that for copyright reasons the selection of books varies from country to country.

In the United Kingdom: Please write to *Dept. JC, Penguin Books Ltd, FREEPOST, West Drayton, Middlesex UB7 0BR.*

If you have any difficulty in obtaining a title, please send your order with the correct money, plus ten percent for postage and packaging, to *P.O. Box No. 11, West Drayton, Middlesex UB7 0BR*

In the United States: Please write to *Consumer Sales, Penguin USA, P.O. Box 999, Dept. 17109, Bergenfield, New Jersey 07621-0120.* VISA and MasterCard holders call 1-800-253-6476 to order all Penguin titles

In Canada: Please write to *Penguin Books Canada Ltd, 10 Alcorn Avenue, Suite 300, Toronto, Ontario M4V 3B2*

In Australia: Please write to *Penguin Books Australia Ltd, P.O. Box 257, Ringwood, Victoria 3134*

In New Zealand: Please write to *Penguin Books (NZ) Ltd, Private Bag 102902, North Shore Mail Centre, Auckland 10*

In India: Please write to *Penguin Books India Pvt Ltd, 706 Eros Apartments, 56 Nehru Place, New Delhi 110 019*

In the Netherlands: Please write to *Penguin Books Netherlands bv, Postbus 3507, NL-1001 AH Amsterdam*

In Germany: Please write to *Penguin Books Deutschland GmbH, Metzlerstrasse 26, 60594 Frankfurt am Main*

In Spain: Please write to *Penguin Books S. A., Bravo Murillo 19, 1° B, 28015 Madrid*

In Italy: Please write to *Penguin Italia s.r.l., Via Felice Casati 20, I-20124 Milano*

In France: Please write to *Penguin France S. A., 17 rue Lejeune, F–31000 Toulouse*

In Japan: Please write to *Penguin Books Japan, Ishikiribashi Building, 2–5–4, Suido, Bunkyo-ku, Tokyo 112*

In Greece: Please write to *Penguin Hellas Ltd, Dimocritou 3, GR–106 71 Athens*

In South Africa: Please write to *Longman Penguin Southern Africa (Pty) Ltd, Private Bag X08, Bertsham 2013*